THIS CRUEL WAR

THIS CRUEL WAR

The Civil War Letters of
Grant and Malinda Taylor
1862-1865

Edited by
Ann K. Blomquist and Robert A. Taylor

MERCER UNIVERSITY PRESS
2000

ISBN 0-86554-654-1
MUP/H487

© 2000 Mercer University Press
6316 Peake Road
Macon, Georgia 31210-3960

∞The paper used in this publication meets the
minimum requirements of American National
Standard for Information Sciences — Permanence
of Paper for Printed Library Materials,
ANSI Z39.48-1984.

Taylor, Grant, b. 1828.
    This cruel war: the Civil War letters of Grant and Malinda Taylor,
1862-1865 / edited by Ann K. Blomquist and Robert A. Taylor. —1st ed.
    p. cm.
    Includes bibliographical references and index.
    ISBN 0-86554-654-1 (alk. paper)
    1. Taylor, Grant, b. 1828 Correspondence. 2. Confederate States of
America. Army. Alabama Infantry Regiment, 40th Biography. 3. United
States — History — Civil War, 1861-1865 Personal narratives, Confederate.
4. Alabama — History — Civil War, 1861-1865 Personal narratives.
5 United States — History — Civil War, 1861-1865 Social aspects.
6. Alabama — History — Civil War, 1861-1865 Social aspects. 7.
Soldiers — Alabama Correspondence. 8. Tuscaloosa County (Ala.)
biography. 9. Taylor, Malinda J. Slaughter, b. 1933 Correspondence. I.
Taylor, Malinda J. Slaughter, b. 1833. II. Blomquist, Ann Kicker, 1948- . III.
Taylor, Robert A., 1958- . IV. Title.
    E551.5 40th.T39 1999
    973.7'461'092 — dc21   99-42544
    [B]   CIP

CONTENTS

This book is dedicated to

Leonard "Scot" Norwood
(1922-1996)

and

Harold Kicker Windsor
(1918-1996)

Southern gentlemen who
served their nation,
honored their heritage,
and
loved their families

and to
Virginia Dair

ACKNOWLEDGMENTS

Anyone who works in the field of Civil War history inevitably incurs debts along the winding road to publication. We wish to thank the late Leonard "Scot" Norwood for finding these letters and making the initial tedious transcriptions. His wife Jeanne had continued to be supportive of efforts to make them available to all students of the Confederate South. Both Scot and Jeanne opened their hearts and home to us and willingly shared their lives.

Numerous librarian and archivists labored to find and provide the material necessary to make Grant and Malinda Taylor's story come alive. Pamela J. Hall of the Florida History and Genealogy Library of the Indian River County Main Library was especially helpful and went far beyond the call of duty. Professional historians like Dr. Jerrell Shofner of the University of Central Florida and Dr. Nick Wynne of the Florida Historical Society offered sage advice and council when needed.

Friends and family also contributed to this project in so many ways. Cordelia Allen, Jim Taylor, Henry Seale, Mell Kicker Newman, Mabel Kicker Wyatt, Mary Tate Kidder, and George and Genny Taylor all gave aid and comfort to two harried editors. Special thanks to Eric, Jason, and Tate Blomquist who tolerated their mother's obsession with the letters of long dead relatives.

John R. Blomquist and Virginia J. Dair provided the necessary life support for us to complete our unique mission. They put up with proofreading, typing, endless historical conversations, and trips to libraries on weekends and holidays. Historian's spouses surely deserve extraordinary commendation for all they endure in the quest to unlock the past.

Lastly, thanks to Marc A. Jolley of the Mercer University Press for seeing the value of the Taylor letters and helping us bring them to light.

INTRODUCTION

On April 13, 1862, Grant Taylor, a newly-enlisted private in Company F (later G), 40th Alabama Infantry Regiment, sat down to pen a letter to his wife and children from a camp in Demopolis, Alabama. Seven days later, his wife Malinda laboriously wrote a reply to her soldier-husband. Thus began a three-year correspondence of some 160 plus letters chronicling the impact of the American Civil War on this Alabama family.

Grant Taylor was born in 1828 as the eighth child of Archelaus and Lucy Taylor. He grew up not far from his birthplace near Pleasant Grove, Pickens County, Alabama. After receiving a fairly good education for the times and location, young Grant wandered west to Union County, Arkansas. His deep religious faith and Bible study probably led him there for missionary work. But by 1850, he was once again living on Alabama soil.

In 1852, Taylor made a happy marriage with Malinda J. Slaughter. Malinda, born 1833 in Richmond County, North Carolina, also called Pickens County home. The Taylors farmed with Grant working, for a time, as a local school teacher. The political crises of the 1850s seemed far away from their corner of west central Alabama, plus as non-slaveholders these troubles did not appear threatening to the Taylors. Yet Lincoln's election, the secession of the lower South, and the firing on Fort Sumter changed their lives forever.

When the war came, the Taylor family was living in Cushing, Alabama. Cushing, in Tuscaloosa County, like much of the northern tier of the state, was not a hotbed of secessionist sentiment. In fact, Tuscaloosa County cast 64% of its votes for cooperationist delegates to the state secession convention.[1] When

---

[1] Ralph A. Wooster, *The Secession Conventions of the South* (Princeton: Princeton University Press, 1962) 63. For more on Alabama during the war see Walter L. Fleming, *Civil War and Reconstruction in Alabama* (New York: Columbia University Press, 1905) and Malcolm C. McMillan, ed., *The Alabama Confederate Reader* (Tuscaloosa: University of Alabama Press, 1963).

North and South came to blows in 1861, Taylor and his neighbors were willing to let those who yearned to volunteer do so while they stayed at home with their families and businesses.

However, predictions of a short war and an easy Confederate victory rang hollow by the spring of 1862. Military setbacks and potential manpower shortages for the rebels forced the new Confederate States to institute the first national draft in American history. An April 1862 law required all able-bodied men between eighteen and thirty-five to serve in the Confederate army for three years or until independence was won. Participation in the conflict was no longer optional for many white male Southerners. Few men wished to have the stigma of being conscripted associated with their names. Plus most wanted a say in their choice of duty. Consequently, many men reluctantly enlisted in new or existing rebel units.

Grant Taylor, at age thirty-four and with four children, certainly had no burning desire to leave his home to learn the soldier's trade. But the real threat of conscription left him little choice. Grant and his cousin Malachi Taylor traveled to Demopolis and signed into the 40th Alabama Infantry, Colonel A. A. Coleman commanding. Malachi was soon discharged, leaving Taylor "buddyed up" with Ide Teer, the husband of Grant's youngest sister. Taylor was in the army now as a private and bound to it for the duration.

How did Taylor feel about the cause for which he was now to fight and perhaps die? In all of his letters home, there are few solid exclamations of support for the Confederacy or any utterances of southern patriotism. Words such as his October 1862 exclamation of being ready to fight against a Union "vandal horde, this destroyer of our peace," faded quickly. Civil War historian James M. McPherson described such semi-patriotic soldiers as typically being "a non-slaveholding Southern married farmer with small children who was drafted in 1862 or enlisted to avoid being drafted."[2] McPherson's description fit Private Grant Taylor perfectly, and as the war went on, his morale only declined. Much of his early correspondence to his wife deals with a vain attempt to secure a

---

[2] James M. McPherson, *For Cause and Comrade: Why Men fought in the Civil War* (New York: Oxford University Press, 1997) 102.

substitute, Malinda also mentions several local men shooting off their trigger fingers to avoid military service. These accounts offset romanticized legends about Southern eagerness to fight.

Grant Taylor would indeed fight in the ranks of the 40th Alabama. The regiment had an active role in several major theaters of war, though it saw relatively little heavy action at first. Until October 1862, the 40th Alabama was part of the garrison of the important port city of Mobile. Pressing Union columns in Mississippi would cause the 40th Alabama to leave the Gulf coast and join the command of General John C. Pemberton then defending Vicksburg. These men would stay until the river fortress surrendered on July 4, 1863. Taylor was one of the thousands of Confederate soldiers paroled after General U. S. Grant's triumph. A glad Pvt. Taylor enjoyed an unofficial furlough until arguments about parole were settled, forcing him to return to what he called his "hated duties as a soldier."

A reconstituted 40th Alabama soon joined the Army of Tennessee in time for the twin disasters of Lookout Mountain and Missionary Ridge in November 1863. Private Taylor was absent for most of the fighting here due to an injury, although he would winter with his regiment near Dalton, Georgia, with the rest of the Confederacy's hard-luck army. After a cold, hungry, and homesick winter in north Georgia, the Alabamians faced the daunting threat of General William T. Sherman's armies on their march into Georgia.

The campaign from Dalton to the gates of Atlanta was gruelling on the rank and file of both armies with its constant movement and fighting. Taylor was so weak from illness that he stayed in Georiga hospitals until May recovering from lingering pneumonia. Once released from the hospital, he went back to his company for more marching and combat. By August, while in line of battle near Atlanta, he recorded "oh how tired I am getting of this thing." His strong religious convictions sustained him as it did for so many Civil War soldiers. These convictions enabled Taylor to keep going in the face of fatigue, slim rations, and the almost constant fear of wounding or death.

The 40th Alabama would, however, miss the final act in the Atlanta drama when it was pulled out and returned to Mobile to bolster that cities' defenses in the face of possible Union attack. In many ways, the winter of 1864-1865 was the hardest of the war. Ill again, poorly clothed and shod, Grant faced slow recovery in a "hole of a hospital." Being stationed in his home state and unable to see his loved ones, including a newborn son conceived while on furlough, "makes my poor heart almost to bursting," he wrote. With gentle urging from Malinda, Taylor promised to come home—leave or not—before the 1865 campaigns began. By mid-December, he admitted that "the boys are generally very much out of heart and say it is no use to fight any longer."

By the fateful spring of 1865, the Confederacy indeed tottered on the brink of destruction. Even the proposal to place slaves into rebel units to increase depleted ranks, which Grant vehemently opposed, did little to raise hopes. When the 40th Alabama received orders to once again leave Mobile for the Carolinas in a desperate attempt to stop Sherman's blue-clad juggernaut, Taylor made his own vote on the Confederacy's chances by marching homeward and away from the last front. By the war's end Taylor returned, albeit slowly, to his regiment after a bit of what Civil War soldiers called "French leave."

The Taylor letters not only show life in the army, but they also give important information on the lives of ordinary Alabama rural folk. Thirty-two of Malinda Taylor's letters to her husband survived. Her letters are a rich source on the war for those left behind on the home front. Although Private Taylor destroyed his wife's letters for the middle period of the conflict, many from 1862 and late 1864 to 1865 remain. Having both sides of a wartime correspondence provided is relatively rare. Malinda Taylor, like her husband, had to make a significant life adjustment with the coming of civil war—the most immediate was being alone on the family farm with only her young children. Nights seemed the worst of it at first, but later she could write that "I am not afraid to stay here of a night at all." Her long days were filled with the work involved in running a farm and caring for the young ones. Her letters are filled with a longing for peace and an easing of her burdens. By June, 1862, she admitted that she was "tired of this way of living." As a non-slaveholder, Malinda did not have a ready supply of servants to assist her as did upper-class Southern women.

Time and necessity toughened Malinda Taylor as she carried on in the face of adversity. She supervised the selling of their farm and the relocating of her family to Pleasant Grove. In fact, as the war continued, she showed a growing confidence in her business capacity and even a degree of pride as her self-reliance increased. Not even health problems and the strain of her 1863-1864 pregnancy caused her to falter, though she depended on a network of family and friends that modern mothers could appreciate. With time, the war wreaked havoc on this kinship system as Malinda sadly reported the death, wounding, and debilitating illnesses of family members to her husband through her letters.

The costs of war are evident in the almost matter-of-fact way such losses are communicated. Malinda lost her brother Atlas J. Slaughter in October 1862, her brother-in-law John Parker in March 1863, and finally her brother Walter Slaughter in September 1864. Grant, in turn, mourned the loss of friends and the death of his own father. Probably the hardest blow was messmate Ide Teer's capture by Federal forces in June, 1864. Malinda could only wonder when she would receive the news that her husband had suffered a similar similar fate. For both of them, the price of Confederate nationalism and Southern independence was too high and, by 1864 each sought the war's end on any terms.

Readers of these letters will come away with a clear sense that the Taylors were a loving couple and not afraid to express their feelings on paper. Their passion for each other is conspicuous in print and is at times surprising for people in Victorian America. Malinda showed her desires in several poignant passages, such as a July, 1862, line that she dreamed "the other night you had come home and I thought we were lying together." The Taylors also had the tensions any marriage faces when partners are separated for long periods of time. For example, they disagreed on the naming of their fifth child, born in May 1864. A sharper exchange occurred in January 1865, when Malinda hosted a party for young adults in her home. Private Taylor rebukes her for what could become an immoral gathering and a source of gossip about her. A natural strain between an absent soldier and a newly-confident wife accustomed to making decisions on her own obviously existed by 1865.

This Cruel War seems a fitting title for a volume of Taylor family letters. Grant Taylor used these words some six times in his wartime writings. In November 1862, he remarked in a letter "what a number of widows and orphans are being left by this cruel war." By April 1863, he wondered "would to God that this cruel war might close," and a year later asked "would to god our people become humble that this cruel war may close." Chances are these references came from a popular wartime ballad "Weeping, Sad and Lonely" by Charles C. Sawyer:

> "Weeping, sad and lonely,
> Hopes and fears how vain!
> Yet praying when this cruel war is over,
> Praying that we meet again!"[3]

Indeed, these letters point out the brutal nature not only of the Civil War but of all wars. For the Taylors' family, and friends, the war brought precious little glory or romantic notions of causes won or lost. Their rough prose provides more evidence of the downside of the war and is both historically significant and emotionally touching.

Editorial Policies

This collection of letters was saved by the Taylors themselves and passed to their daughter Mary Josephine, who was a mere toddler when the Civil War began. It was not until 1988 that the letters were rediscovered in an old suitcase by Leonard L. Norwood, a great-grandson. The originals are in the possession of the Norwood family. Ironically, the co-editor, Robert A. Taylor, is not a relative of Grant and Malinda Taylor despite the common last name.

The letters themselves were written on all sizes of paper in both ink and pencil, Writing paper was a highly-prized commodity for

---

[3] Francis T. Miller, ed., *The Photographic History of the Civil War*. Ten Volumes. (New York: Review of Reviews, 1911) 9:351.

Confederate soldiers and scarce as the war progressed. At time, Private Taylor used medicine prescription forms and public notices for his notes home. Some of the envelopes were "twice turned," used on the outside and then refolded and addressed again with the inside now exposed.

One of the things the Taylors shared with many other Americans of the 1860s was a cavalier attitude toward the rules of grammar and spelling in their letter-writing. Grant Taylor was an inconsistent speller, and his wife was far worse. Without the benefit of an education comparable to her husband's, Malinda must have struggled with every line in her efforts to communicate her thoughts. In preparing these letters, hopefully, an editorial balance has been struck that will let the Taylors speak for themselves in their own way and at the same time let modern readers share their experiences. Paragraphs and periods have been added where needed, and editorial intrusion are marked with brackets. The temptation to "help" Malinda with her composition has been resisted and her words mostly remain as her husband Grant saw them. He never criticized her lack of literary skill or seemed to mind it much.

Grant and Malinda Taylor. Year is unknown, but probably not long after the Civil War.

Grant and Malinda Taylor. Probably early 1880s when
they had moved to Beebe, Arkansas.

Grant and Malinda Taylor on the front porch of their home at 402 W. Illinois Street in Beebe, Arkansas. Their son Lavalgas W. Taylor is with them. Photo taken probably in the 1890s.

Gravestones for Grant and Malinda Taylor in Beebe, Arkansas. He died in 1908, not 1907 as carved on the marker.

The regimental flag of the 40th Alabama. (Courtesy of the Alabama State Archives.)

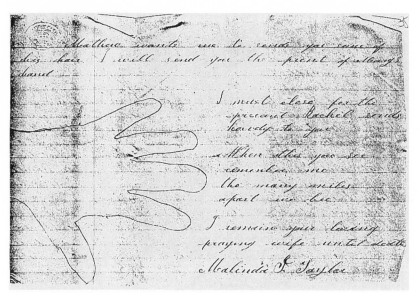

Mary's handprint accompanies letter 35.

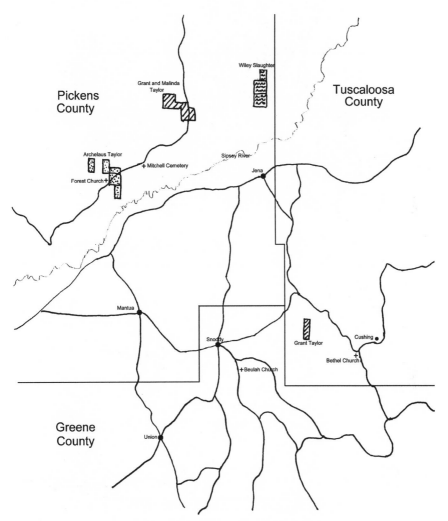

Pickens County, Tuscaloosa County, and Greene County

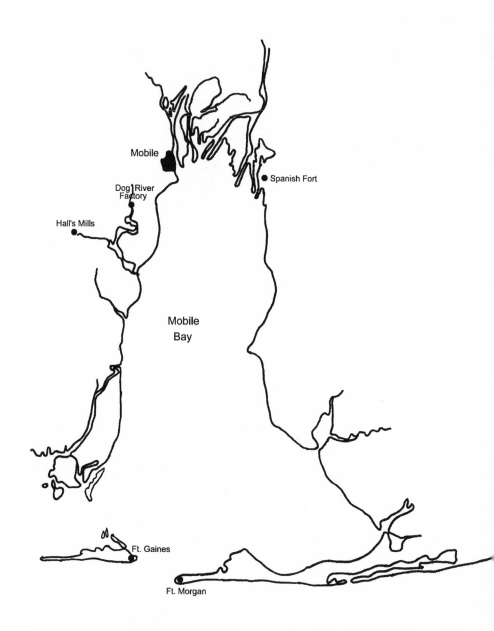

Mobile

Spanish Fort

Dog River Factory

Hall's Mills

Mobile Bay

Ft. Gaines

Ft. Morgan

Mobile Bay Area

Corinth

Decatur

Grenada

Birmingham

Columbus

Tuscaloosa

Buck Creek

Eutaw

Vicksburg

Meridian

Selma

Jackson

Demopolis

Montgomery

Mobile

------- Railroad
——— River

April 1862 - July 1863

October 1863 - January 1865

CHAPTER 1

TRY TO BE RECONCILED

War called Grant Taylor away from home and hearth. Both soldier and wife are optimistic about their future prospects if only they can be reconciled to being separated. Their first letters include daily concerns of food, clothing, health, and family.

1

Demopolis Ala[1]

Apr 13th 1862

Dear and beloved wife & children,

I seat myself this Sabbath morning to drop you a few lines to inform you of matters and things. I am tolerably well and hope that you are enjoying the best of health. I had an attack of diarreah yesterday morning but feel like I am about well this morning.

We landed here Friday evening about 3 o'clock on the 11th and found 5 companies encamped on the fairground. We are very comfortably situated. We have good dry buildings to sleep in. We have a beautiful place to drill in but the regiment is not full and I am told that if [it] is not filled we will not stay here long but I do not know where. I should be very sorry to have to move as we are so well fixed. There is some sickness in camps but I do not hear of but one dangerous case. He is a man from Chocktaw Co.[2]

The men generally appear to be in good spirits. Some few are badly dissatisfied. We get plenty of beef and bread, a little coffee,

---

1 Demopolis was the county seat for Marengo County, Alabama.

2 Choctaw County is south of Pickens County.

flour, pickled pork, rice and sugar and molasses. We have not drilled any yet but will stand our examination on Monday and receive our bounty and then go to drilling.[3]

The news here is that they have been fighting dreadfully. They fought three days. We killed fifteen thousand Yankees and took six thousand prisoners. Our side lost six thousand killed and wounded. They then rested 3 days to bury the dead and were to fight a pitched battle last Friday but I have not heared from it.[4]

I heard over in Pickens [County] that Bud, Jack and John were all exemp[t]ed.[5] I feel like that if it was not for being away from you and the children that I could enjoy myself pretty well but being away from you kills my joy but we must cheer up and do the best that we can. Be sure to write as soon as you possibly can for I want to hear from you before I leave hear [here] if I have to leave here soon.

Kiss the children for me. Pray for me. Tell all enquiring friends howdy for me.

Direct your litter to Mr Grant Taylor, Demopolis, Ala care of Capt H[ugh] Somerville.[6]

Be sure to write and believe me, your loving husband as ever,

Grant Taylor

Malinda, be sure to try and secure some wool before it is all gone. If you cannot get that salt at the Bluff, give Mr. McGifford

---

[3] Men who enlisted, rather than being drafted, were paid a bounty of $40.

[4] On April 6-7, 1862, the battle of Shiloh raged in Tennessee. Total Union losses were 13,047 and those of the Confederates 10,694. See E. B. Long, *The Civil War Day by Day: An Almanac 1861-1865* (Garden City, NY: Doubleday, 1971) 194-196.

[5] Men could be exempted from the Confederate draft based on health, occupation, or to leave one white man on every plantation with twenty or more slaves. See James M. McPherson, *Battle Cry for Freedom: The Civil War Era* (New York: Oxford University Press, 1988), 611-612. Atlas Slaughter, Andrew Slaughter, and John Parker. Atlas and Andrew were Malinda's brothers and John was married to Malinda's sister Mary.

[6] Hugh Summerville (1823-1862) served as a captain in the 40th AL until his death in May 1862.

the money and get him to go for it.[7] It is said we will leave here Friday or Saturday but I do not know. Save your money and do [not] pay debts with it until I advise you. Direct your letter to Grant Taylor, Demopolis Ala care of Capt H Sommerville. Maybe I will get it before I leave here.

Your loving absent husband
Grant Taylor

I have just heard that we will leave here Saturday. Write anyway.

2

Demopolis

April 14[th] 1862
Dear and b[e]loved wife,

We stood our examination today.[8] I was mustered in for 3 years or during the war. Malki was discharged.[9] I send you forty dollars except Malchi will have to pay his way back home out of it.

This leaves me tolerably well and I do hope you and the children are well. Pray for me and try to be reconciled God can take care of me here as well as there.

I am told here that there are sacks of salt at Steel's Bluff at thirteen dollars and 50 cents per sack.[10] I want you to go there as soon as you get this and buy a sack and get Mr. McGifford to take

---

7 Probably Steel's Bluff. Mr. McGifford is unidentified.

8 Physical examinations were performed by the 40th Alabama regimental surgeon Dr. George J. Colgin. See John H. Curry, "A History of Company B, 40th Alabama Infantry, C.S.A.," *Alabama Historical Quarterly,* Vol. 17, No. 4 (Winter 1955) 164.

9 Malachi Taylor, Grant's cousin. Grant referred to Malachi as "Malki."

10 Steel's Bluff was probably a bluff owned by Abner A. Steele in Section 9 Township 24N Range 2W on the Tombigbee River in Pickens County.

care of it until you can send for it. If you cannot go yourself try and get some one to go for you.

I do not know how long we will stay here. I do not expect we will stay here many days longer. Do write to me immediately maybe I will git it before I leave here.

Keep your money until you find that it is going down and then pay my debts with it. Write to me whether you get the salt or not.[11] Be sure to have those shoes made. Mine will be nines. I wrote to [you] yesterday and sent it by mail giving you an account of how we are getting along.

I bought 24 bushels of [from] Kay Taylor for you which he will haul to you.[12] He is paid for it. May God help you and the dear children and your loving absent husband.

Grant Taylor

April 15th. I am rather puny today with diarreah though I am able to go about.

3

Ala Tuscaloosa Co[13]

Apr 20th [1862]

Dear husband,

I am seated to drop you a few lines. We air all well except Mathew and Mary.[14] They had some fever last night. I think it was

---

[11] By the spring of 1862, salt was becoming expensive and difficult to purchase. See Ella Lonn, *Salt as a Factor in the Confederacy* (Tuscaloosa AL: University of Alabama Press, 1965).

[12] Rufus "Kay" Taylor, Grant's cousin and brother of Malachi Taylor.

[13] Grant and Malinda lived on Buck Creek, later called Cushing (now Ralph) in Tuscaloosa County at the beginning of the war.

[14] Matthew (age 3) and Mary Taylor (age 20 months) were the 2 youngest children of Grant and Malinda at the time of this letter.

cold. Rachel is not very well.[15] I hope these lines may finde you well.

We air getting along very well. We planted the ground that was broke up. We air not quite done braking the rest. Mr Salmon is got Clay.[16] He also took your hides.

I recieved your litter yesterday. Oh, how glad I was to hear from you. It gave me Joy and pain. Joy to hear from you and pain to think how fare away you was. Grant I try to pray night and morning when I am by myself. I kneel alone and pray to God for your health and your return home. Mrs Salmon staid with me the first knight.[17] It was a sad night with me but the next morning I arose with newness of life. Why it was, God only knows. I have not felt as bad since you left as I did from the time you valenteered until you went off. I have so many cears [cares] on my mind.

I was at the prayer meating at Mr Salmons. You was r[e]membered in prayer. I have not heard from father since you left home.[18] Sally and Lizer staid with me the next night.[19] I then s[t]aid by my self untill Cousan Lizar Jane came on Sunday.[20] She will stay with me until next Sunday.

Grant, Mr Bollings has moved to Union.[21] Pertiller Barnet is dead.[22] Grant, Jack Leatherwoods company was sent back providing they could get 200 and 50 guns.[23] They had got 200 when the news came that there was a great number of Yankies

---

[15] Rachel (surname unknown) was a hired black cook, not a slave, for the family.

[16] William Salmon of Tuscaloosa County. Clay was a family horse.

[17] Jane Salmon, wife of William Salmon.

[18] Malinda's father, Wiley Slaughter.

[19] Sarah "Sally" F. Frierson Leatherwood, wife of Matthew J. "Jack" Leatherwood. Eliza Louisa Slaughter Parker, Malinda's sister. Malinda calls Eliza, "Lizer."

[20] Eliza Jane Taylor Campbell, Grant's cousin. Here she is referred to as "Lizar Jane."

[21] Mr. Bollings is unidentified. Union is a village in Greene County, Alabama.

[22] Pertilla Barnet (born c1834) of Pickens County, Alabama.

[23] Matthew J. "Jack" Leatherwood, son of Miles Leatherwood.

clost by Tuscaloosa.[24] They was then ordered to go there immediatley. I believe the Almighty is bringing things to a close and I don't care how quick.

The children says they want to see Pa so bad. When I ask Mary where Pa is she says you [are] down on Beck.[25] She hardley ever calls your name. Rachel sends you howdy and says she is getting along the best she can. So I must close so I remain your true praying wife until death.

How often I have looked for you
and often seen you come
but you have departed from me
and I know not when to returne
Malinda J Taylor

PB Eliza Jane sends her best respects to you & says that you must write to her soon.[26]

Hall's Mills, Ala.[27]

Apr 9th, 1862

Mr. Taylor Dear Sir,

I have just received your communication of the 3rd inst stating that you had been sworn into another company, together with the certificate of Judge Nabers.[28] I hasten to write to you informing you of the relation you sustain to my company. You have been duly sworn into the Confederate service as a member of this company and no further oath will be administered to you. No other oath has been administered, or will be, to any of my company. I had legal

---

[24] A possible reference to Union troops under Brigadier-General Ormsby Mitchel moving through northern Alabama in April, 1862. See Long, *Civil War Day by Day*, 198-200.

[25] Mary Taylor (age 20 months), daughter of Grant and Malinda. Beck was a family mule.

[26] Eliza Jane Taylor Campbell.

[27] Hall's Mills was located southwest of Mobile.

[28] Zachariah L. Nabors.

& full authority to muster men into the service and all who signed the muster roll have been duly sworn in, and all you have to do is to report to me at Mobile and you will receive your bounty just as the other men have done. Moreover since my company has been recvd into the regiment I have no power, however much I might desire to do so, to extend your furlough.

Respectfully,
Yours,
[Capt.] N. M. Carpenter[29]

4

Mobile[30]

April 22nd 1862

Beloved wife & children,

I am pretty well today. Have been pretty puny ever since I have been in camps but never confined. I feel better today than I have since I left home. I hope that you and the children are enjoying the best of health. I want to hear from you very badly.

We left Demopolis last Saturday and landed here on Sunday. We are encamped under a cotton shed. It is open on one side and we lie on the soft floor.[31] We have had plenty to eat so far. I do not know where we will go from here, but will go somewhere shortly. I expect to Hall's Mills where Mr Porter is.[32]

---

[29] Captain Nathan M. Carpenter commanded Company B, 36th Alabama Infantry Regiment. See *Alabama 1907 Census of Confederate Soldiers, Perry and Pickens Counties* (Cullman AL: Gregath Company, n.d.) 3:226.

[30] Mobile, Alabama.

[31] Elements of the 40th Alabama were housed in a warehouse on Royal Street in Mobile. See Elbert D. Willett, *History of Company B 40th Alabama Regiment Confederate States Army 1862-1865* (Montgomery, AL: Viewpoint Publications, 1963) 7.

[32] John H. Porter (Co B 36th AL).

I saw Mr Cartee in town yesterday.[33] He and all of our neighbors were well except Tom Salmon.[34] He has been sick with measels for a week. We have one case of measels in our company. If I can keep well I think I can enjoy myself as well as could be expected under the circumstances.

I study a heap about you and our sweet children. Do not neglect their education.

The man that I wrote to you about being sick at Demopolis died that day. I sent you forty dollars by Ki.[35]

Salt is from 13 to 15 dollars per sack here. I wrote to you how to manage about get[ting] you some salt. I think you had better secure some as soon as you can. Goods are higher here than they are up there. Anything like decent shoes are 12 dollars per pair.

If you cannot stay there, I want you to try and stay there until you are done laying-by your crop and then you can hire Ki to help Bud and John build a house near Busters.[36] But stay there if you can. Write to me how you are getting along every way.

This place is crowded with soldiers. Some going one way and some going another. I saw a regiment from South Carolina on their way to Corinth.[37] They have been fighting below New Orleans for 2 or 3 days but not much damage done.[38]

Write to me often. Direct to Grant Taylor, Mobile Ala, care of Capt H[ugh] Sommerville.

Hug and kiss the dear children for me and pray for your loving absent husband.

To M J Taylor [from] Grant Taylor

---

[33] Joseph Cartee (1823-1908).

[34] Tom Salmon, son of William and Jane Salmon.

[35] Malachi Taylor, Grant's cousin. He is also referred to as "Ki", and earlier, "Malki."

[36] Atlas "Bud" Slaughter (Malinda's brother) and John Parker (married to Malinda's sister Mary). Buster was Josiah B. Archibald.

[37] This was either the 10th or the 19th South Carolina Infantry. See Clement A. Evans, ed., *Confederate Military History*, 13 vols., (Atlanta: Blue and Grey Press, 1899) 5:111.

[38] On April 18, 1862, Union navy forces began bombarding Forts Jackson and St. Philip below New Orleans. See Long, *Civil War Day by Day*, 201.

I will write to you what coller [color] to make my cloth[e]s when I find out myself. Be as saving of your money as posible for I cannot save much here. Take Mr P Phillips acct to him and have a settlement with him and if he is owing me anything, take it out in postage.[39] I would send you some stamps and envelops if I could get my money changed.

5

Ala Tusk Co.[40]

April the 26th [1862]

My Dear husband,

I am seated to drop you a few lines this holy Sabbath day at cousin Alsey Anns.[41] I recieved your letter the 24 but it did not find me well. Last Tuesday Dr. Snoddy took out one of my jaw teeth.[42] I found him at Sams.[43] Mrs Cartee went with me.[44] I reckon you know how it felt. It kept me up all Monday night. I have just eat enough to keep me alive tho I kept up. My jaw is better now. I think the jaw bone was injured. The doctor said I was made out of pretty good leather. He took 2 hard pulls at it.

The rest is well. Malky gave me my money today and your letter.[45] I got a letter from [Capt] Carpenter.[46] I sent it to you in my letter to Demopalis. I don't know wether you got it or not.

Grant I got along so slow with my work I have hired Ky's George a month at seven dollars per.[47] I don't know wether it will

---

39 P. Phillips is unidentified.
40 Tuscaloosa County, Alabama.
41 Alsey Ann Taylor, Grant's cousin.
42 Dr. Samuel A. Snoddy.
43 Sam is unidentified.
44 Sarah Caroline Cartee, wife of Joseph Cartee.
45 Malachi Taylor.
46 Capt. Nathan M. Carpenter.
47 George Taylor, son of Malachi Taylor.

suit you or not. Rachel does all she can to get along.[48] Fait Mullings' house got burnt last Friday night.[49] They was gon from hom at the time. I heard some letters read from Hood and Teral.[50] They were well. I engaged 5 pounds of wool from Mrs Bolton.[51] I got a pound Saturday to knit you some socks from her at 4 bits. I will go on [and] send to the bluff for that salt.[52]

Grant, I am not afraid to stay here of a night at all. I am not half so lonesum as I thought I would be. I look to my heavenly Father for protection. Grant pray for me and our sweet little ones. Little Mary has heard me whisper my prayers so mutch that when she comes to me she begins to whisper to me.

Dont make yourself uneasy about home. Enjoy yourself iff you can. I want you to get a furlough, if you can, and come home. I want to see you so bad. I dream of your coming home most evry night. God, grant that my dreams may come to pass. I suppose the North is crying for peas [peace]. I don't know how true it is. I wish it may be so.

Harte is going to have a calf after a wile.[53] Your pigs is not spaid yet. I went to see Mr Norris abought it.[54] He promised to come the next morning but he never done it and has not come yet. I don't think there is but one of them with pigs. I don't think we wil make any wheat at all and I dont know of anybody that will. Ky wants to know how mutch you owe him and wright it to me.

I will have to come to a close for Rachel is reddy to go to mill and the [post] office. This is Monday evening so I remain your humble Praying wife until Death.

Malinda J Taylor

Mr J Leatherwood send his respects to you.[55]

---

[48] Rachel (surname unknown) was a hired black cook for the family.

[49] Hugh Lafayette Mullins, Grant's nephew.

[50] James Hughes "Hood" Taylor and William Terrell Speed. Hood was Grant's cousin and Terrell was the husband of Grant's cousin Martha Ann Taylor.

[51] Mrs. Bolton is unidentified.

[52] Steele's Bluff in Pickens County AL.

[53] Hart was a family cow.

[54] Probably Wilson Norris.

[55] Probably James Leatherwood.

I would wright more if I had time. Dont forget to pray.

6

Dog River Factory[56]
5 miles from Mobile

May 1st 1862

Beloved wife and children,

I seat myself tonight to pen you a few lines. This leaves me in good health except a slight cold and I hope you and the children are enjoying the best of health. I received your letter of Apr 20th 2 days [ago] and the one of Apr 26th today. And Oh the joy it gave me. I could have wept tears of joy over them if I had been alone but being alone here is almost an impossibility. And yet how lonely I feel sometimes when I think of the many long miles that intervene between us and the small probability of our meeting soon but I believe we will meet again for I have prayed with all the faith that I could that we would meet again and I know you have. But as to getting a furlough you need not expect it while I keep well, at [least] not for a long time. But I want to see you as bad as you possibly can me.

I enjoy myself here much better than I expected. I wrote to you from Mobile telling you all up to that time. We left there last Friday and came here. We have splendid houses to stay in but nothing but green pine wood to burn and that we have to carry a long ways. This is certainly the poorest part of the world I ever saw. It all looks like the pine flat at Pate's old mill all over this country.[57]

We drill five hours each day and the ballance is taken up in cooking and doing anything we please so [long as we] behave ourselves. This regiment is not filled yet and I do not believe it

---

56 Dog River Factory was an encampment south of Mobile.
57 Pate's Mill in Pickens County, Alabama.

will be. If it is not I do not know where we will go. I do not like this place. It must be very sickly from the appearance.[58]

I got Capt Carpenter's letter. He came to see me at Mobile and claimed me but I refered him to Capt Sommerville. They talked it over but did not finally settle to which I belonged. But Carpenter acknowledged that he had the least claim on me.

Nearly half of our company is sick. Some with colds and some with measels. I expect from appearances that we will have a time of it for awhile. I do not know that any are dangerous as yet.

It is said here that the Yankees have taken New Orleans and I believe it is so. You need not believe the tale about the north crying for peace. They may be but they are determined to conquer us first and they are doing it pretty fast. The people are moving out of Mobile by droves.[59]

Flour is 20 dollars per barrel there, sugar 30 cts per lb, bacon 45 cts, coffe one dollar.

I went to Halls Mills last Sunday and saw all of our neighbors. Eliza was well.[60] Mr Porter was complaining and so was Jo Leavell and John Henderson.[61] They thought they were taking the measels. Tom Salmon was going about.[62] Jack Norris was confined with measels but was better.[63] I heard from there yesterday about 30 were sick but I did not hear who they were.

I am owing Malchi 80 cts I believe.[64] I wrote to Buster to buy you some wool, but if you have got enough you can let him know.[65] I expect you did right in hiring George but be very saving of your money for I will not make much clear here but I need not caution you about that.[66]

---

[58] The 40th Alabama suffered from a measles epidemic about this time at Cantonment Walter. See Curry, "History of Company B," 7.

[59] New Orleans fell to Union forces on April 29, 1862. See Long, *Civil War Day by Day*, 205.

[60] Eliza is unidentified.

[61] John H. Porter, Joseph M. Leavell, and John Henderson of 36th AL.

[62] Tom Salmon, son of William and Jane Salmon.

[63] Jack Norris is unidentified.

[64] Malachi Taylor, Grant's cousin.

[65] Buster was Josiah B. Archibald.

[66] George Taylor, son of Malachi Taylor.

You need not make me any woolen cloth[e]s yet. But make me 2 shirts and pants and I will write to you when and what coller I want my jeanes clothes made. Be sure and attend to getting that salt if you have not done so yet for salt is mighty scarce here at 14 dollars per sack. And if the enemy get[s] Mobile you cannot get it at all and I believe they will take it before long. You could sell half of it if you should need the money. But do not seel it unless you do.

I expect Lafayette has gone home.[67] He went to Mobile today to get a furloug and has not returned yet. I received a [letter] from Amaziah Teer yesterday.[68] He and Lab were well.[69] He fought through the big fight at Corinth without receiving a scratch, but was shot twice th[r]ough his coat and once through his haversack.[70] Continue to pray for me. Tell the brethren to pray for me at their prayer meetings. I have great faith in the efficacy of your prayers. If you see Brother Smith tell him howdy and tell him to remember me in his prayers.[71] Give my best respects to all enquiring friends. I intend to come home as soon as I can but a man must have a good excuse before he can get a furlough.

Kiss the children for me and try to raise them up in the nurture of the Lord and believe me your Loving absent husband as ever,

To M J Taylor [from] Grant Taylor

Write and direct [your letters] as before.

---

[67] Hugh Lafayette Mullins, Grant's nephew.

[68] Amaziah Teer, Grant's nephew.

[69] Albert "Lab" Iredell Teer, Grant's nephew and Amaziah Teer's brother.

[70] Grant may be refering to the earlier battle at Shiloh.

[71] Rev. J. R. Smith.

7

Ala Tus Co

May 8th 1862

My dear absent husband,

I recieved your letter today. I am seated tonight to answer it after reading it to the children. We air all well and I was glad to hear that you was well and I hope these lines may find you well as me. Jack and Sally went a fishing today to Fillips Mill.[72] I took a bag of corn and brought the meal back. We air getting along. We have got a very fine prospect for a crop. I have not set out any potatoes yet. The bed was covered two [too] deep until I took off some of the top.

Grant, Oh that blesed name. It nearly brakes my heart within me to call it. When you get this letter write to me what you was doing tonight. The children air gone to bed. They know not my troubles. God forbid they ever should. Grant, I believe we will one day meet on earth again. I long for that blesed day to come. Get your likeness if you can and send it to me to weep over.

I was at Beulah last Saturday and Sunday.[73] Thare I saw Mr Cobb. He has got a discharge on the account of his health. Elizabeth and Isabelin Chambers sends thare love and respects to you. Mack Garner allso.[74] I must quit for tonight. I am getting sleepy.

This is Saturday morning. Mr Salmon has just left here.[75] He read your letter. He sen[d]s his respects to you and says they will remember you in thare prayer meetings.

Jack Leatherwood goes into camps next Thursday. They air making up a reg[i]ment to stay thaer at Tuscaloosa. Jack Taylor

---

[72] Matthew J. Leatherwood and Sarah F. Frierson Leatherwood. Phillips' Mill is unknown.

[73] Beulah Church.

[74] Mr. Cobb, Elizabeth and Isabelin Chambers, and Mack Garner are unidentified.

[75] William Salmon.

shot off his little finger to keep from going Waller Stevens shot off 2 of his. Marsh Lee shot off 2 [of] his.[76]

I will keep George 13 days.[77] That is long as I kneed him. His time will be out Tuseday then they will be don hoing the new ground. Its purfectly clean. We planted all the old ground belo to the cross fence. Old Miles told us to do it.[78] I can get a negro to help me when I kneed him. I expect thare is hands sent up to Eutaw evry week or two.[79] I have applide for one. I am now going to preaching at Bethel.[80]

This is Tuesday morning. I went to [church] meeting Saturday and Sunday and to prayer meeting in the evening at Mr Salmonds. Thare you was remembered in prayer. Mr Smith and Mr Jones was thare.[81] I told brother Smith what you told me. He said he would remember you. Mr Heritage is going to make you a pair of shoes at 4 dollars.[82] I am going to get him to make mine and the childrens. Billy and Mack Leavil is dead.[83] I have not got any salt yet. Thare is salt at Tuscaloosa at 15 dollars per sack. I am going to send Thursday by old Miles. I heard the soljers was moved from Halls Mills 40 miles this side of Mobile. I dont know wether you come or not.

I thought I would write any how. Dont forget to pray for me. Tell Ide to pray for me.[84] Grant, I expect I have bin overheard praying many a time for where ever the feeling of prayer overtakes me thare I pray aloud. I dont want you to think I am crazy. If evry body felt like I do thare would be better times.

---

[76] Jack Taylor, Walter Stevens, and Marsh Lee are unidentified.

[77] Malinda had hired George Taylor, son of Malachi Taylor, to work as a farm hand.

[78] Miles Leatherwood.

[79] Town of Eutaw in Greene County, AL.

[80] Bethel Church is located in the community of Ralph (formerly Cushing).

[81] Rev. J. R. Smith. Jones is unidentified.

[82] Henry Heritage (Co G 40th AL).

[83] Probably William Leavell (b. c1840) and Elijah M. Leavell (b. 1841), sons of Robert and Margaret Leavell.

[84] Iredell "Ide" A. Teer, Grant's brother-in-law and close friend throughout their service together.

When ever little Mary sees me in trouble in any way she will say "Ma ly [lie] down on bed."

I want you to keep all my letters, Grant. I believe God will bring us through like he did the children of Isrell. Let us then wait patiently for it. I want you to enjoy yourself if you can. Dont study about home, we air doing very well. Buddy and Jimmy works like Turks.[85] Henry made that colar but did not charg any thing for it.[86] He said he could not take it from me and the children.

I must come to a close, so I remain your humble wife and praying warm of the dust until death,

  Malinda J Taylor

NB I am in the old store house at Fillips [Mill]. I have just recieved a letter from Mary.[87] They air all well. John and Jack and Wat was exempt.[88] Jack was ordered as the malishey [militia] but was sent back provided they could get 2 hundred guns. She says Elizy takes it very hard.[89]

I have just braut [brought] a bushel and a half of corn to mill. Mr Heritage is going to make our shoes. I must now go home to my sweet little children.

8

Dog River Factory

May 9th 1862

Dear wife and children,

I seat myself this morning to pen you a few lines. This leaves me in reasonable health and I do hope that you and the children

---

[85] Buddy and Jimmy are Leonard (age 8) and James (age 6) Taylor, sons of Grant and Malinda.

[86] Henry (surname unknown) was a black man. It is not known if he was free or a slave.

[87] Mary Slaughter Parker, Malinda's sister and wife of John Parker.

[88] John Parker. Malinda incorrectly spells Jake as Jack. She means Jacob Parker, married to Malinda's sister Eliza Slaughter. Walter "Wat" Slaughter.

[89] Eliza Slaughter Parker.

are enjoying the same great blessing. I received your letter directed to Demopolis and one to Mobile which I answered last week. I gave you a detail of events up to that time.

Our company are very sickly at this time. There are about 32 cases of measels and several others down with colds and some with chills. All are mending now as far as I know. I am nearly worn out waiting on the sick. I have not had but 2 nights rest in a week. All the sleep that I got the other nights was taken on a bench about 5 feet long and ten inches wide with nothing over nor under me. But if no bad luck I think I will stand it. Ide Teer is quite poorly and has been for several days.[90] I do not know whether it is cold or the fever.

We have received no arms yet. It is said that we are to be armed tomorrow with pikes. That is a long pole with a kind of knife on the end. The Yankees have taken new Orleans and the head men here are expecting an attack on Mobile constantly. That is why we are to be armed with pikes for the present. Our men are engaged in throwing up breastworks about 2 miles from here. None of our company have gone to work yet, for it has taken what few well men there are to wait on the sick. I have hired all my washing done yet. I get it done at 5 cents per garment.

If you have not got your salt yet nor sent to Mobile for it, you had better not send for it, but write to me immediately for if you send now the likelihood is that you will lose your money. But write to me and I will try [to] get it for you for it is uncertain when Mobile will be attacked. I have no doubt but what the enemy will take it whenever they make the attempt. If nothing more depended on it than just the city, I do not care if the place was a pile of ruins for I believe there are more scoundrels in it than are to be found in the same sized place in the world. But it is to our interest to hold it for many resons.

The regiment that Mr Porter is in has been removed to Mount Vernon about 30 miles above Mobile.[91] Mr Porter was quite sick with measels when they started. I did not hear whether any more of our neighbors in that company was sick or not. Mr Sellers and

---

[90] Iredell "Ide" Teer, Grant's brother-in-law and close companion during their military service.

[91] Mr. Porter is unidentified.

Mr Pearson came over to see me last Tuesday.[92] They were well. James Mahaffey, John and Allec Doigy have joined Carpenter's three years company.[93]

Be sure to write to me every week for Oh how a[n]xiously I wait for a letter from you. I have dreamed twice lately of meeting and embracing you and the children but just as I had done that both times some one came and woke me up and drove away the pleasing phantom. But I feel that I will have that pleasure some day, though it may be a many a day first, for a man can scarcely get a furlough at all.

Give my best respects to all enquiring friends, to Jack and Sally and all the old friends.[94] I try to pray for us all but one has a poor chance to hold communion with his Maker here when he can scarcely get to be alone a minute and on every side hear oaths of the most horrid kind mixed up with every conversation. But still it has no influence on me to turn me from the path of Morality and religion.

Kiss the dear children for me. God bless their sweet little hearts. How I would long to embrace them and you if there were any chance, but I know there is no cha[n]ce soon and I do not suffer my mind to dwell on it. I have not seen but one little babe in 2 weeks and then Oh how my heart swelled in my throat as I thought of sweet Mary. I could weep many a time at the thought of her if I could be alone, but it is no use to write in any such strain to distress you. Do not be distressed at my foolishness.

May God bless you all and your distant loving husband,

To Mrs M J Taylor [from] Grant Taylor

Ide sends his best respects to you.

---

[92] Elijah Sellers (Co B 36th AL).

[93] Privates John P. Doigg and Allec Doigg (Co B 36th AL). See *Alabama 1907 Census of Confederate Veterans*, 5:73.

[94] M. Jack and Sarah Leatherwood.

PS May 9th. There has been some guns sent here today. I heard just now that they were fighting at Fort Morgan.[95]

9

Dog River Factory

May 16th 1862

Dearly beloved wife and children,

With pleasure I seat myself tonight to answer your sweet letter written from the 8th to 13th inst. I had been looking eagerly for one for a week and oh how delighted I was to hear that you were well and doing so well. I do not want you to deceive me but write exactly how you are getting along. I received 2 letters from you 2 weeks ago which I answered. I write to you ever week and you must write to me the same.

I am well except a slight headache and I hope you and the sweet children are enjoying the best of health.

When I received your letter I had my hands up to my elbows in wheat doe [dough] making out biscuit[s], but I had to drop every thing till I read it. You ought to see me making up doe in a big pan for 15 men. I get on my knees and put the pan between my knees and then I work it into a perfect oil. But it is hard work to cook here for we have nothing to burn but pine wood.

We have had so many sick in our mess that I am serving a trade at cooking. There have been 32 cases of measels in our company and several other cases of other sickness. Three of our men have died with measels this week. They were Lyon, Pearce and Noland. Lyon died last Monday in the hospital at Mobile.[96] Allison Pearce died here this morning a while after sun up. Maberry [Mabry] Noland also died here today about twelve o'clock. Jack Pearce has been sent home on a sick furlough with

---

[95] Fort Morgan was a large fortification guarding the entrance to Mobile Bay. See also Arthur W. Bergeron Jr., *Confederate Mobile* (Jackson MS: University Presses of Mississippi, 1991), 55.

[96] J. P. Lyon, Allison Pearce, and Mabry Noland (all of Co G 40th AL).

measels. He came very near dying. He and ten others were sent to the Hospital last saturday. They are trying to get furloughs for all the sick for 15 days. I expect several will get them. Ide is in bad health but not confined. He has applied for a furlough but I am afraid he will not get one.

You ask me to tell you what I was doing last Thursday night. I am pretty certain I was writing a letter to you (God bless you).

We are seeing pretty tight times here. A certain number are sent out to work on the fortification eve[r]y day. We have to work one hour and rest one hour for twelve hours. Some are detailed to cook and some to wait on the sick. I had to cook three days this week. I think if I stay long in camps I will learn something about cooking. I am better satisfied than I expected. But I am bound to study about my sweet family. But I study about you as little as possible for I could not stand to dwell on our separation.

I sent my likeness to bud for you some three weeks since by J.M. Benson.[97] Bud has received it and I expect you have also, but do[n't] weep over it if you can help it.[98] I think it is a very good one.

They are expecting an attack on Mobile constant. We have drawn a few old rifles. Some companies have double barre[ll] shot guns and some have muskets but there [are] not near enough of all sorts to arm all the men.

I wrote to you not to send your money to Mobile for salt as you might stand a chance of losing it but write to me whether you get it in Tuscaloosa. If you do not I will get it for you if I am here. I think I can borrow enough money for that.

We made up money to pay for Pearces coffin.[99] The officers have sent him home. The Government requires a request from ones family in order to send it home clear of transportation fees. I send you a request for you to sign and send back to me so that if I should happen to die in camps I may be sent home without so much charge to you. I want to be buried by my mother.[100]

---

[97] James M. Benson (1823-1904) served in Co C 24th AL.

[98] Bud was Atlas Slaughter, Malinda's brother.

[99] Allison Pearce.

[100] Grant's mother was Lucretia Morris Taylor (1789-1861). She was buried at Forest Church in Pickens County, AL.

I must close as it is growing late. May God bless you and the dear little ones is the prayer of your loving husband.

Grant Taylor

PS Give my best respects to all enquiring friends. Tell Rachel and Henry howdy for me.[101] I want them to take as good care of you as they can.

May 17th

Malinda, There is no salt in Mobile. Get it up there if possible. I cannot get any here. I am quit[e] well this morning. Several of our company have got sick furloughs this morning. Ide applied for one too but could not get it. He is quite poorly and I do not believe he will ever get well here, although he is not confined. I feel quite lonesome this morning there are so many of the boys going home. There is no chance for a well man to come home yet. You need not look for me soon. Pray for me but I need not ask it I know you do it. Be sure to kiss the children all for me. Tell Leonard and Jimmy that Pa still loves them and he says they must be good boys. God bless you all.

Grant Taylor

10

Ala Tusk Co

May 21th [1862]

Dear husband,

I am seated to answer your letter witch came to [me] this evening. We air all well tonight. I do hope and pray that these

---

[101] Rachel was their black cook. Henry worked at Wilkerson's Mill.

lines may finde you well. Cousan Martha Speed is staying with me and her sweet little babe.[102] I have recievd boath your letters that was written since my last. I found some of your dough on your letter that you spoke of.

Grant, I could not get but 8 lbs of salt at Tusk. I baught me a number 1 cow from Mr Salmon at 30 dollars.[103] Old Miles told me to do so.[104] I am abought to sell Speck and Dunny for a big price. I dont know exactly what. Hart will soon have a calf.[105] 1 of your gilts will have pigs. I have just set out 31 roas [rows] of potatoes 50 steps long. Old Miles told me tha[t] Steward was coming with hands this week to work out my crop.[106] What a blessing that will bee. I have turned the hogs into my wheat. Old Miles said that was all the way I could save it. The rust has ciled [killed] the oats.

Last Friday I went to carry George as fare [far] as Alcy Anns.[107] Then Saturday me, Martha and Elizar Jane getherd up and went to meeting at my beloved curch.[108] After we got thair we thaught we would walk over to Goings spring and going along I met Betty.[109] I could not controle my feelings. She showd me Ides likness and told me that Dr Shockly had yours but it was a mistake.[110] Kay Taylor has just hollered at the gait and is gon to feed his horse.[111] I must quit for tonight and talk some with him.

Thursday morning Wat, Bud, John and Jake is in camps at Tusk.[112] Nute Huses wife is dead.[113] Bill Baily is dead. Green

---

[102] Martha Ann Taylor Speed, Grant's cousin, married to W. Terrell Speed. Her baby was Eliza I.C.L. Speed (Feb 1862-Oct 1862).

[103] William Salmon.

[104] Miles Leatherwood.

[105] Speck, Dunny, and Hart were cows.

[106] Daniel Stewart.

[107] George Taylor was working for Malinda as a farm hand. Malinda calls Alsey Ann Taylor, "Alcy Ann." Alsey Ann is Grant's cousin.

[108] Martha Taylor Speed and her sister Eliza Jane Taylor Campbell. Malinda's beloved church is Beulah Church.

[109] Goings Spring is unknown. Elizabeth "Betty" Taylor Teer, Grant's sister, married to Ide Teer.

[110] Iredell Teer. Dr. Thomas W. Shockley (1822-1893) who served in Co B 40th AL. He was discharged in August 1862 due to disease or disability.

[111] Rufus "Kay" Taylor.

[112] Walter Slaughter, Atlas "Bud" Slaughter, John Parker, and Jacob Parker all served in Co A 41st AL. Even though they had been exempted a

Holoman is dead.[114] Grant, you cannot tell my feelings last Saturday when they all began to sing when I looked and could not see you no whair. I thought of whair you was. It was allmost more than I could bare. I went home with Jack for dinner.[115] He asked me if I kneeded any money. He said I should have long as he had any. I told him I had money. I also heard that Capt Sumerville was dead but you said nothing abought it.

Buddy and Jimmy is learning rite away. They say they want to see you so bad they dont know what to do. Jimmy wants me to wright to you that he prays to God to let you come home. Mathew says you have got a heap of Yankes to cill before you can come home. Little Mary is the sweetist little thing I ever saw. How I wish you could see her. Buddy says he tries to bee good and works hard.

Grant I wright you as nigh the truth as I can and I want you to do the same.

Cousin Grant, please recieve my best love. You must write to us all. We would be delighted to hear from you at any time. Be shure to write and we will answer all your letters

Martha A. Speed[116]

Mr Cammel, Mr Speed, Hood and Tom all came home and staid
a week. Ben Franklin also.[117] They said they fard better than they expected. They got plenty to eat. Why cant you come home tow

---

month earlier, these men all soon had to enlist. With the great need for men, exemptions were soon curtailed by the Confederate government. After the 41st was formed in Pickensville on May 6, 1862, they marched to Tuscaloosa where they drilled for a month. See James F. Clanahan, *The History of Pickens County, Alabama 1540-1920* (Carrollton, Alabama: Clanahan Publications, 1964) 43.

113 Newton Hughes. There were 2 men in Pickens County by that name: Newton H. Hughes and Newton R. Hughes.

114 Bill Bailey and Green Holloman are unidentified.

115 Andrew Jackson "Jack" Slaughter, Malinda's brother.

116 Martha Ann Taylor Speed.

117 James Campbell, W. Terrell Speed, James Hughes "Hood" Taylor, Thomas Taylor and Benjamin Franklin Wells.

[too]. Grant, that request is a trying thing. It has bin my long and constant prayer that I could die with you and bee buried in the same coffin. I would leave my children in the hands of my folks to go with you.

I will soon be out of paper.

Jimmy wants me to write to you that one [of] his teeth is out.

I believe I have written all that is worth writing. When you come home I will tell you all I know. Grant, dont forget to pray to almighty God for your health and for your return home. Pray for our beloved Cuntry, that it once mor may abound in peace. Oh that blessed word peace. When will it come. God grant it may come soon is my humble prayer.

I must quit now and get dinner and then carry it [letter] to the [post] office. Oh how I wish you were here to take dinner with us, but it cant bee so. I want you to content yourself as well as you can and I will do the same. So I remain your distant sincere wife until death,

Malinda Taylor

NB I have had my dresses wove some time and have got another peace [piece] ready to weave. We air doing finely. Bee contented if you can.

11

Dog River Factory

May 25th 1862

Dear and beloved wife & children,

I am seated this holy Sabbath morning to pen you a few lines. I am quite well this morning and I do hope this may find you and the sweet little ones enjoying the same blessing. I received a letter from you some 10 days ago which I answered immediately.

From your letter it seem that you thought I was at Halls Mill, but we have never been stationed there. We have been here over four weeks. The name of this encampment is Cantonment Walter.[118] We are about five miles from Mobile. We had good houses to stay in until last Friday when we had to move out into tents. Last night was a terrible night. It rained tremendously and our tents leaked considerably.

The measels are rageing in the other companies and a man dies nearly every day. One died this morning with brain fever. Our company are all able to go about, but several have the diarrhea. Some thirty of our company have gone home on sick furloughs. I wrote to you last week about Allison Pearce being dead and two others. We have also lost our captain. He had the measels the same time with his men, got better and started home some 2 weeks ago and died on the boat.

I also wrote to you that you need not try to get salt from Mobile as there is none here. We are still at work fortifying Mobile. We have to work on Sundays just as any other day. I do not believe the Lord will bless such doings. It has so happened that I have not had to work any on Sunday yet.

The last I heard from Mr Porter was that he and his company was taken some 30 miles above Mobile and Mr Sellers was in Mobile. I expect we will have to stay here all summer. I do not see that it is much warmer here than it is up there [home] in the sun and it is much cooler in the shade.

Last night We were engaged in singing. We sang Halleluiah and it revived me up and made me feel as I have often felt at some of our precious meetings up there. We have preaching twice each Sunday, but the preacher is a reading Methodist and it does me no good to hear him.

Malinda I have dreamed of you and the dear children many times since I left you and Oh how disappointed I was when I awoke and found it a dream. God only knows when, if ever we meet again but I pray daily for it to be so and I have faith to believe that we will. Hug and kiss the children for me and believe me your ever loving husband,

Grant Taylor

---

118 The 40th AL moved there on April 26, 1862.

I sent my likeness by James Benson several weeks ago. I send you an odd leaf of paper. Write whether you can get any paper. It is very high here.

12

Ala Tusk Co

May the 29th [1862]

Dear husband,

I am seated to drop you a few lines. We air all well and I do hope and pray to God that you air enjoying the same great blessing. I am looking for a letter from you. Father and Mother was [here] to see me last Friday and staid until Sunday.[119] They sends thair best respects to you.

They brought your likenes. When Mother told me she had it I came very near fainting. When I open it and got the glimps of it, it fell from my hands. The next I knew I was clapping my hands, hollowing and crying. Grant, I would not take a million of dollars for it if I knew I would never get another. It allmost brakes my heart to look at it. It is so natureal. I showed it to old Miles.[120] He looked at it for a moment and said, "ah poore fellow, hee looks so natureal."

Robbert Leavel died last Sunday night with fever.[121] Cousan Mary Taylor is staying with me.[122] There is a call now for evry man that can bair armes. It is in the papers.

Preacher Scot was ciled [killed] by a tree.[123] Mr Steward has not hepe me any yet but will in a few days.[124] Crouse Garner hepe to burn Pensicolia so he wrote.[125] Carpenters Cavaldry is thair.

---

[119] Malinda's parents, Wiley and Lucy Slaughter.
[120] Miles Leatherwood.
[121] Robert Leavell (Co B 36th AL).
[122] Mary Taylor, Grant's cousin.
[123] Rev. William Scott (1822-1862) was buried at Unity Cemetery in Pickens County.

The little gilt lost her pigs. I have not solde my cows yet. I have got you[r] shoes at home. Our shoes all comes to nine dollars. I think that is very reasonable.

Grant, I am getting tiard of this way [of] living. I want to hear from you so bad. I want to see you so that when I am away from home, I hurry back hoping you air thair. When will all these troubles end. God only knows. Grant I feel that God has revield it to me that we will surv him together on earth again.

Pray earnestly that we may meet once more. Excuse bad writing and spelling. Goodby for this time. So I remain your loving wife until death.

Malinda J Taylor

13

Dog River Factory

Jun 1ˢᵗ 1862

Dearly beloved wife and children,

I seat myself this blessed Sabbath day to pen you a few lines to inform you that I am quite well this morning and I do hope these few lines may find you and the dear children enjoying the same blessing. I received your precious letter of May 22ⁿᵈ on the 25ᵗʰ which gave me much pleasure.

I have no general news that would interest you. We are getting along much after the same fashion as when I wrote to you in my last two or three letters. We have lost no more men since I wrote to you last Sabbath. I wrote to you then that 3 of our men and our captain were dead. Allison Pearc was one of them. The captain had the measels, got better and started home but died on the boat the

---

124 Daniel Stewart.

125 Pensacola was evacuated by Confederate forces on May 9, 1862 after setting fire to various military installations. See Charlton W. Tebeau, *A History of Florida* (Coral Gables FL: University of Miami Press, 1980) 210-211.

time you heard he did. Lieutenant T[homas] O Stone is our capt. now.

I received a letter from Hughs the other day.[126] He was not very well and William had had the flux but was better.[127] Hughs sent his best respects to you.

You stated in your letter that Cousin Elsy Ann's Taylor boys had been home and then you ask why I cannot get a furlough and come home too.[128] Well, they tell me the reason is this, that they are expecting an attack on Mobile constantly and they will not give a well man a furlough to go home at all. Lofton had a severe attack of flux sometime back and he talked of getting a furlough, but he was given to understand that it was hardly worth his time to try even for a sick furlough.[129] So you see that it is useless for me to try now and God only knows whether I ever will get a furlough, but I hope that if we stay down here that I can get one in the summer. But staying here is uncertain for we were ordered to Corinth some 10 days ago but as we were not equiped we were permitted to stay here. Do not be uneasy from what I say for God can take care of me there as well as here.

Write to me whether Kay Taylor has hauled that corn to you or not.[130] I bought 24 bu. from him and paid him to haule it to you.

Tell Laura that I see Jo Maize every few days.[131] He belongs to a Sumter [County] company encamped about 1/2 mile from us.[132] They belong to our Regiment.

Dear Malinda, this day twelve months ago was a sad day to us. On that day you will recollect that my dear mother departed from these low grounds of sorrow and I thought that the day was dark and gloomy.[133] And so it was, but not to be compared to this in relation to our situation. Then we were happy in each others society. Now we are saparated by hundreds of miles by a sterne

---

126 James Hughes Taylor, Grant's brother.
127 William M. Taylor, Grant's brother. "Flux" was dysentery.
128 Alsey Ann Taylor's sons were James Hughes "Hood" Taylor and Thomas Taylor.
129 Thomas Lofton.
130 Rufus "Kay" Taylor, Grant's cousin.
131 Joseph and Laura Mays. Private Joseph Mays (Co C 40th AL).
132 Sumter County is south of Pickens County.
133 Grant's mother was Lucretia Morris Taylor (1789-1861).

necessity with many chances against our ever seeing each other again. Oh dearest wife and children, I never knew how I loved you untill I was forced to leave you. How my heart swells in my throat and tears start to my eyes as I pen these lines and contemplate the present and try to fathom the future. But do not, dear Malinda, think me miserable for I am much better satisfied than I expected, and I try to humbly pray to God and put my trust in him that we will one day meet in life to enjoy ourselves together as in days that are past and gone.

Paper is very scarce and high here. I will send you a little along in my letters and if I get a chance I will send a quantity to you. Write to me as you here [hear] from Mr Porter and our other neighbors.

I sent my likness long ago as I wrote to you. And Bud had it the 3^d of May so he wrote to me. I hope you have received it before now. When you receive it write to me what you think of it. If I had yours and the children's I would not take any money for them but do not want you to have them drawn for we are not able to afford it. I want you to save some of your money if you can for if I should get to come home before I draw, I shall need some to pay my way back to the army.

Watch every chance you can get to get some salt. God only knows what you are to do if times do not change before next winter. Nurse your hogs and try to make your meat for if you do not you will have to do without. Bacon is 60 cts per lb here, corn $2.50 per bu. Molasses $1.50 per gallon, sugar 30 cts per lb. Common writing paper 75 cts to one dollar per quire. I gave 65 cts per pack for these envelopes that go around my letters. They c[h]arge 3 dollars for half-soling a pair of shoes.

Give my best respects to cousin Elsy Ann and family. Mr Leatherwood and family. Mrs Porter and aunt Henny and Mr Salmon and family, and all other e[n]quiring friends, if any.[134] Write to me how you are getting along with your crop and how it and the neigbors crops look.

---

[134] Alsey Ann Taylor, Miles Leatherwood, Mrs. Wm. Jasper Porter, and William Salmon. Henrietta Moore (1814-1886) lived with Jasper and Adline Porter. She was called Aunt Henny, so she was probably a relative of the Porters.

Direct your letters to me care of capt T O Stone, Col. [A. A.] Coleman's Reg. Mobile Ala.[135] I will close by saying to the children that I still love and weep over them and I want them to be good children and mind their ma and try to please God and that maybe God will someday bring their pa home to see them. Tell Rachel and Henry howdy for me. So I remain your loving distant husband,

To M J Taylor [from] Grant Taylor

14

Ala Tusk Co

June the 7th [1862]

Dear and beloved husband,

I am now seated to drop you a few lines. We air all well and I hope these lines may finde you well. I recieved a letter from you last Saturday. I was glad to hear that you was well. I am getting along very well with my crop. Mr Leatherwood come and ploughed 2 days for me last week.[136] I will get mor help when I want it.

Ky was [by] to se [me] last Sunday and braught a letter.[137] It stated that you wanted a pair of pants. I had a piece of cloth in the loom to make the children. So I made you a pair [out] of that.

I am now at Bettys wrighting this to you.[138] I came over to bring your pants. Cousan Elizar Camel came with me.[139] I am going this morning to see Dady. We had fried chicken this morning for breakfast. Mee and Betty thought of you and Ide.

---

135 Colonel Augustus A. Coleman was born in Camden, South Carolina in 1826. A Yale-educated lawyer, he became an Alabama state judge in 1853 and sat as a delegate in Alabama's secession convention. See Evans, ed., *Confederate Military History*, Vol 8, 529-530.

136 Miles Leatherwood.

137 Malachi Taylor.

138 Elizabeth "Betty" Taylor Teer, Grant's sister.

139 Eliza Jane Taylor Campbell. Here Malinda calls her "Lizar Camel."

Grant dont neglect to pray. The enemy cant deprive you of that privilidge. So I remain your humble praying wife,

M J Taylor

[The following letter was written by Elizabeth Taylor Teer, Grant's sister, to her husband Ide Teer and her brother Grant Taylor.]

Dear Husband and Brother,

I am seated to write you a few lines informing you that I think my health is improving some. Thomas Lofton sent me word that you were well which I was very glad to hear. I spent the day at Wm Davis' yesterday and in the evening Mr Barnes came driving up with George looking more like a dead man than a live one.[140] He has had the fever for 12 days. He was a week getting from Corinth home. He said he walked some and rode some —— on the [train] cars and the balance of the time he was bumping along in an old waggon. He had a verry high fever and a verry bad cough. He says that they have Charles under arrest for leaving camps and going home without a furlough.[141] George says there are a great many sick at Columbus.

Ide I sent your things by Mr Brandon which I hope you have got.[142] Ide you requested me to become reconciled. Well, I am better reconciled than I ever thought I could be without you. I want you both to pray for me and also for yourselves. Pray that you may forebeare the temptations of a camp life. I would be verry glad to see you both but I recon it will [be] some time before I do.

---

140 William Davis was married to Grant's sister Unity. Mr. Barnes and George are unidentified.
141 Maybe Charles McCartney Taylor, Grant's cousin.
142 Probably John R. Brandon.

Little Mary is still verry puny with her bowlels.[143] Write often. Nothing more only I remain your truly affectionate wife and sister.

Elizabeth Teer to

I. Teer and G. Taylor

Linny and Eliza are going to stay with me tonight and if you were only with us, how happy we would be.[144]

* * * * * * * * * * * * * * * * * *

[The following letter was written by Eliza Jane Taylor Campbell, Grant's cousin.]

Much Beloved Cousin,

I will write you a few lines informing you that I am in tolerably good health. Cousin Grant, I have not much to write that would interest you. I thought as Cousin Malinda & Betty were writing I would write a few lines. Mr Campbell, Hughs, Tom & Terrell and [have] been at home once since you left on a furlow but made a verry short stay.[145] They only s[t]aid 7 days with us. We havent received but one letter from them since they left. I suppose they have gone to Florida.

Rufus has not volunteered yet.[146] His crop looks verry promising indeed. Ma's family are all well.[147] Cousin you must write to me on the reception of this. You cant imagine the gratification it would afford me to receive a letter from you. Present my kindest respects to Iredell. Please excuse my short & bad writing as my pen is so bad until I can scarcely write at all.

I will have to close as we are all a going a visiting today. It is now half past 9: oclock. Farewell, dear cousin,

E J Campbell

---

143 Mary Dulcena Teer (born 1860), daughter of Ide and Betty Teer.

144 Linny was a nickname for Malinda. Eliza Jane Taylor Campbell.

145 James Campbell (Eliza's husband), James Hughes (Hood) Taylor, Thomas Taylor, and W. Terrell Speed.

146 Rufus "Kay" Taylor.

147 Alsey Ann Taylor is Eliza Jane's mother.

15

Dog River Factory

Jun 8th 1862

Dear Wife & children,

I take my pen this Sabbath evening to write you a few lines to inform you that I am well except cold. And I do hope that these few lines may reach you all well and doing well. I received your letter giving an account of receiving my likeness some days ago but as I had started one to you the day before I have not answered it till now. I am glad that you got it and to hear that you were all well but sorry to know that you took it so hard. But trust in God and I do verily believe he will one day bring us through all our troubles.

I have no general news to write. Everything is going on here about as usual, only we have quit working on the fortifications and devote our time to drilling, though the work on them is still going on. I wrote to you in my last why I could not get a furlough. The reason is this, that they are expecting an attack on Mobile and they want every available man to stay here.[148] God only knows whether I ever will get one or not but I hope so sometime during the summer. But even that is very uncertain.

Ide received a letter from Betty yesterday stating that she was in tolerable health except cold and Betty stated that you had the name of being the smartest woman on Buck creek.[149] Oh Malinda, how glad I am to hear that of you. Although I knew it before, yet to hear it from other lips gives me more pleasure than anything I have heard for a long time. May God enable you to bear that character through.

There is a heap of sickness in this regiment. There are one or 2 deaths every day here. The measels and their affects are the

---

[148] Confederate leaders feared a Union attack on Mobile as a follow-up to the fall of Pensacola. See Bergeron, *Confederate Mobile*, 55-56.

[149] Buck Creek ran through the community of Cushing (now Ralph) where the Taylors lived.

principal causes.[150] Malinda, there is more to impress solemnity on my mind here than any place I was ever in and fell [feel] more determined to live accord[ing] to the will of my dear savior than I ever did before. May God enable me to do so is my prayer. And if we never meet on earth any more, I humbly hope that we will meet in heaven to part no more.

Paper and everything is very high. This paper cost me 50 cts per quire and is very sorry you see. Bacon is 50 cts per lb so I am told and everything in proportion. Someone stole a half quire of paper from me last week much better paper than this. You had better go or send to Union and get you some paper and envelops.[151] Give any price for it if you can get it. If I had any chance I would send you some frome here. I will send you a sheet in each letter. But I cannot send envelops in that way.

I have picked out two verses which I think is applicable to your case. And pay particular attention to the last vers.

Direct your letter to me care of Capt T O Stone, 40th Reg, A V Mobile Ala. The A V stands for Ala. Volunteers.

Kiss the dear children for me and believe me your loving and devoted husband as ever,

Grant Taylor

The Widowed Heart
Poor desolated heart!
If yet one joy remain
If in thy lonely path so drear
One lingering uncrushed flower appear
To bid the smile again
Who now partakes
The smiles it wakes
On culling it for thee, of tenfold value makes?

Earth yields no cure but Heaven has given
A balm for hearts bereft and riven.

---

[150] Measles and typhoid fever were running rampant in the 40th Alabama at this time. See Willett, *History of Company B*, 9-10.

[151] Union is a village in Greene County.

A balm ne'er tried in vain:
That volume Bright
Where beams of light
Illume the eternal words reveals it to thy sight.

16

Ala Tusk Co

June the 11th 1862

Dear and beloved husband,

I am now seated to wright you a feu lines. We air all well and I hope and pray these lines may finde you well. I recieved your beautiful letter of June 1 yesterday. It gave me pleasure to hear you was well. Oh when I can hear that you air well I can bare my troubles very well. Ky was here the first day of June. We was talking of your dear Mother and that we thought it was a sad day but not to be compaird with this. Remember this is God's will and try to be contented. All these troubles is only for a few days. I say to you again I believe that God has reveild it to me that we will prais him together on earth again.

Grant, you said for me to be saiving of my money. I tell you I have got lots of it tho I am as saving as I can be of it. Mr Hirum Colvin was here yesterdee and gave me 25$ for Dunny and 22 and a half for Speck.[152] He also wanted Harts yearling and said he could not take the other 2 without him. I stuckout for a good while that I could not let him go but concluded the other one would make as mutch beef as I had salt to go on so I let him have it at 16$ and a half. Grant he tolde me to wright to you that he wanted to by your oxans. He said tha [they] was worth 80$. I think he will give mor than that. He wants to by your Cotton also.

The crops all looks very well. I am getting along finely with my crop. I am don planting Potatoes. I have got a bully patch and they look fine. Grant, I wish you could se my newground corn. Its

---

[152] Hiram Colvin (1831-1887) of Greene County.

as black as my old hat. I tell you I am getting to be a splendid farmer. All I like [lack] beeng a man is the pants and something els.

Grant, Kay will hall my corn when I kneed it. I have got enough to last me until August yet. My hogs looks fine. Another one of the gilts is with pig. I hope she wont loose them. I take good care of them as I can. Harte has got a calf. We get plenty of milk and butter now. Old Mr Hamer is expected to die evry minute.[153]

Grant I saw poore old Dady last Saturday.[154] He is nothing but skin and bone. I dont think you will have a father long. I showed him your likeness. He said it was his poore old father and then he asked if it was Hughs.[155]

I was at Davises a few minuts. I showed it to Uny.[156] I saw the tears come into her eyes as she looked at it. Lucreta burst into tears when I showed it to her.[157] I have to weep with evry one that I see a weeping.

Mr and Mrs Ritcherson spent the day with me last Thursday.[158] He said if I kneeded help call on him. My first swarm of bees came out that day and he hived them for me.

Grant, little Mary can talk almost as plain as I can. Evry man she sees she will say yonder is Pa. That soon fills my eyes with tears. She dident know your likeness. I showed it to Mathew. I asked him who it was. He said it loked like Pa. I felt like my heart would breake.

---

[153] Mr. Hammer is unidentified.

[154] Archelaus Taylor (1783-1862) was in poor health at the end of his life. The 1860 census recorded him as "insane." When his wife died in June 1861, the newspaper reported that "she leaves a poor idiotic husband." *Pickens Republican* (Pickens County AL) July 4, 1861. He was about 78 years old and was probably senile.

[155] Archelaus Taylor's father was George W. Taylor (c1759-1843). George was born in Virginia but led a pioneer life after the Revolutionary War, living on the Georgia frontier 1785-1806, unsettled middle Tennessee 1806-1812, and northern Alabama prior to its statehood 1812-1843.

James Hughes Taylor, Grant's older brother.

[156] Unity Taylor Davis, Grant's sister.

[157] Lucretia Taylor Mullins, Grant's sister.

[158] Mr. and Mrs. Richardson are unidentified.

I am staying this week by myself. I am not very lonesum and not afraid at all. God is with me. He reveiles himself to me plainer now than he ever did before.

I have knit you 2 pair of new socks. One stran of them is cotton. I am ready now to make you some more clothes if I knew what color to make them. Ky said he would come and take your place for a month when he was don laying by if they would have him. I heard Mr Porter was coming home. I dont know how true it is. The measels is at Mr Porters and Bill Parkses.[159]

Grant the men that came from your company told Betty and Lucreta that you was the best man in the world. You air so good to the sick. I hope God will bless you and make you usefull for time to come.

I have just s[t]rung and put on a large mess of beans for dinner. Grant, if you was only her[e] to help eat them. Oh the pleasure it would gave me toung [tongue] cant tell. Remember evry day brings these troubles nearer to a close.

Bud is at home with measels. Pap, Mother, Mary and Elizy was going to Town last Monda to see John and Jake. Mrs Pearcon has a fine boy.[160] Mrs Sellers a fine girl.[161] Jane Leatherwood has a boy.[162]

Grant I want you to wright to me what you have to eat and wright me the truth.

Wash Leatherwood has got up a little school to keep from going to the army.[163] Your school would of kept you from going. A thousand times do I regret your quitting it but I have given all things with myself up to the hands of God. Thare we must put our trust. Enjoy yourself if you can. Dont bee uneasy about home. Take care of yourself and we will do the same, but dont forget to

---

[159] Mr. Porter is unidentified. William S. Parks (1838-1918) who married Nancy Jane Leavell (1838-1904).

[160] Mrs. Pearson is unidentified.

[161] Nancy Jane Drummond (1829-1913), wife of Elijah Sellers.

[162] Jane Leatherwood is unidentified.

[163] Probably George Washington Leatherwood. Teachers having 20 or more students were exempt from the Confederate draft in 1862. See Albert B. Moore, *Conscription and Conflict in the Confederacy* (New York: Macmillan, 1924; Columbia, S.C.: University of South Carolina Press, 1996), 53.

pray to God. Lishe & Dully went to Columbus after Ammy and brought him home sick.[164]

I keep your watch running yet.

June 12th Mr Porter was her[e] today.[165] He has a ferlow for 15 days. There is a heep of the soldiers come home. Old Miles told me yesterday the soldiers was all dismiss for 60 days.[166] My heart like to flew out my mouth but Mr Porter says it is not so. My hops is all dashed to the ground again.

Grant, if you air not pleased with my traid I reckon he wold [trade] me back. The cows will stay her[e] until fall.

John Porter, Dick S, Brantly G, George S, two Howard boys, Lifus H is all at home and a heap more.[167] Maybee it will be your time next. God send it may.

I must close for the presant. I expect I can get paper her[e] but if you can get [some] send some any how. So I remain your same humble praying wife until death,

Malinda J Taylor
Dont forget to pray.

17

Dog River Factory

Jun 15th 1862

Dear & beloved Wife & children,

Again I am permitted to pen you a few lines this holy day. I am well except cold and headache. I have had the worst cold for 2

---

164 Elisha "Lishe" Teer, his wife Dulcena "Dully" Taylor (Grant's sister), and their son Amaziah "Ammy" Hughes Teer (1841-1863). Amaziah Teer was later killed at Missionary Ridge.

165 Mr. Porter is unidentified.

166 Miles Leatherwood.

167 John H. Porter (Co B 36th AL); Richard Smith (unknown); Brantley W. Garner (Co F 11th AL); George Stewart (Co E 18th AL); Henry H. Howard, James Howard, and Leonard Howard (all Co I 40th AL); Lifus H. is unidentified.

weeks that I almost ever had. Although I have not stopped from duty. Whenever I b[e]gin to mend I am put out to stand guard and that throws me back again.

I hope you and the dear sweet little ones are well and doing well. I received your letter and pants yesterday. I was very glad of my pants and still gladder to hear from you as it had been nearly two weeks since I had heard from you.

I have nothing new to write. There is still a heap of sickness among us but mostly measels. There are some cases and even deaths from Typhoid fever and Pneumonia. Josh Pate is lying quite low with measels here in the hospital.[168] I think he is very dangerous unless he could be better attended to than he can be here. Some one or two dies here almost every day.

I wrot to you that a well man could not get a furlough and now they will not give sick furloughs unless the doctor will certify that he believes that it will save a mans life or constitution to let him come home. They will not even let a man go home with a corps[e]. Although they will let the corpse be sent home but no person to go with it.

A recruit that came to us about 4 weeks ago died last week with measels. His name was Thomas Carver and lived not far from Mullins.[169] I do not wish to dishearten you by what I write about furloughs but to keep you from being disappointed if I do not come home soon. I intended all the time to come sometime this summer but as the thing now stands God alone knows when I can come home.

I received a letter from William and Emmaline yesterday dated June 2nd.[170] They were all well. They have left Hughs and moved to within 2 miles of Memphis.[171] They never stated the cause why they had moved. They sent their best love to you and siad they would write to you soon. I am as well satisfied as could be expected

---

168 Josh Pate is unidentified.

169 William Mullins (Grant's brother-in-law) or his son Hugh Lafayette Mullins.

170 William "Wick" M. Taylor (Grant's brother) and his wife Mary Emmaline Gammill.

171 James Hughes Taylor (Grant's older brother). Memphis, a village in Pickens County, Alabama.

under the circumstances. But God and myself only knows how bad I want to see you & the children. But I feel more resigned to the will of my dear savior than I ever did before.

Give my best respects to Mr Leatherwood and Family.[172] Tell him that I am very much obliged to him for the assistance he has rendered you that God's blessing on him and his and that I pray that we may both live so that if we never meet on earth we may meet in heaven.

I sent you 2 sheets of paper in the last two letters and will send you one in this. I believe I have gone throug[h]. Tell Leonard and Jimmy that pa says they must be good boys and mind you and love the good man. May God bless you all is the prayer of your loving Soldier husband.

Grant Taylor

PS I heard from George Davis 3 days after you were over there he was better.[173] Write often.

To Mrs M. J. Taylor, Pleasant Grove, Pickens County, Ala.

18

The following letters are from the Slaughters, Malinda's parents and brother.

June 17th 1862

Dear son,

I am permited this morning to seat myself to write you a few lines in answer to your kind favor which came to me the 16th inst.

---

[172] Miles Leatherwood.
[173] Probably George Davis, Grant's nephew.

It give all great satisfaction to read it. It found us and all the connection well except Wats family.[174] There is eight down at his house with measles. (James Shirleys family and Wats are liveing together.)

Grant I hope the these few lines may find you in good health and in fine spirits. I have nothing of interest to write you. We were over at your house three weeks ago and found Malinda and all the children well and in fine spirits. John & Jacob has had the flux in camps but they are well now or was when last heard from.[175]

Oh the troubles of War is upon [us]. Try and be as cherful as you can. You requested an interest in our poor Prayers. Dear son we will try. And we beg an interest [in] yours for we are in trouble too. Lord grant us all grace for our day trial and grant that we may enjoy each others presants one time more on earth. And if not grant us all a happy admitance arount thy throne where we shall never be seperated no more forever is the Prayer of your loveing and affectionate Parents. Write soon.

To Grant Taylor Wiley and Lucy Slaughter[176]

* * * * * * * * * * * * * * * * *

Dear Brother,

I will drop you a few lines myself. I am at Fathers this morning. It may be for the last time for I have to go back to camps next monday. But I can hardly walk yet. I am very weak. The measles fell on my bowels and they brought me down very low. But I am improveing slowly. My old cronic disease is hurting me at all times but not so bad as it has bin. Grant I find a camp life disagreeable indeed but it is God a chastizing us for our sins and let us be as humble as we can for if He chastised us not, we are not

---

174 Walter Slaughter, Malinda's brother.

175 John Parker and Jacob L. Parker, brothers who were married to Malinda's sisters.

176 Wiley S. Slaughter (1805-1883) and his wife Lucy Ussery (1805-1866), Malinda's parents.

Try to be Reconciled   41

sons but bastards. Grant I would be glad to see you but as we are deprived of this satisfaction let us try to pray for each other as long as we have breath.

So Dear Brother Farewell

Write soon

But I cannot tell you where to direct your letter for I may be in Columbus in less then a week. If I am, I will write to you. So I remain your loveing Brother as ever,

Atlas. J. Slaughter[177]

Grant Pray for me.

19

Ala Tusk Co

June 19th 1862

Dear affectionate Husband,

I take my pen in hand this evening to answer your kinde letter whitch I recieved the 14th. I had just started you a letter the day before I recieved it. We air all well except Mathew. He was taken day before yesterday with fever. It cools a little of a morning. I gave him 2 doses of blewmas but he throwed it up.[178] He appears to be some better this evenin. He has throwing up and running off of the bowels. I don't think it anything serious.

I have got old Wiley her[e] laying by my corn in the way of paying his de[b]t.[179] I have never got only 2 days help yet but thank God I can do without it. I am not beholding to any body. It

---

[177] Atlas J. Slaughter (c1829-1862).

[178] Blue mass was a pill composed of mercury and chalk and was used as a standard Civil War-era treatment for diarrhea. See Bell I. Wiley, *The Life of Billy Yank, The Common Soldier of the Union* (Baton Rouge: Louisiana State University Press, 1978) 137. Malinda incorrectly calls blue mass, "blewmas" in her letter.

[179] James Riley (born 1820-1824) lived in Greene County, Alabama. Malinda incorrectly spells his name as Wiley.

don't hurt old Miles to make a promase and then break it at all and as for old Dan Stewart he may go to shit.[180]

I have sent to Union for some paper and envelops. I was at Beaulah last Sunday and to prayer meeting at Mr Po[r]ter's in the evenin. Brother Smith sends his love to you and says he remembers you in his prayers. Mr Porter, Adline and Aunt Henny spent the day with me last Tuseday and he robbed my bee gums [trees] for me and got 3 pecks of honey out of them. It was very nice honey. Old Mr Hamer is alive yet.[181]

Grant that was beautiful poetry you sent me and suited my case very well. I recieve a portion of that balm evry day. I feel like a pore desolate heart but I have a friend that sticketh closter [closer] than a brother that watches over me and you. Grant thare is some of the most feeling prayers sent up to heaven in behalf of the soldiers I ever heard. Shurley God will hear and answer prayer.

Eddingses Company will start to Columbas Mississippi tomorrow. Mr Cartee is at home. Jimmy is gon in his place. Bud Henderson is at home very sick. Tom Parkes is at home. Bill Browning is dead.

This is Friday Morning. Mathew is abought like he was yesterday. He has some fever yet. Old Rily has just told me he was not going to charg me any thing for his work.[182] We air running 3 plows, Rilys horse and my 2. When tha [they] get done ploughing they air going to hoe it all over. I made a fine chance of onions abought 3 pecks. I have had thirty 4 yds of cloth wove since you left home and have got another peace on hand for you some cloths but I hope you wont have to stay thare for me to send them to you.

Grant, Mary is a sweet little girl. When I ask her whare Pa is she will say way down in the field. When I wash her face she will say "oh Pa come kiss a me." If she sees Buddy or Jimmy with a green apple she will say "Ma, Buddy and Jimmy bin pulling green apples." I know you want to see her. Rachel dreamed last

---

[180] Miles Leatherwood. Daniel Stewart.

[181] Union, a village in Greene County AL. Beulah Church in the community of Cushing in Tuscaloosa County. William Jasper Porter. Rev. J.R. Smith. William Jasper Porter, his wife Adline, and their aunt Henrietta Moore. Mr. Hammer is unidentified.

[182] James Riley.

night that you was maried to a Yankey lady. Mabee that is a sine [sign] that we will bee maried again shortly. Oh how I wish it was.

Grant, I have just contented myself and I am waiting patiently for your return. I believe God has told me to wait. That is what I have to do wait for his all wise time. We air kneeding rain very bad. I have got 100 and 13 hills of tobacco set out for you to chew.

I will rite some on an old letter.

I recieved a letter from Mrs Beely and Caty Frieson. The old husy wanted meat and lard. Caty said for me not to bee troubled about you going off that the girls had to give up thair bougs [beaus] two [too]. Betty Garner has left Eadeses. They would not let Mack come thair for some purpose or other and they fell out. She is at Crouts Garners. I was glad of it for she gave me a black nam[e] so I heard. She talked abought me to Morning and she told Cousan Elcy An.[183]

Mathew wants me to wright to you that he is sick and he wishes you was her[e]. Buddy dose [does] all my milling and going to the [post] office. He went with me to Beaulah last Sunday and rode Beck by hisself. I tell you he felt big.[184] The boys still loves thair bo[o]ks and learn very fast.

Iff you meet with troubbles
and trials on the way
Cast your care on Jesus
and dont forget to pray.

I am going now to the [post] office myself so I must close for this time. Tell ide howdy for me and to pray for me.[185] So I remain your distant praying wife,

Malinda J Taylor

---

[183] Mrs. Bailey is unidentified. Caty Frierson, daughter of Samuel and Frances Frierson. Elizabeth Garner (age 19) was listed as a domestic in the household of James Leavell in the 1860 Pickens County AL census. Mack is unidentified. Crouse Garner may be Charles Garner. Mourning Taylor, Grant's niece. Alsey Ann Taylor, wife of Grant's cousin George Taylor.

[184] Beck was the family mule.

[185] Iredell Ashcraft Teer, Grant's brother-in-law.

[The back of the following letter was used as the last page of the letter above. It was written by Malinda's sister Mary Slaughter Parker to Malinda, but the date of Mary's letter is not known. "Wat" is their brother Walter S. Slaughter.]

Dear Sister,

I seat myself to write you a few lins in fine health. We are all well at this tim as far as I know. Wat had liked to laust [lost] his baby last weeke by poison. Little Lisy touck down Wats shot bag and spilt the caps out and the baby picked them up and swaled them.[186] Thay sent for the doctor in haste. It throud them up before the docter got there. He sede if it had not throde them up it would have dide [died] in one hour.

I went to the Mason Walk yesterday.[187] It was very ser[i]ous. There was a sight [of] folks there. There was forty eight Masons dreast in uniforme.

We all are going tomorrow to Martons to have our likness takon. In my locket me and Jhon will be takon in one side and Milt and Poney in the other. Jack and Lisy, Bet and Quene is all going.[188]

So nothing more for this tim. Yes there is. I have got a new frock. I bote it with socks. Hesterran Caley is marr[i]ed. She got a man by the name of Harres.[189]

So nothing more. Write to me. Tell Gra[n]t that all I like [lack] being a docter is the lisons [license]. Jhon ses tell him that he is most don[e] laingby and then he is going a fishing.[190]

Mary E Parker

---

186 Eliza A. Slaughter (born c1857), daughter of Walter Slaughter and Serena Webb.

187 Mason Walk was a parade of some sort.

188 Martin was a photographer. Mary and her husband John Parker are having their photographs made with their children Noah Milton Parker and Joseph Napolean Parker. Jack, Lisy, Bet, and Queen are unidentified.

189 Hester Ann Calley and Mr. Harris are unidentified.

190 John Parker, Mary's husband.

20

Dog River Factory

June 22nd 1862

Dear wife & children,

Once more amidst death and trouble am I permitted to pen you a few lines this holy Sabbath morning to inform you that I am well and doing well. That is doing as well a[s] could be expected and I do hope these lines will reach you and the dear little ones enjoying the best of health. I received your precious letter of 11th and 12th inst the other day which gave me much pleasure.

There is still a heap of sickness here yet. 2 men died in the hospital last night which makes about 40 out of this Regiment. since we came here. Josh Pate died with measels last Tuesday. There is a talk of moving some 5 miles from here but I do not know how true it is. I hope we may move if we can get to a healthier place.

I am glad you have sold the two cows but I had rather you would keep the yearling if he will take the two cows without him. But if he will not agree to take the cows without the yearly you can lett him go too but I rather think it a bad trade for beef will be mighty high this fall. If he will give you one hundred dollars for the steers let him have them but for no less. I do not care to sell them no how and under the circumstances that is none too much.

Well as to my clothes I hardly know what to say. They have never determined what coler our uniforms will be but you can make the jeanes a grey mixed rather dark. You [need] not make it up until you hear further from me. As to cotton clothes I shall not need more than one more pair of pants this summer. Make me 2 shirts as to coler make them as you please. Under the present orders I can never get them from home unless some one comes from up there to bring them to me. For as I wrote to you they have stopped furloughing entirely. But I am in hopes that order will not stand long.

You said you want to know what I got to eat. Well I get plenty of corn bread and loaf bread. I get 1 pou[n]d of bacon and 5 pounds of fresh beef per week. A very scanty allowance of sald [salt] about one fourth enough sugar and molass[es], not a bit of coffee. A plenty of rice and pease [peas], no vegetables unless we buy them ourselves and they are so high that we cannot afford to buy them. Cabbage, very small, are 10 cts per head, beans and Irish potatoes 20 cts per quart. C[h]ickens large enough to fry are 50 cts. Common water mellons in Mobile are $1.50 each and a good sized one $4.00.

I was there last Tuesday and saw Elijah Sellers, Mr Pearson and Mr Nix.[191] Their time will be out this next Thursday. I put one quire of paper and a package of envelops in their hands for you. I want you to hold on to your money untill you are supplied with provisions for another year, except you may pay old Mr Porter 5 dollars.[192] Write whether you paid for your cow or not. If you[r] money does go down in value you can still pay debts at its full value if [it] is Confederate money and I would advis you not to take much of any other sort except our own state money.[193]

Give my love to all the neighbors and enquiring friends. S W Owens is in the hospital here very low with the fever.[194] We have a very good preacher here now but he is a Methodist. He preaches twice each Sunday and holds prayer meetings twice a week, Sunday and Wednesday nights.[195]

Malinda let those nights be especially devoted to prayer for my return home. For at those times I think most of you and the dear children. Learn them all you can. Kiss them for me and believe me your true loving husband, as ever,

Grant Taylor

---

191 Elijah Sellers, Pearson, and Nix (all of 36th AL).

192 Perhaps D. Porter, age 73 in the 1860 Greene County, Alabama census.

193 As early as 1862, the South was being flooded with Confederate money that declined in value. See McPherson, *Battle Cry of Freedom*, 438-439.

194 Private Starling W. Owens (Co A 40th AL) from whom Grant bought land in November 1854.

195 Josiah Barker of Co F served as the 40th Alabama's chaplain.

PS I saw old Mrs Hatchett in Mobile the other day. Also, Ann.[196] They are low down in the world. Write to me if you get all my letters. I write every week. Do you do the same?

21

June the 22 1862

Dear and beloved husband,

I am permitted tonight to drop you a few lines. I recieved a letter from you yesterday stating that you had got your pants. I was sory to hear that you was not well. I had rather you would keep well there than to come home sick. We air in reasonable health. I do pray these lines may finde you well. Mee and Buddy has bin to Prayer meating this evening at Mrs Sellars.[197] Thare was some eloquent Prayers put up in behalf of the soldiers.

I heard this evning that Thomas Cobb saw you as he was going down.[198] Oh Grant how I want to see you. God only knows. Sometimes I feel like I cant stand it and then I will cher up with the thought of the pleasure it will bee to me when I see you. I dream of you nearly evry night coming home but I dont feel disappointed when I awoke.

I heard a letter read from John Mahaffy.[199] He stated he only got one small piece of bread and a small piece of beef once a day. He has bin in a big battle at Ritchmon.[200] Grant, Ruthy Barton died Fridy night.[201] I never herd what was the matter.

This is Monday morning. We air in tolalerable good spirits this morning. I heard yesterday that all the states had gon back into

---

[196] Mrs. Hatchett and Ann are unidentified.
[197] Nancy Jane Drummond Sellers.
[198] Thomas W. Cobb (1844-1911), perhaps Co G 5th AL Cavalry.
[199] John H. Mahaffey (Co C 11th AL).
[200] Probably a reference to the Mar 31-June 1, 1862 battle of Seven Pines fought near Richmond VA. See Long, *Civil War Day by Day*, 218-220.
[201] Ruth Barton (born 1843), probably daughter of Elias and Catherine Barton.

the Union but I don't know how true it is. I sent to Union and got a dolars worth of paper and envelops.[202] It is not very good as you see. We air don plowing the new ground. I had plenty peas to so [sow] it and Rachel, Mr Rily and Thomas is hoing it.[203] When it rains I will plow the Corn at home again and then I will bee done laying by. The big men in Tuscaloosa says — weeks dry wether now will bring peace. Grant I am willing for peace on any turmes. I had rather live on bread or meat by itself than to live the way I am living.

I am going to Fathers the latter part of this week.[204] Oh how I wish you was her[e] to go with me. It wont bee mutch pleashure to me to go over thare without you. Next Wednesday will be 11 weeks since you left home. Can it bee posable you will have to stay 11 more weeks. I pray not.

Grant when you get this, if you think a letter will meet [reach] me at Pleasant Grove by the 5 or 6 of July direct it thare.[205] Mr Rily eats at your place. When little Mary wants anything she will say pa I want more coffee or anything els. It makes me so sorry for her. She calls evry man Pa. When she sees your likeness she will say I want kiss a Pa. All this is trying on my feelings. I will send you a little lock of her hair for you to look at. Mr Norris was to see me Saturday evening how I came on.[206] He said he would bee shot before night iff it would bring peace in our land.

So I must close. I remain your unworthy wife until death,

Malinda J Taylor

---

[202] Union, a small community in Greene County, Alabama.
[203] Rachel, a hired black; James Riley; Thomas is unidentified.
[204] Wiley S. Slaughter, Malinda's father.
[205] Pleasant Grove, a small community in Tuscaloosa County, Alabama.
[206] Probably Wilson Norris.

22

Dog River Factory

June 27th 1862

Dear wife and children,

I seat myself this morning to answer your loving letter of June 22nd which came to hand yesterday. I wrote to you on the same day but as you requested me to meet you at the Grove by letter I will start this. It leaves me in fine health and I hope that it may reach you and the dear children enjoying the same blessing. I was uneasy about little Matthew until I received it as you wrote in your other letter that he was sick.

I wrote in my last that you might make me some jeans but you need not be in a hurry about it for the government has forced a heavy coat and pants on us for a uniform instead of paying us our 25 dollars for clothing and I do not expect we will get anything for the clothing and blankets that we have furnished. You can make the cloth at your leisure and if I do not need it you can put it to some other use. You may make me some shirts and drawers and have them ready. I shall need them or the shirts at least between this and winter if I have to stay here so long. But I do not know of any chance I will have to get them from there for as I wrote to you in the last two letters they have stopped furloughing only in extreme cases and that almost entirely among the officers. I hope that order will not stand always but God only knows.

I wrote to you in my last what we got to eat but provisions are getting scarcer. This week we had scarcely anything some days but corn bread and soup made by boiling ham bones and thickened with meal. But now we are getting tolerably plenty again. I believe we will suffer before the end of the year. They have not suffered much for rain here yet.

I think sickness is diminishing here. I do not know of any deaths since last Tuesday. James Love died that day. He was brother of Josh Pate's wife and Josh died the Tuesday before as I wrote to you. S W Owens is very low and from what I can learn it is a dangerous case. I did not see Thomas Cobb on his way down here but I went to see him in their camp between here and Mobile. We are nearly South of Mobile and they were encamped between here and there. His Reg. is gone to Chatanooga Tennessee. I think they started yesterday.

I put one quire of paper and pack of envelops in the hands of Mr Nix to carry to you. I expect they will start home today as I wrote to you. I saw him and Sellers and Pearson last week in Mobile. I could not find Elijah when I went to start or I would have given them to him. But you will get them anyway before you need them. I gave $1.50 for the paper and 60 cts for envelops.

I met up with Lige Kinny in our camps here the other day. He lives in Mobile and came out here to se[e] Jo Lancaster.[207] He looks quite natural.

We have pretty hard times here this week. We have to start at 3 o'clock and march over two miles and drill till after sundown dressed up with our coats buttoned around us. The heat is very severe on us. There are five Reg. meet there. It is a fine sight. I saw General Beauregard there the other day.[208]

Malinda nothing has stirred the deeps fountains of my soul so much since I left home as the sight of that precious little lock of hair. Oh how natural it looked only longer than when I saw it last. My eyes are swimming in tears as I wright this at the thought of the distance between me and that dear sweet little creature and the impossibility of my seeing her soon if ever in this life. I thought I loved you all before I left you but I never knew half the depth of my love till I had to be torn away from you all. But my trust is in God that he will not let me die before I see you all once more.

You seemed to be more dejected when you last wrote than usual but dearest wife cheer up. God doeth all things right. And then we have a blessed hope that if we never meet again on earth we will meet in that Glorious home above. Where there will be no more wars and partings and sighings but where it will be one bright Summer always & storms do never come. So take courage and do not forget to pray.

---

[207] Private Joseph Lancaster (Co B 40th AL).

[208] On June 25, 1862, General P. G. T. Beauregard reviewed the 40th, 32nd, 38th Alabama, 3rd and 4th Florida, and the 27th Mississippi. See Willett, *History of Company B*, 9.

I have named it to my officers about putting Ky in my place but they have given me no answer yet. I do not think they will have him from the fact that he was rejected in his own place. Give my best love to all inquiring friends. Alwa[y]s read my letters to the children and tell them that I write to them too whenever I write to you. So no more at present from your loving Husband,

Grant Taylor

PS When you back [address] your letter to me back them in this form
Mr Grant Taylor
Co. F. 40th Ala. Reg.
Mobile Ala.

Keep this as a model. If I move from here all you will have to change in the backing will be to put the name of the [post] office and state in the place of Mobile Ala. I am as well satisfied as could be expected. I would be willing if you are to give my land for a substitute to take my place for my term of service. I want you to talk to old Rily and see if he would be willing to come for that. Be sure to do so.

23

July the 5 1862

Dear husband,

I am now seated to pen you a few lines. I am well at presant and hoping you air the same. I am now in camps at Tusk. Mee, Mary and Elizar came her[e] last Thursday.[209] Jack came with us.[210]

---

[209] Mary Slaughter Parker and Eliza Slaughter Parker, Malinda's sisters.
[210] Andrew J. Slaughter, Malinda's brother.

I read the letter that Mr Peebles braught to Jack.[211] I was glad to hear from you. I left word at Cushing for my next letter to be sent to Pleasant grove. I will get them tomorrow.[212]

Grant I have had awful feelings since I have been her[e]. I have met with a heep of friendes and acquaintence but I could not meet you. I cant tell you anything about my feelings. Grant you must excuse my short letter. We are going back this morning. I left the 3 boys with mother. When I came over I found Father very poorly with rumatism in his hips.

So I must quit,

Malinda J Taylor

---

211 Mr. Peebles is unidentified.

212 Cushing, a small community now called Ralph, in Tuscaloosa County. Pleasant Grove in Tuscaloosa County.

Chapter 2

I Would Give My Land for a Substitute

After the first few months the novelty of military life had all but worn off. Both Grant and Malinda were desperate for him to return home. They wrote extensively to each other about a substitute and worked feverishly to recruit one.

24

Cantonment Walter

July 7th 1862

Dear Wife & Children,

I seat myself this evening to drop you a few lines. I am very well and feel quite comfortable after dining on corn bread and water. We do not get half enough to eat of nothing except bread and pickled beef and we cannot eat the beef to do any good. I tell you it is tight times for me to come down to such fare but I keep my spirits up finely with the hope that it will not be so always and with the knowledge that you and my dear children have plenty. I can bear almost anything for myself as long as I know you are provided for. I do hope that you are all well and doing well.

The health of Reg. is getting better since the measels passed through but the mumps are spreading now pretty fast. We were all marched to Mobile on the 4th and paraded through the streets. There were seven Reg. met there besides a goodly number of cavalry and artillery. It was a grand sight, but not a very pleasant one. The heat was so oppressive.[1] I see in this morning's paper that France has acknowledged the independence of the Confederate States. I hope it may be so. The papers also states that our forces have gained a great victory at Richmond. They had fought eight days at last accounts and the enemy had been cut of[f] from their gunboats and they had burnt all their military stores and were retreating. It was thought that nearly the whole army would be captured.[2]

I started a letter to meet you at Pleasant Grove. It started the 27th June. I hope you got it. I wrote to you about your cows some time ago. I do not want you to take less than one hundred dollars in cash for the oxen. You need not try to sell my cotton as you cannot get near what it will be worth next winter.

I wrote to you in my last that I would give my land for a substitute if you were willing and for you to see old Rily and see if he will come for that.[3] If he will not come for that I will give him in addition to the land 50 dollars each year to help support his family. But do not offer the $50 extra untill he refuses to come for the land.

Dear Malinda I got the letter containing that sweet lock of hair. Oh how I yearn to press the sweet head it grew on to my aching heart. I cannot bear to study about home no more than I can help. But I pray to my dear Savior and toil on with the hope that I shall one day be permitted to meet you all on earth and I firmly hope that we shall one day meet in heaven where we shall enjoy each other's society through the never ending ages of a blessed immortality. There is quite an interesting prayer meeting and sometimes preaching going on in camps here almost every other night. Quite a number present themselves for prayer whenever an opportunity is offered. The Chaplain of the Regiment is a

---

[1] General John H. Forney reviewed all the troops in his Mobile army on that date despite the heat. See Elbert D. Willett, *History of Company B, 40th Alabama Regiment, Confederate States Army 1862 to 1865* (Montgomery, AL: Viewpoint Publications, 1963) 9.

[2] During the Seven Days battles around Richmond (June 25-July 1, 1862), Robert E. Lee defeated George B. McClellan's Army of the Potomac and forced its retreat. See Stephen W. Sears, *To the Gates of Richmond: The Peninsula Campaign* (New York: Tickner and Fields, 1992) 179-336.

[3] James Riley.

Methodist though an interesting preacher and seems to be much devoted.

Tell Rachel and Henry howdy for me.[4] Give my best love to all enquiring friends. Pray for your absent one and believe your loving distant husband.

Enclosed I send the 3 boys thumbpapers.[5] Farewell for the present.

To Mrs M J Taylor [from] Grant Taylor

I want to get a letter from you very badly as it has been ten days since I got one.

25

Ala Tusk

July the 13th 1862

Dear and affectionate husband,

I am again permitted to pen you a few lines. I am at Cousan Elcys Anns on my way home.[6] I aimd to go home last Sunday but on that day Mathew got snake bit. He has never walked a step since. Grant I cannot tell you what he suffered. His leg and thigh, groin is perfectly black. It bit him on the top of the foot. Dont bee uneasy about him. He dont suffer any now. He is mending very fast. Father sent him her[e] in his buggy. Negro John will carry him home on a pillow.[7] Grant you dont know how I felt when I did not know wether he would live or no, and to think whare you was.

---

[4] Rachel worked for the Taylors and Henry worked at Wilkerson's Mill.

[5] A thumbpaper is probably a flipbook of drawings that shows motion when fanned.

[6] Alsey Ann Taylor, Grant's cousin.

[7] "Negro John" is unidentified.

I recieved your letter today. It came to the [post] office the 5th but cousan Elizar Jane was at the office and took it out for me.[8] So I never got it until today. Grant, Teral Speed was braught home a Corpse last Tuseday and was beried at Mitchels.[9] Crouse Garner was also brought home today was 2 weeks ago. Young Jerarde Grigry died this morning. You have herd of George Davises deth.[10]

Wright to me what colar to mak your clothes. I rote to you of my being in camps. While I was thare me and Wat closed the war that was between us.[11] You dont know how mutch happier I feel about it. I wrote Mary a letter some time ago and tolde her to tell him that we could close the war that was betwe[en] us.[12] So she gave the letter to him and John said he cried like a childe over it.[13] I went to him and told him I wanted to speak to him before we diede. He appeard to bee perfectly friendly with me.

Grant it is thought that peace will bee made in the corse of 2 months. Oh how fervently I pray for it.

Old Rily was talking of going in your place for a month. He wanted me to hire him. He never said what he would take. I am willing to give the land, houses and all if he would go.

I saw Mr B Peebles this morning.[14] He sends his love and respects to you. The Regiment at Tusk will start to Merion next week on the account of provision.[15] They get barely enough to eat. John, Jake and Wat came home last Tuseday and went back Friday.[16] All can come but you. I had rather do without seeing you than to ever part with you again.

---

[8] Eliza Jane Taylor Campbell, Grant's cousin.

[9] William Terrell Speed (Co C 2nd AL Cavalry) died on July 4, 1862, at Bluff Springs, Florida. Mitchell's Cemetery is located in S18 T22S R13W in Pickens County. Terrell was buried without a marker.

[10] Crouse Garner and Gerard Gregory are unidentified. George Davis was Grant's nephew.

[11] Walter Slaughter, Malinda's brother.

[12] Mary Slaughter Parker, Malinda's sister.

[13] John Parker, Malinda's brother-in-law.

[14] Probably William Battle Peebles (Co D 8th Confederate).

[15] Marion in nearby Perry County, south of Tuscaloosa.

[16] John Parker, Jacob Parker, and Walter Slaughter.

Cousan Mary sendes her respects to you.[17] I was at Zion yesterday.[18] Mr Briant preached a great sermon.[19] Pap thinks there will bee peace in 60 days. You know he is a proffit.

Grant they air offering from 11 to 17 cents for cotton.

George Stewart wright[s] that peace is bruing fast as it can. I feel like peace will bee made soon. I want you to pray with all your heart to God that he may bring peace to our distress land. I herd Mr Falls read in a late paper that some big man I have forgot his name said that he knew something and if the South knew it it would cause a shoute all over the Sothern states.[20] The man said he believed evry soldier that was encamped on the fielde would bee permited to return to thir peaceful homes in 30 days. God grant it, I pray is my humble prayer.

Morning sends her love to you.[21] I am wrighting by candle light so I must close. Give my love to Ide. Tell him to pray for me. Grant my faith in God is strong. I believe he is working for our good. So I remain your lonely wife and humble Christian.

Malinda Taylor

Cousan Elcyan sendes her love to you.

26

Cantonment Walter

July 14th 1862

Dear Wife and children,

Gladly do I avail myself of the present hour to pen you a few lines. This leaves me in fine health for which I thank my God and I do hope that these few lines may reach you and the dear children

---

[17] Mary Taylor, daughter of Alsey Ann Taylor.

[18] Zion Church in S22 T22 R13W now in Greene County.

[19] Rev. Briant (Bryant?) is unidentified.

[20] Thomas W. Falls.

[21] Mourning Taylor, Grant's niece.

enjoying the best of health. I received your little letter from Tusk for which I was thankful, but was somewhat disappointed, for I had not received one from you before in over two weeks and when it came it was so short. But I can excuse it. I wrote to you the 29th June and directed it to Pleasant Grove and I wrote to you since then. When you write always state the date of the letters you get from me and then I will know more how to write to you.

I have but verry little camp news to write. Sickness is increasing in camps. Several cases of fever now in the hospital. Wiley Horton is in there.[22] He has been quite sick, but I think he is a little better. Lafayette Mullins came back the other day but he is quite poorly yet.[23] Ide is well.

There is talk of moving us nearer Mobile. But I hope it is not the case. I fear though that we will be ordered to Tennessee or Virginia before I get to come home. They furloughed two of our men yesterday and it is thought by some that they will furlough two at a time for ten days regularly. But they are going to take our name[s] alphabetically and my name beginning with a T will put my time a long way off. I want to see you mighty bad but there is no chance yet. I pray [to] God for the time to come soon.

I wrote to you in my last that we were suffering for something to eat as we had to live over half our time on bread. But they are feeding us a little better this week. We get bacon 4 days out of seven and beef the other three. We get plenty of corn meal and loaf bread and rice, and but a small allowa[n]ce of sugar and molasses. That is what we get to eat this week.

Do not sell my steers for less than $100. I wrote for you to see old Riley and offer him my land to take my place and if he would not do that offer him fifty dollars a year extra. The first fifty to be paid to his wife as soon as I get home. He will also draw his pay from the Government in addition to the above. If he will agree to come write to me immediately. I will pay his expenses down here of course. If you failed to get my other letters with the above in it go to see him as soon as you get this and let me know what I may depend upon, but I do not expect he will do it.

---

[22] James Wiley Horton (Co B 40th AL).
[23] Hugh Lafayette Mullins, Grant's nephew.

Malinda I wrote to you some time ago for us to pray every Wednesday and Sunday night especially for my return home. Well last night I went to prayer meeting and oh how earnestly I prayed for that thing. I feel like God will answer our prayers.

We have a considerable revival going on here among the soldiers. Quite a number presented themselves last night for prayer. Several have professed since the meeting commenced. It is held every other night and on Sundays, our duties preventing us from assembling oftener. Oh Malinda you do not know how my poor heart is revived. Sometimes I get almost shouting happy. And then I feel that I have such a humble reliance on my blessed Savior. I never felt so humble it seems to me in all my life.

I feel this morning that come sickness, sorrow, pain or death, I can trust my all in the hands of my dear savior. Oh how I long to be with you that you might participate in my joys. It is said that in camps is the place for one to backslide and become wicked. But I have not found it so thus far. But rather it is the most befitting place to inspire solemnity than any place I was ever in. For here you see nearly all the miseries that the world is heir to in miniature and how can a man be so callous so hard hearted as to not feel solemn and naturally turn his thoughts to higher and purer things than earth affords for pleasures to satisfy the cravings of an immortal mind. But there are some here that seem determined to heap up wrath against the day wrath. Malinda still continue to pray for me. Never cease praying.

I shall soon need my shirts and shoes and socks for my shirts are beginning to break now and all my socks are in holes. But I do not know any chance to get them yet. In fact, I shall not need them under a month or so yet.

I wrote to you that they had forced a heavy uniform on us. You need not be in any hurry about making any jeans for me. You m[a]y make it between now and winter. Maybe I will need it then, if not you can sell it. Instead of making it a dark grey make it a light grey. That is if you have not commenced it. But if you have commenced making it a dark grey you can continue to make it of that coler.

I received that sweet little lock of hair. Oh how sweet and natural it looked only longer. How I want to see her and all of you.

I have given directions several times how to direct your letters. It is not worth while to do it in this.

May God bless and protect you all is the prayer of your humbled loving Soldier husband,

Grant Taylor

PS Kiss the children for me and call it Pa's kiss and tell them that Pa wants to see them mighty bad, that he studies a heap about them and prays to the good man to bless them and make them good children. Encourage them to learn their books. I sent you a quire of paper and pack of envelopes by Mr. Nix some time ago. Hope you have got them. I now send you two rings that one of our men made. Wear them to remember me.

27

Ala Tusk

July 19ᵗʰ 1862

Dear and beloved husband,

By the goodness of God I am permitted to pen you a few lines on[c]e more. We air not very well. My jaw is trying to rise. Mathew is stil on the mend. He can walk but cant straiten his leg. I hope these lines may finde you well. How it chears me up to hear you air well. I got your letter of July the 14ᵗʰ last Thursday, written on Monday, that is pretty strait news. I also got one last Tuseday July the 7 stating you was living on cornbread. Grant it was the most distressing letter I ever got from you. Little Leonard cried like his heart would breake to think you was living on bread. We all took a good cry abought it. But the last letter was the most chering one I ever got from you. It was all I could do to keep from holl[er]ing while I was reading it. I pray for you daily, for your health and for your return home. I pray with all the faith I have. I believe God will answer our prayers when we pray believing.

Grant thare is no chance for Rily to come in your place. Thare is 1 or 2 after him evry day. I went to see him last Monday. He said he could not tell then so I went this morning again and who should I finde thare but old John Crim.[24] I was very mutch supprised to see him thare. He was trying to hire Rily to go in some mans place. So it is not worth while for me to try any more. He said when he went it would bee in his own place. He would liv on bread the rest of his days before he would try to do any better, that is my notion. Grant almost evry one says tha [they] would not do it if tha was you. That peace will bee made soon. To holde on a little while yet. I would freely give all we posess for a substitute to take your place.

The People are dying her[e] very fast. Dave Brooks is dead.[25] In a few days after he died his wife misscaried and died in a few days.[26] Jeff Night was wounded and diede. Henry Lam was ciled [killed]. Neacy Jennings has got a fine bastard boy.[27] Dunny will have a calf in 2 weaks. I don't reckon Colvin will want her now.[28] One of the gilts has got 3 nice pigs, a month old. 2 more will have pigs in a few days.

I paid for my cow the day I got her. I also paid for our shoes but heritage cant get leather to make them.[29] Grant we have plenty of peaches and apples now but I have no appetite for them because you air not her[e] to help eat them. We air suffering for rain. If I could get one more rain I would make corn enough to do me. 4 weaks yesterday since we had any [rain].

I have got 13 letters from you.[30] I get them all. Thair was one her[e] for me when I got home from Fathers. I got the one that you sent to Pleasant Grove as I rote to you in my last. My jaw aches like it would burst so I must quit for this evening.

---

[24] Probably John Crimm (born c1814) of Pickens County.

[25] David S. Brooks (Co F 41st AL) died Jun 1862.

[26] Lucy S. Hagood married David Brooks on December 4, 1854 in Greene County, Alabama.

[27] Jeff Knight, Henry Lamb, and Neacy Jennings are unidentified.

[28] Hiram Colvin (1831-1887).

[29] Henry Heritage (Co G 40th AL).

[30] All 13 letters are extant in this collection.

This is Monday Morning the 21. I feel better this morning. My jaw got easy some time las night for the first time since Friday. It is swelled very bad. Mary Ritchey diede yesterday about 11 o'c.[31]

Grant I want to see you. God only knows how bad. I dream of you coming home almost evry night. What joy thair will bee when you come. Grant how it revives me to hear that you enjoy religion so well. Last night I was in so mutch misery with my jaw that I forgot to Pray for you. When I awoke this morning I thought of it. I felt ashamb of it but I asked God to forgave me.

I believe little Mary would know you. Evry time we sit down to the table she says poor Pa wants dinner. If I ask her whare Pa is she will say "gon down to the field." Grant content yourself if you can. All this is for our good. It has done me good alredy. It has made me humble enough to do any thing that is right.

I had no idie that little lock of hair would [have] such an effect on you. Grant, you dont know the company She is to me. She stays in the house with me all the time. I must close for this time and when you come I will tell you all. So I remain your obedient Praying wife until death.

Malinda J Taylor

28

Near Mobile

July 22nd 1862

Dear wife and children,

I seat myself this morning to pen you a few lines in answer to your loving letter of July 13th written at cousin Elsy Ann's. I was mighty glad to get it for with the exception of that little note from Tusk I had not received one from you in nearly 4 weeks and oh how anxiously I awaited one from you.

---

[31] Mary A. Richey (1831-1862) was buried at Beulah Cemetery.

I am very sorry that sweet little Matthew got bit by that snake but I hope it will not injure him.

I am well except cold. I have had a very bad cold for several days. I hope you and the children are enjoying the best of health.

We moved in about 2 miles of Mobile yesterday.[32] I like our new encampment very well, but I fear we will be moved nearer the city and made to guard it. 2 Reg. are to leave here today for Chattanooga in Tennessee and it is believed that we will have to go there shortly but none of us know anything about it.

I wrote to you in my last to make my jeans a light grey but befor that I wrote for it to be dark grey. I still want it a light grey. But you need not be in a hurry about making for they have forced a heavy coarse suit of stuff on us and I shall not want yours before fall. I will soon need shirts, shoes and socks but I do not know how to get them unless you could take them over to Jack's or Mullins's and maybe they could send them to me. If we get to stay here I think several of our men will get to go home. But the captain takes their names alphabetically and it will be a long time before it reaches me.

As for hiring a substitute for a month, they will not give leave of absence for so long a time and then I cannot afford to pay what it would cost me for a shorter time. For by the time that I paid his expenses down here and back and his wages and my own [way] home it would cost fifty dollars and it would cost nearly as much for ten days as it would for 30 for the expenses in traveling would be the same.

I feel that I shall one day be permitted to return home. I am getting mighty tired of this way of living, but ought not to grumble for I believe that it is for our good. Maybe we did not tha[n]k God in our hearts enough for the pleasure and the happy days we lived together. I feel utterly humbled and feel my dependance on my blessed savior more than I ever did before. Oh those hapy days we enjoyed together will they never return. Yes, I believe they will and I am pretty certain of one thing that when we leave this troublesome world we shall meet in that glorious

---

[32] On July 21, 1862, the 40th Alabama moved to Camp Marshall Austell, one and a half miles from Mobile. See Willett, *History of Company B*, 10.

home above where parting will be known no more. Then why, my beloved wife, should we complain. We who have such a blessed eternity before us. May God bless and comfort you my dear one is the fervent prayer of your loving absent husband,

To Malinda. J. Taylor [from] Grant Taylor

Do not direct your letters to Company F as the letter of our company has been changed. Direct it to Mr Grant Taylor, care of Capt T O Stone, 40ᵗʰ Ala Regt, Mobile, Ala.[33]

P.S. I hear mighty distressing news from Pickens [County] about rain. How is it with you. You have not mentioned it in none of your letters. Lafayette Mullins returned to camps some 10 days ago but very feeble. He is now in the hospital at our old encampment but he is not much sick only too feeble to bear moving about. Ide is well and sends his best respects to you. Give my best respects to all enquiring friends and Brother Smith especially. You stated that Crouse Garner was brought home. Was he dead?

G. Taylor

Do your best to get a substitute for my whole term of service and let me know the result soon for if I get one it must be done before we leave here. I am in hopes that we will stay here all summer. It is not so hot here as you might think. There is almost always a brisk breeze stirring here. Our company has but three in the hospital and but one of them much sick. S W Owens is getting well. He has been down nearly six weeks.

---

[33] Thomas Oswald Stone (1834-1864).

29

Ala Tusk

July 27 1862

Dear distant husband,

I am again permitted to pen you a few lines. We air all well
and I hope these lines may finde you well. I mist [missed] getting
a letter from you last week. This makes too [two] I have written
since I got one. I havent mutch to write this time.

Grant it is Suffrony Barton that is dead instead of Ruthy.[34] Jack,
Sally and Elizar spent the day withe me last Friday.[35] Jack is at
home on a ferlow. I spent the day at Mr Salmons today.[36] We air
kneding rain very bad. My Corn looks abought as well as any I
have seen. Down on Brush Creek they air making nothing at all.

Mr Ritcherson is going to carry my wool to the factory next
Tuseday.[37] If I knew you would not kneed the jeanes, I rather
make plain cloth for the children.

If they air giving furloughs in the way you wrote try to swap
names with some of them for fear you air ordered to some other
place. The children air laying up apples for you now. I dont allow
my hopes to bee bilt up on any thing I hear these days. I
understand the soldiers can all come home provided they will go
for regulars for 5 years after this war closes. I had rather you would
stay during this than to go for 5 years afterwards. George Robuck
is at home for the first time since he left home.[38]

I want you to go beg like a prety boy for a ferlow. I dremed the
other night that you had come home and I thought we were lying
together talking. Oh how happy I thought I was and at that
moment I was awoked by one of my dogagues.[39] How
disappointed I felt to think you allways had bin her[e] to help

---

[34] Suffrony (b. c1897) and Ruth (b. c1843) are probably daughters of
Elias and Catherine Barton.
[35] Jack and Sally Leatherwood and Eliza Slaughter Parker.
[36] William Salmon.
[37] Mr. Richardson is unidentified.
[38] George N. Roebuck (born c1840).
[39] An ague was a fever followed by a chill.

warm me up. I had then to ly thar and shiver it out by myself. What awful feelings I had. Try your utmoste for a ferlow.

You said for me to encourage the boys to learn thair books. They kneed no encouragement. They air after me with thir booke constant[ly]. I learn them all I can. I shal look for a letter Tuseday.

I have 8 prety little pigs now and will have some more in a day or 2. I think the old sow is dried up. I thought after a while I would have the old sow and 3 of the white sho[a]tes spaid. I saw Mr Nix and Mr Percon and Mr Selars.[40] I asked them if you was very mutch dissatisfide. They said you was in good spirits as anybody they had seen. Grant evry body inquires about you. All ways at the next word after howdy is when did you get a letter from Mr. Taylor. I got my paper and envellops that you sent me.

Giv my love to Ide and Lafait and take a full portion yourself.[41] And believe your loving wife until death,

Malinda Taylor

30

Camp Marshal Austin[42] near Mobile

July 30th 1862

Beloved wife & children,

Through the mercies of a kind providence I am once more permitted to pen you a few lines. I received your affectionate letter of July 19 and 21st last Friday the 25th which gave me great pleasure to hear from you, but sorrow to hear of your suffering with your jaw. I am not so well as I have been. I was taken night before last with fever and yester morning with diarreah. They both held on to me until last night. I was quite sick all day yesterday but I feel tolerably well today only I am weak. I think if

---

[40] Elijah Sellers, Nix, and Pearson (all of the 36th Al).

[41] Iredell Teer and Hugh Lafayette Mullins.

[42] Camp Marshall Austell.

I can get a day or two of rest I will be all right. I have enjoyed fine health for some time past and 10 days ago I was heavier than I ever was at this season of the year. Yesterday was my day to write to you but I did not feel able but do not feel uneasy about me. I feel that whether I live or die I shall be well. It is true I want to see you all very bad if it is God's will and I believe I will one day see you on earth, but not my will but God's be done.

As I wrote to you in my last we have moved nearer Mobile and a pretty hard time we have of it now. For it takes half the well men in the Reg. to guard the city, one half goes one day and night and the other half the other day. So you see we have to stand guard every other day which is hard times.

There are a great many soldiers passing through here from Tupelo Miss to Chattanooga Tenn. or to Richmond Va.[43] The company that Emmy Teer belongs to passed through to-day.[44] But as I did not see them I do not know whether he and lab were along or not.[45]

Old Squire Horton is down here waiting for Wiley to die or get able to go home.[46] Wiley is very low and has been for some time but thought to be on the mend. Lafayette Mullins has not been able to do any thing since he came back and I do not think ever will be of any service in the army. He has a disease of the heart and the doctors dont seem to do him any good. He is in the hospital in Mobile. I do not know how many this Reg. has sick as they are scattered over the city in different hospitals. Our company has only four there but there are some 20 puny ones in camps.

I got a letter from Wick & Emmaline last week.[47] They were in tolerable health. Hughs was not very well.[48]

---

[43] These troops were part of a large movement of Confederate troops from Mississippi to Chattanooga via Mobile to reinforce General Braxton Bragg's planned advance northward to Kentucky. See James M. McPherson, *Battle Cry of Freedom: The Civil War Era* (New York: Oxford University Press, 1988) 516.

[44] Amaziah Hughes Teer (c1841-1863).

[45] Albert "Lab" Iredell Teer (c1844-1889).

[46] Squire Horton, father of James Wiley Horton (Co B 42nd AL).

[47] William M. Taylor, Grant's brother, and his wife Mary Emmaline Gammill.

[48] James Hughes Taylor, Grant's brother.

Have four of your gilts and the old sow spaid this fall if you can. If you do not you will not have any meat. Get Elijah Sellers to do it. I recon he has come home before now.

I saw pork selling in the market last Saturday at 35 cents per pound. Coffee is $2 per pound and coarse domestic [cloth] 50 cents per yard, calico 75 cents and everything else in proportion. Flour is 32 dollars per barrel, bacon 60 cents per pound by the retail. A decent pair of soldiers shoes are 20 dollars per pair. Water mellons that will weigh ten lbs [$]1.50 cents and a large size sometimes as high as five dollars. These prices look fabulous but I know them to be so. Tobacco that is fit to chew is from $1.25 to $1.50 per lb. I am nearly out of money but I hope we will be paid soon.

I will soon need my shirts and shoes but I do not know how to get them. Perhaps if you could take them over to Jacks or Mullin's they might get a chance to send them. I think Kates brother John will get off on a furlough in a week or so and if he had them he would bring them to me.[49] They only furlough 2 at a time and then wait till they come back before furloughing any one else. That is two out of each company. And as the captain takes the names alphabetically it will be a long time before it reaches me, but I do not despair.

I sometimes hope that peace will be made shortly or at least I pray that it may cheer up my dear wife. Remember that though we may never meet on earth again we have that hope that [we] will meet on the bank of sweet deliverance.

Kiss the dear sweet children for me. Teach them to pray and tell them that Pa often thinks of them and prays for them and sheds tears for them. Oh I never knew half how good I loved them and you until I was separated from. I want to see you all so bad but I do not pine.

I took dinner at Elijah Kinneys last Monday.[50] He lives a half mile from our camps. God bless you all is the prayer of [your] loving husband and father,

Grant Taylor

---

[49] John (surname unknown), brother of Catherine (who is married to Andrew Slaughter).

[50] Elijah Kinney is unidentified.

I often dream of seeing you and the children and how glad I feel. I have just read nearly all of your letters and I could not help shedding tears over some of them. God bless you.

31

Camp Marshal Austin near Mobile

Aug 1st 1862

Dear Wife and children,

I seat myself this evening to drop you a few lines. I wrote to you day before yesterday but as I was not well then and as I received your loving letter, written last Sunday yesterday I thought I would write you again lest you be uneasy. I have got well again and I hope you and the children are enjoying the best of health. I was glad I got your letter as I always am. As to my jeans I shall not need any this winter unless I lose what I have except a pair of pants and you can make them strong plain cloth if you had rather.

As to swaping time with anyone to let me come home that is impossible for all want to come home as bad as I do. I believe that if I had a substitute here I could get to come home for twenty [days] if not more, but if you are not making corn enough we can not pay what it will cost. But if you see old Riley ask him what he would come a month [for]. If you can get any one for 15 or twenty dollars. Write to me if you think you can stand to pay at least fifty dollars to see me. I have written to Wick and offered him that note to come a month in my place so by the time I hear from you I shall have heard from him.

Lafayette has been taken about 5 miles from Mobile to a hospital. I do not think he will do any good here. He has a disease of the heart.

I want you to dry as many peaches as you can. If I should get to come home I want some to bring back with me. If I can not come to see you, could not you come to see me this fall. If I stay here maybe you could get Jack to come with you.[51] But do not try to come unless I write for you. I want to see you mighty bad but then if you should come I could not see the children and that would nearly kill some of them. May God watch over us for good is the prayer of your loving husband and father,

To M J Taylor [from] Grant Taylor

PS Excus bad writing as I have to write on my knee seated on my pallet. I hope you can read it. Instead of directing your letters to Company F direct this way Mr Grant Taylor, care of Capt T O Stone, 40th Ala Reg, Mobile, Ala. The letter of our company is changed from F to G. Ide is well and sends his best love and wishes to you. I had nothing to write but I see that I have nearly filled out my sheet. May God bless you. Goodby dear ones.

G. Taylor

Try Jim Jacobs.[52] See if he will come for 15 dollars if he is about there.

32

Ala Tus Co

August 5th 1862

Dear and mutch beloved husband,

I am again seated to pen you a few lines. We air all well hoping these lines may reach you in fine health. I recieved 2 letters from you yesterday for the first in nearly 3 weeks. God only knows how glad I was. One was July the 22 and the other the 30. It almost kills me to hear of you beeing sick.

Grant I write these lines with a sad heart. Old Rily has backed rite square out from taking your place. Last Thursday Leatherwood

---

[51] Andrew J. Slaughter, Malinda's brother.
[52] Jim Jacobs is unidentified.

and Noris and Rily and his wife came her[e] and fixed it all up and he was to start next Sunday.[53] I wil send you what he was to go for. Old Miles wrote it down. I was to help get his cloths so I rode all day yesterday trying to get cloth. I got 2 shirts, 1 pair pants, 2 pair drawers and took them up thare this evening. One of his children was sick. If it had not bin for that I would give him just what I thought of him. I wish he had to eat dry bread the balence of his days. But try to think it as all for the best. You might get to come home and then we would have all we have got. God says all things works together for good to them that loves God. I gave Hirum Colvin back his money for them cows to help make the trade between me and Rily.[54]

Grant, Crouse Garner was brought home a corpse. He picked out the text he wanted his funeral preached from, it was Prepare to meet thy God. Milly Bounds is dead.[55] She died with pneumony. Little Jim Fra[n]klin deserted and came home and is now scouting abought.[56]

I had a very good rain last Friday and 2 nice showers since. Grant try to bee contented. I felt yesterday evening like I had rather bee dead than alive. I cried and prayed all the way home. I prayed more earnest than I ever did in my life. This morning I feel very well reckonciled. Grant continue to pray for peace that is what I want now. Tell Ide to pray for me and for peace.

Wright to me if you think it would bee prudent for me to try to come to see you. Cay Taylor wood [would] go with me anytime.[57] I could leave my children thare. I will do it iff you air willing. I am very ancious to go.

I read a letter from Sally Taylor last Monday. Her and Gilbert has got relegion. Gilbert is in the army.[58] Tell Wick and Emaline to wright to me.

---

[53] Miles Leatherwood; probably Wilson Norris; James Riley and his wife Sarah.

[54] Hiram Colvin (1831-1887).

[55] Milly Bounds (c1841-1862), wife of Daniel T. Bounds.

[56] James D. Franklin (Co F 41st AL).

[57] Rufus "Kay" Taylor, Grant's cousin.

[58] Gilbert Taylor, Grant's nephew, married Sarah Stewart in 1856 in Greene County.

Jack Leatherwood has just left hear. He says Co Newton tolde him in Tuskloosa last Monday that it was a bad trade that me and Rily had made.[59] He said all the men from 18 to 50 would bee cald [called] out before a month. They were going to pass a law to that effect and that substitutes would not clear a man.[60] There has been 30 thousand past through Tuscaloosa lately.

Rachel is breaking up the turnip patch this morning. I have driede some peaches and apples. I want to dry a heap more. I got my wool carded. It is a nice gray. I bought 2 shirts from Mrs Cartee ready made whitel, I will keep for you.[61] I bought them for Rily.

I must quit for Leonard is now on old Beck to go to the [post] office and to the mill. Farewell.

I remain your affectionate wife until death,

Malinda J Taylor

The following was the agreement for James Riley to serve as a substitute for Grant Taylor. It is in the handwriting of Miles Leatherwood. However, as seen, Riley changed his mind.

August 1 1862

This instrument is such that I James Riley doth agree to take Grant Taylor plaise [place] as a substitute in the Confedreat war for the term of 3 years or during the war for the sum of eight hundred dollars which is to be discharge in the following property, viz 160 acres land including the buildings with the crop of corne that is on this place at six hundred dollars.

---

[59] Co Newton is unidentified.

[60] The Confederate Congress dealt with the substitute system in August 1862 by making men who sent substitutes liable for conscription. See Albert B. Moore, *Conscription and Conflict in the Confederacy* (New York: MacMillan, 1924) 34-35.

[61] Sarah Caroline Cartee, wife of Joseph Cartee.

7 hed of cattle at 130 dollar
1 sow & pigs & 2 head killing hog
at 30 4 bee gums at 6 dollar
1 pr shooes at 4 dollar
   land   600.00
   cattle 130.00
   hogs   30.00
   bees   <u>6.00</u>
       766.00[62]

33

Camp Marshal Austin near Mobile

August 6th 1862

Dear Wife and Children,

I received your letter of July 29th yesterday. Well, if you can fix any way to pay Riley $800 you can send him on but do not pay him anything until he comes down here. He will have to come here to be examined by the doctor and it may be that he will not be received. My captain says he is willing to receive him if the doctor does. I would rather he would take all the land and less of the [live]stock, but make the best trade with him that you can. Have someone, Leatherwood if you can get him, to witness the trade and take down a list of what you are to give him with their prices annexed.

You can let him have one suit of clothes and I can let him have my uniform suite down here at a heap less than he will have to pay the government charged me as I have worn it some. You will also have to let him have fifteen dollars in money to pay his way

---

[62] Interestingly, the written agreement states the total value will be $800, but the numerical total is only $766. Even with the $4 for shoes added, the total would still only have been $770, making an unexplained difference of $30.

down here and mine back home if I am not paid off. Pay out as little money as you can help and try to keep enough [live]stock to live on next year. You had better get Leatherwood to price your things as he knows better what they are worth than you do.

He [Riley] will have to come here and be examined before I can know whether he will be received and I hereby pledge all that I possess to fulfill all you promise him when I come home for I will have to come home before I can make him a deed to the land. I will also give his family possession by the first of Jan. I say again make the best trade with him that you can. I will fulfill all when I come home. He can come to Gainsville and there take the railroad and when he gets to Mobile he can find his way to where the 40th Reg. which is near the new grave yard about 3 miles from the depot. Send him as soon as you can. Hiring him will ruin us but we are ruined anyhow. Two suits of clothes is a plenty for him to have and I can let him have my b[l]ankets at a reduced price.

I am not well. I have have the diarrhea for several days but I think I am better. I am still able to go about. I wrote two letters to you last week. I hope you and the children are well.

[Letter ends here without his usual closing.]

34

Camp Marshal Austin

August 8th '62

Dear Wife & Children,

I am seated again to drop you a few lines. I wrot to you day before yesterday giving you full directions how to hire Riley. I would say again try to get him to take all the land and less of the [live]stock. Try to keep enough to live on next year. Get Leatherwood to price the things if you can as he will know better what they are worth than you do. Get him to take down the articles and the price and I will comply ply [fully] with any contract you may make when I get home. For Riley will have to come down here to be examined and sworn in and I will have to be up there to make him a title to the land. You will have to let him have fifteen dollars which will pay his way down here and mine back home. I will give his family possession by the first of January next. Make the best bargain with him that you can and I will fulfill the contract when I come home.

If you fail to get Riley I want you to take my shoes and two shirts over to Jack's and get him to take them to John Boon's to bring to me.[63] Boon starts home today on a furlough of fifteen days which will give you time to see what you can do after you get this and if you fail to go over there. Also, if you send my clothes send me five dollars as I am near out of money and I have no idea when I will be paid off.

I am on the mend and think I will be able to go on service in a day or two. I have been able to wa[l]k about all the time. I hope you and the children are all well.

Mr Porter's Reg. is encamped not far from here now.[64] I spent part of last monday with them. Mr Porter was well. Jo Leavell was in the Hospital but not very sick.[65] James Mahaffey was said to be dying that morning.[66] He had been sick 3 weeks. I did not see him nor Jo. I do not know whether Jim died or not. Richard Smith's Reg is encamped 3 or 4 miles from here but I have not seen any of them yet.[67] Lafayette Mullins has applied for a discharge. He ought to have it. Ide is well. He is in the city on guard now. I do not know whether there is much sickness in the Reg. or not, as the bad sick are all carried to the city. We have only one man in the hospital from our company.

Goodby dear wife and children for the present,

To Mrs M J Taylor [from] Grant Taylor

PS For your eye alone. Be very careful or Riley will fool you. Do not put any more in his hands than you can help until I get

---

[63] Andrew J. Slaughter. John Boone (Co A 40th AL).
[64] Both William Jasper Porter and John H. Porter were in Co B 36th AL.
[65] Joseph M. Leavell (Co B 36th AL).
[66] James M. Mahaffey (Co B 36th AL).
[67] Richard Smith is unidentified.

him fastened down here. You know him. If [he] has a mind to, he can back out after you pay him part and [there will] be no chance to get it back.

I think it would be a good plan for you to get a buggy and take Leonard with you to ride his horse or Beck back and come with him to Gainsville and see him off. You can have as an excuse that you want to come and see Matilda.[68]

And then even if he were to act ever so strait, he may be refused here and then there would be no chance to get anything back from him. One suit of clothes is enough to bring with him as he will have to be uniformed, 2 shirts and 2 pair of drawers, as many socks as he wants. I say again to make the best trade you can and I will stand up to it. Let no one see this. Be careful that he does not find out that you doubt him. I can let him have my blankets. I do not think we will leave here soon. I expect he can get a transfer if he wants one but that may be uncertain.

Give my best love to all inquiring friends.

G Taylor

35

Ala Tusk Co.

August the 9th 1862

My Dear husband,

I seat myself this Saturday evening to wright you a few lines. We air all tolaberable well. I have a ketch in my shoulder that pesters me very mutch. I hope these lines may reach you in good health. I have just returned from Bethel.[69] It is the Destrict [meeting] thare now. Mr Ashcraft Preached today and a great

---

[68] Matilda Morgan Sanders Taylor Woodard, remarried widow of Grant's brother Leonard.

[69] Bethel Church in the community of Cushing (now Ralph) in Tuscaloosa County AL.

sermon it was.[70] It gave me more relief than any sermon I have heard since you left hom. His subject was to show that this ware [war] is all for air good. Grant I believed that long ago. Thare is a happy day ahead for me and you if we continue in faith.

This is Sunday morning and what a beatiful morning it is. Oh Grant if I only could see you this morning and talk with you. I feel like I cant live this way mutch longer. I feel so humble this morning that I could get down in the dust in behalf of a soldier and you esphely [especially].

I got a letter from Betty yesterday.[71] How glad I am to get a letter from anybody. Grant I reckon you have heard about Wiliam Mulens beeing ciled [killed].[72] How awful that was. He has got the reward he has always bin striving for.[73]

Grant you said for me to ware them rings to remember you. I can remember you without wareing them. I think they air very nice. I ware them all the time. Little Mary says they air pas. I know you want to see her. She is mighty sweet.

I saw Hilery Crouch yesterday.[74] He is as fat as a bare [bear]. Both of Tom Brookses boys is dead.[75] Old Miles sent Wiot [Wyatt] yesterday, and halled rails and made the cross fence between the potatoes and orchard.[76]

I have returnd from Bethel again. Mr Jones Preached Blunt Abbernathy and his sisters funeral today and then Mr Ashcraft preched also and then took the Sacrament.[77] Grant I thought of you that you was deprived of that greate privlidge. You have no idie the Prayers that they put up in behalf of the soldiers. Old

---

[70] Rev. William Ashcraft.

[71] Elizabeth "Betty" Taylor Teer, Grant's sister.

[72] William Mullins, husband of Grant's sister Lucretia.

[73] Malinda's meaning is that he has reached heaven and his reward there.

[74] Hillary Crouch is unidentified.

[75] Tom Brooks is unidentified. Perhaps David S. Brooks who died in June 1862 is one of these sons.

[76] Wyatt may be a slave, hired hand, or a son.

[77] Rev. R. Jones; Thomas S. Abernathy; the sisters are unknown; Rev. William Ashcraft.

Uncle Mathew believes that the melenium is not fare [far] of[f].[78] Oh how I pray for the blessed time to come.

Martha and Hariet Drummon took dinner with me today.[79] Rebecca Mahaffa started [to] Chacktow Bluff last Friday after Jim.[80] He was alive and that was all.

Grant when I hear you air bad sick I am going to start to you or dy in the attempt. If you get sick I want you to write me word immediately. I am going over to Forest [church] next Saturday to meating and to carry you some clothes to send of[f] by the first one that will carry them.

Kys George staid with me last night.[81] Ky has been out to Huses and Wicks.[82] Wick and Huse had a falling out. Jasper is living with Wick now.[83] Grant I dream of you nearly every night comming home. How overjoide it makes me feel. Mee and God only knows how bad I want to see you.

August the 11th. My shoulder is no better. It is all I can do to write. Cay Taylor is gon to see Hood at Florida.[84] He was dying very to the last they heard from him when I went to Town. Jack drove Clay to town in Paps buggy.[85] He worked as good as any horse. Mary went in the buggy with him.[86] Me and Elizy worked Buds mewl to her buggy.[87] So we had a fine time of it. Bill and Nain Parks joinde the church last Saturday at Bethel.[88]

---

78 "Old Uncle Matthew" is unidentified but probably a slave.

79 Harriet Drummond (born c1841) and Martha Drummond (born c1835) were daughters of Thomas J. and Margaret Drummond.

80 James Mahaffey married Rebecca A. Thomas in 1861. Jim died in Aug 1862 in Confederate service. Rebecca married James Hallman (Hollman?) in Feb 1864.

81 George Taylor, son of Malachi Taylor.

82 James Hughes Taylor and William M. Taylor, brothers of Grant.

83 Perhaps Jasper Taylor (born c1847), son of Malachi Taylor.

84 Rufus "Kay" Taylor went to see his brother James Hughes "Hood" Taylor.

85 Andrew J. Slaughter; Clay is a family horse; Pap is Malinda's father Wiley Slaughter.

86 Mary Slaughter Parker.

87 Eliza Slaughter Parker; Atlas "Bud" Slaughter.

88 William S. Parks and Nancy Jane Leavell Parks. They were later listed as members of Prairie Baptist Church in Greene County.

Grant see if some of the young men wont swap names withe you so you can come home before you have to leave thare. I have got your likeness her[e] to look at but it is not you. It only grieves me to the depths of my soul to look at it. I look at it and read your letters again and again. Excuse this bad spelt and awkward written letter for my eyes is allways full of tears when I try to write to you. The children says they want to see you so bad. You aught to see them how they listen when I go to read a letter from you. Buddy cryes over nearly evry letter. So farewell for this time,

I remain your humble praying wife,

Malinda J. Taylor

The children sends howdy to you. Little Mathew saide the other day Ma if you was to see Pa coming woulddent you run rite at him. I expect to go to Alcy Anns tonight and to Forest [church] tomorrow.[89]

Grant you dont know how I miss you. When I go over thare it seemes to me that I miss you worse thare than I do at home. If we air ever permitted to live together again I want us to live more Devoted to the will of God than we did when we had that greate and Glorious privilidge.

Grant if you should happen to see a lady someday that looks like me down thare you nednot to bee supprised.

Wilkersons Mill is burnt up whare Henry stays.[90] They don't know who done it. They think it was a runaway negro. Grant I have let my doors stay open all the summer so you see I ante [ain't] afraide at all.

Matthew wants me to sende you some of his hair. I will send you the print of Mary's hand.

I must close for the present. Rachel sends howdy to you.

When this you see remember me
tho many miles
apart we bee

---

[89] Forest Church in the community of Benevola in Pickens County.
[90] Wilkerson's Mill is no longer found in Pickens County.

I remain your loving praying wife until death,
Malinda J. Taylor

36

Camp Marshal Austill

Dear Wife & Children,

I embrace one more opportunity of dropping you a few lines to inform you that I am well and doing duty but my puny spell made me fall off 11 pounds. I do hope that these few lines may reach you all well and doing well.

I received your letter giving the sad news that Riley had backed out. Sad more on your account than my own. It is true that I had some hopes that he would come but they were very slim for you know I have no confidence in him. But never mind God will still take care of us and every thing works together for good to them that love the lord and I trust that we both love him.

I have written four letters to you and this is the fifth in a little over 2 weeks. I wrote to Wick some time ago offering him his note to come a month in my place but have not heard from him yet. If he does not come and you fail to get any one to come I want you to come the first of September. Capt Stone says there is no impropriety in your coming and that he will fix it up so that we can be most of our time together. But if you cannot sell your cows again I do not know what you will do for money as you ought to bring 35 or 40 dollars with you. I do not think you can afford to pay Kay Taylor's expenses for from what I can hear you will have both corn and meat to buy. And you ought to save all you can for that purpose.

I wrote to you in my last to carry my shirts and shoes over to Jack's for John Boon to bring to me.[91] He will start back about

---

[91] Andrew J. Slaughter; John Boone (Co A 40th AL).

tomorrow week which will be the 22nd inst and also five dollars in money. But if you have not sent the money you need not as I think I can do better without it than I think you can and then they say that they will pay us before long. Now if you do not get to take my things over in time for Boon to bring them you can take them over there and send them by Tom Lofton as I expect he will start home in a day or two on a 2 weeks' furlough.[92] But if you are coming yourself I can wait a little longer but think the safest plan would be to send them as you may not get to come.

I spent last Sunday with Brantly Garner, Zeke Sanders and the rest of that set of boys.[93] They were generally well but they passed through rough times at Corinth.[94] They are well pleased that they have got back to Mobile again. I was with Joe Heath and Jim Hollman part of the day yesterday on guard in Mobile.[95] Mr Porter's Reg is encamped at our old camp ground at Dog River Factory. I have not seen any of them in more than a week.

James Mahaffey died the fore part of last week. I think sickness is on the increase in our Reg. We have 5 in the hospital from our company, 2 of them are dangerous. Rabe Parker is one of them.[96] Mullins was waylayed and shot last Su[n]day evening was a week ago and died shortly.[97] I expect you will hear the particulars before you get this. Lafayette was discharged on the account of his health and started home day before yesterday. 4 others also from our company went at the same time, Jack Pearce among them.[98]

I do not think we will go from here soon but I do not know. Our guard duty is very hard here around Mobile. We have [to] stand every other day.

Give my best respects to all enquiring friends. Kiss the dear children for me. O how I want to see you all. There is a crushing weight around my heart this evening to think of the long, long

---

[92] Capt. Thomas Lofton (Co G 40th AL).

[93] Brantley Garner (Co F 11th AL); Ezekiel Sanders.

[94] Confederate forces evacuated Corinth, Mississippi, on May 30, 1862. See E. B. Long, *The Civil War Day by Day: An Almanac 1861-1865* (Garden City NJ: Doublebday, 1971) 218.

[95] Probably Joel Heath; Jim Hollman (Hallman?) is unidentified.

[96] Probably C. R. Parker.

[97] William Mullins, Grant's brother-in-law.

[98] John "Jack" Pearce (Co G 40th AL).

days and nights before I get to come home but I pray and you must pray that God may lighten my troubles. When I think of the long long time to the end of my enlistment my heart almost dies within me and I sometimes feel that if it were not for you and the children and it were the Lord's will death would be a welcome messenger but I know that Repining is wrong and I strive against it all I can. Not my will o Lord but thine be done.

If old Riley has entirely backed out and no chance to get him to come I want you to spurn him from your presence and have nothing more to do with him in any way. Not because he did [not] come but because he put you to so much trouble and expense. For he will cheat you out of all you have got if he can.

God bless us all is the prayer of your loving distant husband,

To M J Taylor [from] Grant Taylor

37

Ala Tusk Co

August 14th 1862

Dear and beloved husband,

Th[r]ough the goo[d]ness of God I am permitted to write to you again. We air not very well. I have had another spell with my jaw and neck. I have got on the pewny order somehow or other, but I hope these lines will finde you in good health.

I recieved 2 letters from you today. One written the 6[th] the other the 8[th] giving directions abought Rily. I wrote to you that he had backed out some time ago. I have not seen him since I was thare nor I dont care if I never do again.

I read a letter from Mr Porter yesterday stating that James Mahaffy was dead and that he met up with you the other day. He said he felt like he had met a brother.

Mr and Mrs Sellers spent the day with me today. He told me about ketching you by the leg, I forget whare it was. He said he would write to you soon. Cay Tayler halld my corn a month ago but I could never think to write it. Mr Salmons folks and Mr Porters folks is at daggers point with each other. When Tom came home, it was ten oclock in the night when he came by thare he come hooping and howllowing calling for Jasper and liked to sceared Aunt Henny and Adline to death and they fell out from that.[99]

The Destrict [meeting] will bee at Forest [church] next year and the Assosiation [meeting] will bee at Bulah [church]. Oh how I hop you will bee at home then. Grant I have not rised my voice in curch but once since you left home. I am allways so full that I cant sing to think whare you air.

I also got a letter from you last Monday that you wrote on your pallet on your knee. This letter wont start from the [post] office til Monday, but I thought as I was going over the [Sipsey] river I might not get back in time to write on Monday.

Harrison Leavel has got a discharge, but he says he is going back.[100] I will sende you 5 dollars with your Cloths. Grant if you ever get back again to live with me I will never bee the wife to you that I have been. I will try to discharge my duty better than I ever have. I feel now that I never have done half enough for you.

I will write you some of little Marys talk. When she wakes up in the night, she says "Ma the children wants cover." When the flyes pester her, she says "dogon the flyes." She says Pa is gon to the ware. She tells Rachel she will knock her head over and a thousand more things that I cant write.

This unsigned letter is incomplete.

---

[99] William Thomas Salmon (Co B 36th AL); William Jasper Porter (Co B 36th AL) and his wife Adline; Henrietta Moore who lived with the Porters.

[100] Harrison Leavell is unidentified.

38

Camp Marshal Austill

August 17ᵗʰ 1862

Dear wife and children,

I wrote to you day before yesterday. This leaves me in reasonable health and I hope that you are allso too. I write to you now to tell you that you need not try any farther to get any person to come in my place for a month as they have stopped that way of substituting.

I wrote to you to come to see me about the first of Sept. if you have money. You ought to have 35 or 40 dollars. They say they are going to pay us here tomorrow but I think it uncertain. It seems that fate is against my coming home soon.

I have no news to write as this is six letters I have written to you in less than three weeks. Ide sends his best respects to you. I am in a hurry to get this in todays mail. So nothing more at present from your loving husband.

Grant Taylor

PS As to swaping names that is impossible for all want to go home as bad as I do so we will have to endure it.

39

August the 24th 1862

Dear and mutch beloved husband,

It is through the kinde mercies of my dear savior that I am permitted to pen these lines to you. We air not all well. I have just got home from taking your Cloths to Jacks. I went over thare last Saturdy and aimd to come back on sunday. The children was all sick with hy fever for 3 and 4 nights and so I never got back til now. Jimmy was rite sick this morning. They all have got the worst caughf I ever heard but they air better now. Rachel carried evrything on just like I was hear. Grant she is as good a negro as evr was.

I hope these lines will reach you in good health. God has blesst you since you have been thare. I hope he will continue to do so. Jack is going to start to join your Company next Monday. I sent you $5 with your Cloths. I saw Jack Pirce yesterday.[101]

Your letter came to the office Tuseday, but I was not here to read it. One started to you last monday. I will start this tomorrow.

Old Rily is gon to the ware in a big mans place. He got one thousand dollars and a fine horse. His family is living at Jack Leather[wood]s place. He has baught it for five hundred dollars. But I dont intend they shal ever pester me.

Grant you have heard of the death of Daddy.[102] Dont grieve after him. I staid all night with Lucreta last Monday night.[103] She is in a heep of troubble.

I saw Mr Loftin last Saturday.[104] He tolde me a heep about you.

Mary Taylor is staying with me now to dry peaches.[105] I have got 2 bushels and a half dried. They air selling for $5 a bushel in Tus. I am going to send a bushel up thare Tuseday.

Mem Jacobs is dead.[106] Preacher Roberson is dead.[107] Jim Stags is dead and Narcis Wier and Jim Bensons little girl is dead.[108]

I saw Wick last Sunday. He thinks he will have to go to the army and if he dont, he wants to come and live on your land. Grant it wont do and I want you to oppose it in your next [letter] to me. His family is on sufferance. You weigh the matter and you

---

[101] John "Jack" Pearce (Co G 40th AL).

[102] Grant's father, Archelaus Taylor (1783-1862).

[103] Lucretia Taylor Mullins, Grant's sister, recently widowed at the death of her husband, William Mullins.

[104] Capt. Thomas Lofton (Co G 40th AL).

[105] Mary Taylor, daughter of Alsey Ann Taylor.

[106] Memory Jacobs (Co G 41st AL) died August 6, 1862, at Chattanooga, Tennessee.

[107] Rev. Roberson is unidentified.

[108] Jim Staggs (Co G 41st AL); Narcissa Winn, wife of David Wier; James M. Benson (Co C 24th AL).

will se it wonte do. My horses will have his riding to do. The waggon and steers all the hauling to do. Grant it wonte do.

I know Grant you said for me to come to see you. Oh how it makes my heart beat with the thought of seeing you. All I lik [lack] starting is somebody to go with me. I dont have any idie who I could get to go with me. May[be] I can get someone to go with me.

This is Monday morning. Jimmy is rite sick this morning. I gave him a dose of blew mas last night and he throwd up a heep of phlegme just now.

I dremd of you coming home last night. Why is it that thare is so many coming home and I can never see you. Grant it will bee your time after awhile. I am confident of that. God has told me so and I am waiting for it with patients.

Grant try to bee contented with your lot. Think how mutch worse it could bee. Look at the thousands that air dead and gon. You might bee better off if you were dead but dont think of dying. I believe thare is happy days on earth for us yet. Trust in God. He is the only helper. I have tride him and found him a greate helper in time of kneed.

Come as soon as you can. You will bee as welcom a visiter as evr enterd my doore. Grant try to bee contented. I dont think that peace is fare [far] of[f]. The darkest time is just before day. I have given all things into the hands of God.

Davis and Casper and severl more is making up money to go to the salt works and make salt.[109] Davis put down $10 and I thought 5 was enough for me so I put down $5. I can sell my cows any time I want to. Lizy Sellers wants one of the little steers for beef.[110] Mr Salmon is helping me to pull fodder.[111]

Grant try to get off as soon as you can have some excuse. Tell a little fib rather than miss.

I must close. May health, prosperity and peace crown you is the

---

[109] Perhaps William Davis, Grant's brother-in-law; perhaps James P. Cosper (c1821-1886).
[110] Lizy Sellers is unidentified.
[111] William Salmon (born c1812).

prayer of your lonely wife. Goodby for this time, Dear husband. Dont forget to pray.

M J Taylor

40

Camp Marshal Austill

August 26th 1862

Dear wife and children,

I seat myself this evening to pen you a few lines in answer to yours written just before you started to Forest [church] which I was glad to receive. I am in tolerable good health but not as stout as I was some weeks back. I still keep on duty. I stand guard every other day and night. I hope you and the dear children are all well and doing well. There is a heap of sickness here but I have no means of knowing how many are sick. They send all the bad cases to the city hospital.

Jack landed here last Saturday and has been rejected and thrown back among the conscripts.[112] If he wants to be discharged he will have to go to Wetumka [AL] and be examined. He expects to start home tomorrow. I drew 33 dollars the other day before Jack got here. I had 50 cts when I drew my money. If I can get some changed I will send you some money.

I think you had better sell your cattle again if you can but do not let any one have them for less than they are worth. I do not want you to loan my oxen any more for I want them to get fat and then you can sell them. Do not take less than one hundred dollars.

Mr Porter told me the other day that Leatherwood had let my wagon get in a bad condition by standing in the sun. I think you had better shut down and not loan it to no one for if you do you will soon have no wagon.

If you come down here I reckon I can get board for you at Elijah Kinney's if you will stay. It cost nearly $2 per day for board. I fear

---

[112] Andrew J. Slaughter, Malinda's brother.

it will be a bad chance for me to get to stay with you much. But if you want to come I shall not say for you not to come for I want to see you very badly.

Tell Matthew that I was mighty glad to get that little lock of hair. How I do want to see him and the children but I do not see any chance at all to come home this year. It looks hard if it is fair. I was in Mr Porters reg. last Sunday. Their reg. is nearly sick.

Mr Porter has been in the hospital and was still in there but was well only weak. The three Henderson boys were all in there but were better except little John. I expect he is dead by this time. Bud Holley was in Mobile not expected to live.[113] Jo Leavell has got well but is [not] strong enough to leave the hospital and go to camps.[114] I have not seen him yet. The boys say that he looks tolerably well. Jo Park, Will Barton and Tom Hood were well.[115] Peter Burns was lying very low in Mobile.[116] I saw Dick Smith and Zeke Sanders yesterday on guard in Mobile yesterday.[117] All that set of our acquaintances were well. Their reg is in fine health. Jack Parks is well as is everyone -- ----.[118]

I got 2 letters from Bud and John the other day.[119] They and Jake were well but Wat was quite sick.[120] They are at a place called Charleston in Tenn. 40 miles the other side of Chattanooga.

I am in better spirits than when I wrote last. Continue to pray for me that the day may come when I can get to come home and stay there. But I cannot see any chance for the war to close soon. May God bless you all. Kiss the children for me and believe me as ever your loving husband and father,

To Mrs M J Taylor [from] Grant Taylor

---

[113] Bud Holley is unidentified.
[114] Joseph M. Leavell (Co B 36th AL).
[115] Joseph Park (Co B 36th AL); Will Barton and Tom Hood are unidentified.
[116] Peter Burns (Co B 42nd AL).
[117] Richard Smith and Ezekiel Sanders.
[118] Jack Parks is unidentified.
[119] Atlas "Bud" Slaughter, Malinda's brother; John Parker.
[120] Jacob Parker; Walter Slaughter.

PS Did you ever get the letter containing the children's thumbpapers. Tom Salmon has gone to where his wife is on a sick furlough of twenty days. I saw him in Mobile yesterday on his way. He looked tolerably ---- but did not seem to me that there was much the matter with him. I was very glad to get my shirts and shoes but I was not needing my socks yet but if I get to stay here I can keep them all. I suppose those are the shirts that you bought for old Riley. Did he get any of the clothes that you got for him? Tell old Heritage that he must make your shoes if he gets leather to work at all.[121] He can make yours and ought to do it first as you have paid him for them.

G. Taylor

I sent my winter coat to John Boones. I expect it is at Jack's now.

41

Camp Marshal Austill

August 29th 1862

Dear wife and children,

I seize the present moment to pen you a few lines. I am tolerably well except a crick in the back of my neck. I recei[ved] your letter of August 24th yesterday and was glad to hear from you but sorry to hear that Jimmy was sick. I wrote to you this week giving you all the news. I wrote to you that I would send you some money by Jack but when he left here he did not know but what he would be conscripted bifore he got home and so I did not send it. – -- I write to you that ---- he was rejected here and sent back amoung the conscripts.

Malinda I am almost afraid to write it to you for fear that we may be disappointed. I was promised today a furlough sometime between the fourth and fifteenth of next month if one of our men returns in time who is out on furlough. I do not want you to make

---

[121] Henry Heritage.

to[o] great calculations on the promise for everything of that sort here is very uncertain. I should not have written to you at all about it but you might get a chance to come to see me about that time and we might both start about the same time and miss each other. So if you have any chance to come put it off til after the 20th of Sept. If I do not come by that time I do not expect to come soon. And then by waiting till then you will see whether you caught the measles at Jack's besides the weather will be cooler.

I am coming home to administer on Dady's estate. If I can I can do it and appoint an attorney to attend to it. If I do not do it, Davis has the right and you know Malachi cannot do it.[122] I do not want you to say anything about why I am coming home for I do not want Wick to come there to live for the reasons you named for he has made enough off me already. It seems that he won't do when he has the chance, but keep this to yourself also.

Now Jack said that you talked like you wanted to break up [housekeeping] this winter and move over Sipsey [River]. In that case I would have no objections to you renting the place to him provided you moved all with you. If you think that you can be better satisfied by moving over there, I shall not object seriously but I think you had better stay where you are for these reasons.

First it would be a heavy expense to move and then as there is scarcely anything made over there it would throw you entirely out of reach of getting corn from the Warrior [River].

Do not sell nothing you have on a credit to no one it makes no difference who it may be.

Do not look for me too hard, you may be disappointed but I will come if I can.

I cannot grieve over the death of Father.

Good[by] for the present, Dearest wife and children. Continue to write as usual. Still pray for your loving,

Grant Taylor

Ide sends his best respects to you.

---

[122] William Davis, Grant's brother-in-law; Malachi Taylor, Grant's brother.

42

August the 31st 1862

My Dear beloved Grant,

It is through the kinde mercies of God that I am permitted to write to you again. We air all well and I thank God for it and I humbly hope these lines will finde you well. I am a little pestered tonight. The reporte is that you air dead. I cant believe it is so but it makes me feel sad and lonesum. I have prayed with all the earnestness of my sole that you might bee spared and I believe that God will hear my prare. Saint Jorden is dead.[123] Oh what a distressing time it is. God send us peace I humbly pray.

We air kneeding rain hear. I have sowd my turnips but expect to have to sow again. I have got all my fodder saved. My corn will bee very light but it is all for the best.

I am writing by candle light. Little Mary is sitting up eating Molasses and bread. The boys is gon to bed. Grant I would give one hundred dollars to see you tonight. I intend to see you as soon as I can. Mr Salmon is talking of going down to see Tom.[124] If he dus I intend to go with him.

I got your short letter stating that I nead not try any longer to get a man for a month. Wash Leatherwood has to go to the army. Me and Mary Taylor went to old Mrs Ingrums.[125] She says that peace is made now with the headmen but they will have to bee 2 more big battles yet and at the coming of cool wether all the soldiers will come home. God, send it may bee so.

I solde Speck last week for $30 to Bill Parkes.[126] He paid me $15 down and would pay the rest when he got a 50 dollar bill changed. I have dried 3 bushels and 3 pecks of peaches. Pap

---

[123] Saint Jordan is unidentified.
[124] William Salmon and his son Tom Salmon.
[125] Mary Taylor, Grant's cousin; Mrs. Ingram is unidentified.
[126] Speck was a family cow; William Parks.

bought Mr Alen's [slave] Cap at 1 thousand dollars. Mrs Allen then backed out and would not let him have him.[127]

This is Monday Morning again. We had a fine rain last night. If I can get plenty of rain I will make a heap of potatoes. I expect to draw something from the public. Next monday Mr Salmon is going to Tusk and says he will see to it. Cay Taylor is been gon six weeks to whare the Boys is. He is down thare sick and cant get home. Thedore Phillips is dead and no chance for Nute.[128] Jack Leatherwood tolde me to give you his love when he was hear. He is now in Chatanuga.

Rachel is now getting breakfast and Buddy is fixing a yoke for his calvs. He says he is going to have him some oxons of pinks and Hartes calves.

Grant I dreamed last night that you was dead for ceartain. I thought I went crazy and that will bee the way it will turn out if it is the case. I believe I had rather dye and leave my sweet little ones in the hands of a merciful God and go with you. I feel humbled down in the very dust this morning.

I must close as Buddy is going to the office. So I remain the same humble praying wife until death.

Malinda J Taylor

When this you see remember me tho many miles apart we bee.

During this time period, Grant went home on leave and his letters resumed when he returned to camp near Mobile.

---

[127] Mr. and Mrs. Allen are unidentified.

[128] Theodore Phillips is unidentified. There were two men named Newton Hughes in Pickens County: Newton R. Hughes and Newton H. Hughes.

CHAPTER 3

AND ME BOUND TO STAY AWAY FROM YOU BY A STERN NECESSITY

Grant had been away from home for more than four months before he received his first furlough. Despite having a ten-day furlough he stayed home at least fourteen days from September 8 through September 21. When he returned late to duty, he was concerned about the consequences of his tardy arrival.

While he was home, Grant and Malinda discussed the idea of selling their farm in the Cushing community of Tuscaloosa County. The next few letters include a discussion of which farm to buy and when Malinda would move.

From the letters, it seems that Malinda and Leonard took Grant to Demopolis for transportation to Mobile and that their parting was upsetting and difficult for all of them. Grant's letters resume when he returned to camp near Mobile.

43

Camp Marshall Austill

Sept 22nd 1862

Dear wife and children,

I landed in camps this morning in good health except the headache from the fatigue of last nights journey and I hope that you are enjoying the best of health. I found Mobile in a state of considerable excitement about the Yankees making an attacking on the city. They have stopped furloughing again on the account of it. I do not believe there is any danger yet, but of course I do not know.[1]

It was left to a vote the other day whether our regiment would go to Richmond or stay here and they voted to stay. So I reckon we will stay here for some time at least. There is no yellow fever here. They have moved the most of the sick away from here. Some of our company were sent to Selma. John Staggs died yesterday in Mobile with fever.[2] He was sent there before I went home. The health of our company is better than it was when I left.

I got a letter from Bud today.[3] It was dated the 9th of Sept. Bud was complaining. Watt was able to walk about the house a little.[4] John had gone to his company.[5] He started the 5th. I saw William Barton today.[6] He was well and said that Mr Porter was well. Brantley Garner was sent to Selma with the other sick.[7] I saw him to-day. He was well. Ide is well and sends his best respects to you.

Captain Lofton says he will not do anything with me for being over my time. Malinda, when you left me yesterday I stood and watched you till the buggy did not look larger than a dog. And Oh how lonesome and far from home I felt. It seemed for awhile as if the light had all died out in my heart, but I thought of all the mercies of God and lifted my heart to him in prayer for further protection and I soon regained composure of mind and today feel very well reconciled to my lot, believing that it is God's will and what he does is right. Still continue to pray fervently for our health and my safe return home.

So goodbye dear wife and children for the present.

To M J Taylor [from] Grant Taylor

---

1 Confederate leaders feared a Union strike on Mobile was imminent due to Federal activity in nearby Pensacola. See Bergeron, *Confederate Mobile*, 58.

2 John Staggs (c1836-1862) of Co G 40th AL.

3 Atlas "Bud" Slaughter, Malinda's brother.

4 Walter Slaughter, Malinda's brother.

5 John Parker, husband of Malinda's sister, Mary.

6 William Barton (36th AL).

7 Brantley Garner (Co F 11th AL).

44

Camp Marshal Austill

Sept 24th 1862

Dear wife & children,

I am seated again to pen you a few lines. I am very well and hope that you and the children are in the best of health.

I write to you to tell you that Frank Parker says that he will take eight hundred dollars for his land.[8] $600 cash and $200 on a credit. Now I want you to see Pap and if he thinks it is worth it you had better buy it but [only] if you have money enough to pay for it all by letting my debts lie and to buy your provisions and have pocket money besides. I would rather you would pay for it all and get a title to it at once. I want you to make Buster tell you exactly what he thinks of it.[9] I do not know the place well but what I do know I think it pretty high. But I am willing to go by what Buster says about it. Tell him I want him to exercise his own judgment just as if he were trading for himself. There are 280 acres of it. Jim Yearby will not sell his place.[10]

I wrote to you the day before yesterday giving you all the news and of John Staggs having died last Sunday. Do the best you can and may God bless you and the dear children is the prayer of your loving absent husband,

Grant Taylor

PS Write as soon as you determine what you will do, but do not attempt to move on the place untill all things are fixed up.

To M J Taylor [from] G. Taylor

---

[8] Frank Parker is unidentified.
[9] Josiah B."Buster" Archibald (born c1824).
[10] James E. Yearby (Co B 40th AL).

45

Ala Tusk Co

Sept 29th 1862

[from Malinda J. Taylor]

It has come to the same thing again. But I thank God that you are alive so I can write to you. We are all well as common. Mary looks bad yet. I hop[e] these lines will finde you in good health. I recieved your welcom letter today. I was glad to get it. I was glad to hear that you would stay thare. Me and Leonard got home safe. We got to Mr Ritches an hour and a half [late] be[cause] Clay start[l]ed 2 or 3 times.[11] We got to Clinton by 12 o'clock.[12]

I am going to move next Friday. Cay Taylor is going to hall one load. Jim Teer is going to bring his steers to pull my wagon.[13] I am going to see old Miles tomorrow abought hawling. I went over to Busters last Wednesday. Pap said he thought I had better move to Daddes place for this year and then I would have more time to suit myself in bying a place.[14] Mr Mitchell said he would fix the kitchen for nothing and he would bee a husband and Father to me while I staid thare.[15] Thare is lots of fodder thare but I did not see Ves to know if I could bigh [buy] it.[16] M[a]ry said Pap was very ancious for me to move over thare.[17]

Grant, Pap thought we were coming back thare from Marys. He hates it so bad that he did not tell you goodby. He said he wanted to ta[l]k more with you. I baught 4 hogs, 2 years old, from Mary at seven dollars and a half. Pap said he thought that 4 would bee enough. Pap seems wiling to do all he can for me. I went to

---

[11] Mr. Rich is unidentified. Clay was the family horse.

[12] Clinton, a community in Greene County AL on the way from Demopolis back home to Tuscaloosa County.

[13] Jim Teer is unidentified. There were many Teer families in the area.

[14] Pap is her father, Wiley Slaughter; Daddy is Grant's father, Archelaus Taylor, who died in August 1862.

[15] Mr. Mitchell is unidentified.

[16] Probably John Ves Peebles.

[17] Mary Slaughter Parker, Malinda's sister, and Malinda's father Wiley Slaughter.

see Parker about that corn.[18] He had sold some but had not gethered all. He said I could have some at 1 dollar and a quarter per bushel. Pap said he would try at Speeds Mill for some.[19]

We have just eat supper. I went to the newground this evening.[20] Today was 3 weeks ago me and you went down thare. When I came to the log whare we sit down to rest I could not help but take a cry.

Mr Phillips is going to let me have [corn] meal for what he ows me.[21] He took that paper and said he would get what your emploirs owed you if he could.[22] Grant I had very solemn feelings today on my way from the [post] office when I thought of you requesting me to pray for your health and return home. I tride to pray [for] you. I believe we will meet again on earth. I pray for that daily and all most hourly. Mary says you are gone to get apples for her and wants you to make haste and come back.[23]

The day I left you I knew that you was looking after us. Leonard cried for several Miles before we got out of sight of you. He would say poore Pa is standing there yet. I thought I would venture to look back. I looked back just as you turned to go back. Your beeing at home seemes like a dream to me. Grant, I don't think I can feel any wors when you are dead than I did when I got home and opend the doors and saw your coat and hat and the rest of you[r] things that you had wore while you was at home.

I am up by myself wrighting by candle light. I feel that God is ever presant with me. This is the last letter that I ever expect to wright in this house to you. Send your next letters to the Grove.[24] I reckon Mr Percon will take Beck.[25] I am going to see him. Dont

---

[18] Probably Frank Parker, from whom she is considering buying a farm.

[19] There is a Speed's Mill on Bear Creek in in Pickens County.

[20] The "newground" is unknown. Perhaps land that Grant plowed while he was home.

[21] Probably the owner of Phillips' Mill.

[22] This is probably in reference to the school where Grant taught and the money that was owed to him for his work.

[23] This Mary is their 2-year-old daughter.

[24] Pleasant Grove is at the border of Tuscaloosa County and Pickens County.

[25] Beck was a family mule.

bee uneasy about me and the children. We will get along. God will provide for us if we trust in him. Mrs Jones husband was her[e] Sunday looking about.[26]

If you stay at Mobile this winter I am coming to see you if God will admit. Grant, I think I will bee better contented over the [Sipsey] River than I am hear.

I must close. Excuse bad wrighting and spelling. May health, Peace and prosperity Crown you is the Prayer of your loving wife.

I dreamed of sleeping with you last night.

Malinda Taylor

46

Camp Marshal Austill

Oct 4th 1862

Beloved wife and children,

I am again seated to the pleasing task of writing to you again. This leaves [me] in good health except cold which causes me to have a pretty bad headach. Although, I am on guard to-day and am writing near the guard tent on a log. I hope and pray that these lines may find you all enjoying the best of health and spirits. I received your loving letter of September 29th to-day which made me glad to hear that you and the sweet children were well. But it made me feel sad when you said that this is the last letter I ever expect to write in this house. Sad to think of the many happy hours we have spent together there and that you are now homeless and your loving lawful protecter so far away from you. But God's will be done.

You ought to have taken a receipt from Phillips for that paper, for that is your showing for what is owing to you or me and if he has the mind to he can keep all he collects, unless you had a receipt. I wrote twice to you last week one of which you received.

---

26 Mr. and Mrs. Jones are unidentified. Mr. Jones was probably considering the Taylor home for purchase.

In the other I gave you a full account of what Frank Parker will take for his land and what for you to do. I also wrote to Buster this week giving him the same statement. So it is not worthwhile to write it all down here.

We will move from this camp next week, I expect. We will move about 3 miles north of this and 4 miles from the wharf on the bay. It is about 2 miles from the outer edge of the city.[27] This Reg. Mr Porter's Reg and Dick Smith's and another are ordered to assemble there and form a brigade. So I will be close to all my neighbor boys in the diffirent Reg.[28]

It is rumored that the Small Pox has appeared about 3 miles above Mobile on the railroad but I do not believe it. There is no yellow fever here yet. The health of our reg. is improving.

John Powell was here in camps to-day on his way to his Reg.[29] He has been a prisoner ever since the battle of Shiloah and has been exchanged. His brother was wounded and has gone home on a furlough. I saw Mr Porter last Sunday. He came over to see me and looks as hearty as I ever saw him. John has got a discharge and has gone home.

Salt is said to be selling at 75 cts per lb by the retail in this city. I sold 11 lbs yesterday belonging to the mess for $7.50 in cash. Sweet potatoes are from 3 1/2 to 4 dollars per bushel and 25 cts by the quart. We bought potatoes with our salt money. I saw a man yesterday from the salt works yesterday who says that Ely Going had made the best arrangement of any man here.[30] [He] bought a claim ready fixed up for two thousand dollars and went immediately to making salt. He made 8 bushels the first day he

---

[27] On October 8, 1862, the 40th Alabama moved to Camp Forney on the Spring Hill Railroad four miles from Mobile between Government and Dauphin Streets. See Elbert D. Willett, *History of Company B, 40th Alabama Regiment, Confederate States Army 1862 to 1865* (Montgomery, AL: Viewpoint Publications, 1963) 12.

[28] The 40th Alabama was brigaded with the 18th, 36th, and 38th Alabama regiments. See U.S. War Department, *War of the Rebellion: A Compilation of the Official Records of the Union and Confederate Armies.* 128 vols. (Washington, D.C.: Government Printing Office, 1880-1901) Series I, 15:850.

[29] John Powell is unidentified.

[30] Eli T. Going (1816-1889).

worked. I hope you will not be bothered about getting salt. I wash [wish] you had 20 dollars in the company. Salt is selling there at 16 to 18 dollars per bushel by those who are making for sale.

Poor little Mary: I fear it will be many a weary hour before poor Pa comes with her apples. I can immagine that I can almost hear her sweet prattle now. As you say, my visit seems like a dream. I feel like that I did not pay as much attention to the little boys as I ought, but my mind was so occupied that I could not pay the attention to none of you that I wished to. But God knows it was not for any want of love on my part.

I have heard that our Lieut Col. who has just returned from Richmond Va. offers to bet $1000 that peace will be signed by Christmas but I do not know that he has made the offer and further I can see no reasons why he should have made the offer for I can see no prospect of peace.[31] But God can bring order out of confusion very quick when he sees fit. Cheer up beloved wife, let us put our whole trust more firmly in our blessed Savior.

I want you to kiss the children separately for me and tell them it is for me. I am very well satisfied and I think will be as long as you are provided for. Give my best respects to all enquiring friends and may God bless you all with all needful blessing is the prayer of your devoted loving husband and father.

To Mrs M J Taylor [from] Grant Taylor
& children

PS I send you a conversation that is said to have taken place between a Confederate officer and a family in Tennessee.[32]

---

[31] Lt. Col. John H. Higley.
[32] Perhaps this letter included a separate piece of paper with an article but it is not in the collection.

47

Ala P[ickens] C[oun]ty

October 10th 1862

Dear and beloved husband,

I am now seated to drop you a few lines at my new home. We are all well except Leonard and Mary. They got into a pewny way. Mary has not got any better yet of the bowel complaint so I got Mr Sumerville to come and see them.³³ He did not say what was the matter with them. He left them some medicin. I hope these lines will finde you enjoying a portion of go[o]d health.

We came her[e] to Dadies old place last Monday. I aimed to move last Friday. Cay Taylor and Jim teer was to hall me a load last Friday, but sickness pervented them. I waited for them til saturday then I got Mr Salmon to hall 1 load for $5. Wash Leatherwood to hall 1 load with 4 mewls for 10$ and a negro to help drive the cows for $2. So it all cost me $16.³⁴ I left the waggon and another load over thare. I am going after them next week. Jim Teer will take his steers and go with me. Mrs Jones moved on Thursday and we all staid together til Monday.

Grant I thought I wanted to see you before I moved hear but I knew nothing about it. I feel like I would give evry thing that we posess if you could come home and stay. I dreamd the other night that Mr Porter said that you was detaild to come home and take care of your family. The next morning when I got up I felt so disappointed. God Almighty grant for the time to soon come that you can come home to stay. I want you to pray with all your heart for that one thing and that we all may live to see each other again.

Grant death is a brand in the hand. Elizar Jane Camel died last Thursday was a weak ago and Martha Speed's oldest childe diede yesterday with flux.³⁵ Thare is seven more down with it. Thare is

---

³³ Mr. Sumerville is unidentified.

³⁴ Malinda's addition is incorrect. The total of the expenses she names is really $17.

³⁵ Eliza Jane Taylor Campbell, Grant's cousin, died Oct. 2, 1862 about age twenty-five, leaving two young children while her husband was away

Martha, Mary, Margaret, Lee, Olly, Mayie and the baby is all very low.[36] Elizar Jane diede shouting happy. She was perfectly in her senses until the last. Pap came after Shockly yesterday for mother.[37] She had rising in her head.

I sent to the [post] office this evening for a letter. 2 weaks next Monday since I got one. I think I will get 1 tomorrow. I want to hear from you as bad as I ever did in my life. I like to live her[e] very well but it looks like you ought to bee abought her[e] some whare. I think of the pleashure mee and you have seen hear but now whare is it. I can hardly bare to think of it.

I have not bought any place yet. Mr V Peebles lets me have fodder at [the] cu[s]timary price.[38] It belongs to Jack. I have a good paster for the cows and Clay to run in. Old Beck run away a weak before I moved.[39] When I heard of her, she was at Solestal Williams.[40] Mr Drummon said he would get her for me.[41] Mrs Jones wants to bye her.

This is Saturday morning. Leonard is better. Mary is about like she was. She looks very pail and bad. Grant, next Saturday the big Meeting begins at Farast [Forest church] but I dont think I will enjoy it when I think of you. Oh how I wish you was hear to attend it with me.

Thare has been a big battle near Corinth. Bob Wels and Thomas Leneer was cilled [killed].[42] Reportes say the Yankes cut us all to peaces.[43]

---

completing Confederate service. Sarah Albina Speed, daughter of Martha Taylor and Terrell Speed, died on Oct. 9 at age five years.

[36] Alsey Ann Taylor's family was stricken with dysentery: Martha Ann Taylor Speed, Mary Taylor, Nancy Margaret Taylor, Lee Taylor, Olive Taylor, George Mai Taylor, and the baby Eliza Ida C. L. Speed.

[37] Dr. Thomas Shockley (1822-1893) also served in Co B 40th AL, but was discharged.

[38] Probably John V. Peebles.

[39] Beck is an old mule.

[40] Celestial Williams (1814-1894) of Greene County.

[41] Probably Thomas J. Drummond.

[42] Robert K. Wells (Co B 42nd AL), son of Absolom Wells. Actually Thomas C. Lanier was not killed and he lived until 1891.

[43] At the battle of Corinth (October 3-4, 1862), Confederate forces failed to dislodge Federal forces from the key railroad junction at the cost of over 4,000 casualties. See E.B. Long, *Civil War Day by Day: An Almanac 1861-*

Rachel came with me. She was willing to come. Grant you must excuse this bad letter evry way for I had no place fitten to write on. So I must close for this time. May Peace, health and prosprity crown you is the prayer of your unworthy wife.

Iff you meet with troubles and trials on the way Cast your care on Jesus and don't forget to Pray.

Malinda J Taylor

48

Camp Forney

Oct 12th 1862

Beloved wife & children,

I seat myself This holy Sabbath day to pen you a few lines to inform you that I am in fine health and I sincerely hope that these lines may reach you and the dear children enjoying the best of health. I have not received but one letter from you since I came back but I suppose your moving is the cause. I am getting mighty anxious to hear from you. Always write your letters so as to start them from the Grove on Friday as that is the only day the mail passes down by there. I fear we shall not hear from each other as regularly as we used to.

We moved to this place last Wednesday. We are about one mile from Camp Beulah where R Smith and his Reg. is encamped and 4 miles from the city.[44] Mr Porter is encamped in sight of us. I have seen him once. He was in fine health also Jo Leavell. I do not like our Present camp ground. It is too low and level. And then we have to walk to Mobile to guard the same as we did when we were nearer. The health of the Reg. has improved considerably.

1865 (Garden City NJ: Doubleday, 1971) 274-273 and Peter Cozzens, *The Darkest Days of the War: The Battles of Iuka and Corinth* (Chapel Hill: University of North Carolina Press, 1997).

44 Richard Smith.

Our army has suffered a dreadful defeat at Corinth. I am very anxious to hear from Jack.[45] His Col. who is in Mobile wounded, says that at the end of the fight no more than 10 or 12 of his Reg. could be found. He does not know whether they were all killed and wounded or part taken prisoners and part had straggled off. There is no doubt but that many were killed as they were in the hottest of the fight. Bob Wells, Cas Mitchell and Cal Upchurch were missing when the Col. left.[46] Birt Upchurch got wounded in the ancle.[47] James Williams was sick and was not in the fight.[48] There were upwards of five hundred of the Reg that went into the fight. One Reg has left here to reinforce our army up there and it is said that others are to follow on soon. Some think it will be ours, but we do not know. They have quit giving passes to go to the city. It is said for fear that they don't know what minute we will be ordered away. I hope and pray that we may not have to go.

Do not try to come down here until I write to you to come. If we stay here and everything keeps quiet I want you to come the first of Nov. You can make your arrangements and be ready by that time. So if all things work right you can come along when I write to you.

I want you to buy your corn as soon as you can, for corn will be much higher than it is now. It is worth $1.00 per bushel in the Prairies now. Do not entrust Bill Davis with any of your business on no terms.[49] Find out as soon as you can about that land and let me know so that I can have it fixed up before I leave here, if I have to [leave] here at all.

Continue to pray for me. Give my best respects to all enquiring friends, and tell the children that Pa wants them to be good children and do every thing you tell them. That he wants them to love the good man and meet him in Heaven. Tell them that I study a heap about them and think how pleasant it would be to

---

45 Andrew Jackson Slaughter, Malinda's brother.

46 Robert K. Wells; Cas Mitchell is unidentified. Calvin Upchurch (1828-1902).

47 Capt. Burton Upchurch (1838-1895) of Co B 42nd AL.

48 James Williams is unidentified but probably served in 42nd AL.

49 William R. Davis, Grant's brother-in-law. It is obvious from Grant's letters that Grant does not trust Davis in money matters.

have some of them on my knees and the rest around me, these cool nights. Much pleasanter than to be hovering around a little smokey fire out of doors made of such trash as we can gather up and green pine logs, and when I go to bed I have to crawl in to my tent and stretch my weary limbs on my hard pallet. May God save them from the fate of their Pa. And may he hasten the time when I may be permitted to return home to stay in peace. May God bless you all is the prayer of your devoted absent Husband,

Grant Taylor

P.S. Do not think from the above that I am any worse dissatisfied now than when I was up there. I feel that I have trusted my all in the hands of my Blessed Savior and what he does is right. Although sometimes I cannot help feeling very lonesome and a long ways from my loved ones.

Even now while I am engaged in writing, some are singing some of those good old tunes that we have sung together so much, which carries my mind back far away to bygone days and happy scenes which are never more to return which makes me feel very sad and lonesome. Though those happy days themselves can never return yet I have an unshaken confidence that there are happy days in store for us on earth yet. More ripe and full than we ever enjoyed, rendered sweet and delicious from the bitter draught that we are now drinking.

Oh I never know how to appreciate the pleasure we once enjoyed until deprived of that pleasure. I sometimes think who it is that has brought this distress on us and I get almost desperate and feel that I should not fear to meet them in the deadly conflict and am almost a[n]xious to be led against this vandal horde, this destroyer of our peace. Once more may God bless you and may he bring order out of confusion.

To his wife and children [from] Grant Taylor
in Pickens County Ala

2[nd] PS If you conclude to take that land and pay all the money for it, Get a deed drawn and send it down here. I think I can get

Parker to sign it in Mobile which will do as well as if he were up there and then he can send it back to his wife to sign and hold until the money is paid to her.[50]

49

Ala Pickens Co

Oct 16th 1862

When this you see
remember mee
tho many miles
apart we bee

My Dear Grant,

It is with pleashure that I pen these lines to you. We are all well one time more and I thank God for it. I trust these lines will finde my beloved one well. I recieved a letter from you last Saturday daited the 4th containing the conversation whitch took place in Tennessee. It was a good piece. I never got the letter that you wrote befor this last one but I saw the one you sent Pap. I think I would like [to] live at Franks place very well.

Mee and Jim Teer went after the rest of my things Wednesday. My move cost me just $20. I have paide all we owe on Buck Creek.[51] Olde Beck is at the widow lewissis whare she was raised.[52] She says Beck is 27 years old. They are willing to give $25 for her so I told Mr Drummon to sell her for that. I had to leave my sow and pigs but they did not pay me for her and my fodder. Charly Garner has not paid me yet. I did not bring my yearling when I brought the cows. It broke back and we let it alone until this time and I cilled [killed] it over thare. It waid [weighed] 200

---

50 Frank Parker from whom Malinda is considering purchasing a farm.

51 Buck Creek is the creek that runs through the community of Cushing (now Ralph).

52 The Taylor's mule Beck has gone to the Lewis farm. The Lewis' are unidentified.

lbs. I only kept 100 lbs of it. I thaught that was enough at one time. Mr Leatherwood took 100 lbs. He did not pay me for it so I will have to go over thare again before long and I intend to have what is owing to mee or have a fuss.

Alsy Anns Family is in greate distress.[53] Lee and Martha's oldest childe is diad and thare is 6 down yet.[54] Thare is no hopes for Olly and Marthas baby.[55] Bills Hines wife and boy diede this week.[56] Bob Jordens childe was buried over her[e] at the curch this week.[57] Mary and Mathew had a tech of the flux last week but they get well and how thankful I feel to Almighty God for his mercy. How earnestly I praid for thare health and I want you to pray for us all to have health while you are so fare [far] away. Grant, I want to see you wors than I ever did it seemes to me.

Grant, Davis wants me to write to you to know wether you are willing for the negrows to bee sold or not.[58] A majority of the children wants them solde. Thats it iff you do dully dont want it done and I donte know whether Hughs and Wick dose [do] or not.[59] Davis says he dont care no way. Pap says he thinks it would bee the best to sell them.

Mother has been very sick with rising in her head. I read all [a] letter from Bud writen for himself and several more to Zion Curch. It was a feeling letter as I ever read.

When I ask Mary whare Pa is she says "its Pappy it ante [ain't] Pa." She says you have left her more times she dont call no man Pa now.

Grant, Jack is taken a prisner.[60] I dont know how many more. I can write to you when Mr Mitchel comes back. He is gon to Carrinth.[61] He heard Cas was cilled.[62]

---

[53] Alsey Ann Taylor's family continues to battle dysentery.
[54] Lee Taylor, about age eight, and Sarah Albina Speed have died.
[55] Olive Taylor (about age 4) and Eliza I.C.L. Speed (age 8 months).
[56] Maybe William I. Hines of Co E 18th AL.
[57] Bob Jordan is unidentified.
[58] William R. Davis, acting as executor of Archelaus Taylor's estate.
[59] Dulcena "Dully" Taylor Teer (Grant's sister), James Hughes Taylor and William M. Taylor (Grant's brothers).
[60] Andrew Jackson Slaughter, Malinda's brother.
[61] Corinth MS where the battle was fought October 3-4, 1862.
[62] Cas Mitchell.

I have not baught any Corn yet and I am nearly out. Pap said he would devide with me if I could not get any. I think I can get some at Speeds Mill. I solde my wheat to cay Taylor. Thare was 2 bushels of it at 4$ per bushel.

So I will have to come to a close. Leonard is going to the office. I expect thare is a letter thare for me. Maybee the one I did not get. So farewell for this time for the big meeting begins tomarrow and I have a heep to do. Oh how I wish you was her[e] to go with me. I shant enjoy it.

I remain your loving Praying wife until death,

Malinda J Taylor

50

Camp Forney

Oct 18th 1862

Dear wife & children,

I take my pen this morning to perform the pleasing task of writing to you again. I am enjoying fine health and am in hopes these lines may reach you all enjoying the best of health.

I received your loving letter of Oct 10th which gave pleasure to hear that you had got moved and was well but sorry to hear of L[eonard's] and little Mary's sickness. I hope it will not prove serious.

I have written to you twice to Pleasant Grove before this. I hope you have received them. In those letters I gave you an account of Frank Parker's land. Since then I received a letter from Pap stating that he did not know how I could do any better than to give $[—] for the place if I could not do any better. Frank will not take any less and wants all the money down. I have bought it provided his wife is willing and he can get a place up there that he wants and provided further if you want the place and have money enough to pay for it by letting my debts lie and have plenty of money to buy your provisions and have plenty left for pocket money. I do not want you to run yourself too near out of money.

I started a letter to Buster this morning how to manage it. The way [--- ---- ---- ---- ----] his wife about it and if it suits all [——] have a deed drawn and sent down here for Frank to sign. He can sign it in Mobile and send it up there and his wife can sign it there and then you can pay the money to whoever Frank may direct. In the meantime you had better be looking around for another place as you may miss that one. You had better get some one to see about paying my taxes for this year on the land I sold. I forgot to tell you anything about it when I was up there.

I wrote to you in my last to buy your corn as soon as you could for it would rise shortly.

I think Wash Leatherwood and Eatman showed their patriotism in the charges they made on you for hauling.[63] That shows what would become of you if you had no money. I wish all such men had to go into the army and have to stay there and not get to go home the first time till the close of the war and that shows the necessity of your keeping a right smart of money on hand. The best I can say is to go by Buster's advice.

You need not save any more dried peaches for me if you can sell them for you will need it more than I do. And then what you would send would do but very little good among so many. I only got four little messes out of the ones I brought. The mess had borrowed and eaten up nearly half as much as I brought while I was gone and I had them to pay back.

I will write to you in my next what to do about coming to see me but I fear from present appearance the chance is bad. We keep hearing that Mobile will be attacked shortly and it is said that we are ordered to be ready to march at a minutes warning to Pollard [AL] near Florida. I hope though times may be so that you can come. I send you some dispatches giving an account of [Gen Braxton] Bragg's fighting in Kentucky. They are rather conflicting.[64] But there is no doubt but he gained a great victory. I

---

63 Eatman is unidentified.

64 General Bragg's abortive invasion of Kentucky ended with a confused clash at Perryville on October 8, 1862. Neither side won a decisive victory despite over 7,600 combined casualties. See James M.

do not think John and Jake were in it as one of our men got a letter from that Reg. this week stating that they were stationed somewhere in Tenn. We have heard here that Jack Slaughter, Bob Wells, Cas Mitchell and Jim Going were killed in the battle at Corinth but do not know the truth of it. I am very anxious to hear. Tom Lanier was not killed there, only slightly wounded in the head.

Sickness somewhat increased in our company since we came here. Several are down with fever among them John Boon. There have been several cool nights here. Some say that Frost has been seen in Mobile. Continue to pray for me. Give my best respects to all enquiring friends and believe me your ever affectionate husband and father,

To Mrs M J Taylor [from] Grant Taylor
& children

Oh how I would like to be there with you to attend that meeting. I feared you would be more lonesome there than at the other place, but cheer up, God can be with you there the same as at the other place. By the way did Garner pay you that money before you moved, and you ought to get the receipt from Mrs Jones that I gave her for that money as soon as she was put in possession of the things mentioned in the receipt.

P.S. If you have any fruit or anything to sell, do not let Bat Peebles have it unless he pays you the highest market price and I would rather you would not let him have any thing if you can sell to any one else for he brings them down here and speculates off of us.[65]

G. T.

McPherson, *Battle Cry of Freedom: The Civil War Era* (New York: Oxford University Press, 1988) 519-520, and James L. McDonough, *War in Kentucky: From Shiloh to Perryville* (Knoxville: University of Tennessee Press, 1994).

[65] William Battle Peebles (1824-1884), a merchant in Pickens County.

October 19th I feel much better today than I did yesterday. I understand we are to start day after to-morrow for Meridian and where else God only knows.[66] I sent you a shirt and a pair of drawers that I drew yesterday. The shirt you can make for a gown and the drawers you can fix for Leonard as they are too small for me. Yours affectionately,

G Taylor

51

Ala Pickens Co

October 21st 1862

Dear and beloved husband,

I seat myself to drop you a few lines one time more. We are well and I hope and pray to God that you are enjoying the same greate blessing. I have not got but 2 letters since you went back. I wrote to you last Saturday but I dont know that you will ever get it. I understood today that your Reg was at the depo[t] waiting for the cars at Corrinth. I hope it is not so. Grant, we have a co[–] Meeting going on at Farest [church]. I cant enjoy myself with the thaught of whare you are. God grant that these troubles would come to a close is my daily Prayer.

Grant, you will recollect tonight was 10 years ago we was married. Oh what Pleashure I enjoid then to what I do now. Not once did I think that in ten years that you would bee in the army. I feel like my pleashure was all done in this world. Sometimes I am allmost ready to give you ugp forever and then I fe[e]l like that god will answer my Prayers in due time if I faint not. I will try to continue to pray as long as I am permitted to live. Grant, we must not look for happiness in this world for I dont think we will see it soon, if ever, but I can look at the happiness of heaven and that I will bee permitted to see it when I dy and I can bare [bear] the

---

[66] This rumor of a move to Meridian by the 40th Alabama was incorrect.

troubles of this world very well. I want you to bare your hardships as well as you can and trust to God to bring you through.

Elsy Ans Olly diede Saturday evening.

Oct the 22nd

Dear Grant, I went to Church last night. My poore broken [heart] was peeved a little. Mr R Jones Preached last night. His text was bring all your ties [tithes] into the storehouse. I triede to do that thing. Oh how earnestly I praid that you might one day return home safe. Grant, I can hardly bare to hear any one begin to sing base [bass] because you allways sung base. But we must not take it so to heart.

Mary has not heard from John and Jake since they left Noxvill.[67] She is allmost deranged. John and Jake is now in Kentuckey. Wat and Bud is at Noxvill Tennessee. I dont know soon you and Ide will bee thare. Sally hearde last week that Jack was very sick.[68] She is going to him or get old Miles to go after him. Mr Cay is dead.[69] Jack Leatherwood said he was treated like a dog.

I will have to close. It is gett[ing] time to go to Church. Oh how I wish you was he[re] to go with mee. The children sends howdy to you. Give my love and respects to Ide. Tell him to pray for me.

May health, Peace and Prospirity crown you is the prayer of your loving wif[e],

Malinda J Taylor

Oh! that this unholy war would cease and we would live as the poet says

No, never from that hour to part
we'd live and love so true
The sigh that rends thy constant heart
Should break thy Linny,s too.
M J Taylor

---

67 Knoxville TN.

68 Sally Leatherwood and her husband M. Jack Leatherwood.

69 Rufus "Kay" Taylor, Grant's cousin who had helped Malinda after Grant first departed.

52

Camp Forney

October 25th 1862

Dear Wife & children,

Once more am I seated to pen you a few lines which leaves me quite poorly. I have been on the grunts for nearly a week though I am still able to walk about camps. I feel worse to-day than common.

The Doctor has just pronounced that I have the Jaundice which is very prevalent in camps. But it is not very dangerous. I have no stomach to eat and less that is suitable for a sick man to eat. Dont be uneasy about me. The Lord will do what is right. I received your kind letter of 16th inst. a day or two ago and yours and Betty's by the hand of Mr Stevens.[70] I was truly glad to hear from you that you have all got well once more. But I am puzzled to know why you can not get letters as regular there as at Cushing. I was fearful of that thing when you moved. Oh how disappointed I am when I miss getting your letter at the right time and I know you are too.

How I would have enjoyed that meeting with you. It hurts me to think how we used to want to live over there together but could not get the chance and when we were separated you got the chance to move over there. You mentioned our wedding day and the pleasures we then so [-----]! I thought that all over on that day and that you were living in the very same house that we staid in then. Those were happy days, departed never to return. Father & Mother gone to the land of Spirits and me bound to stay 200 miles away from you by a stern necessity.[71] Oh how changed our condition indeed but if there is no more pleasure for us on earth, I feel that there is happiness in store for us beyond this vale of tears in that bright world where wars and parting, sickness, pain and

---

[70] Elizabeth "Betty" Taylor Teer, Grant's sister. Mr. Stevens is unidentified.

[71] Grant's parents have both died in recent years: Lucy Taylor in June 1861 and Archelaus Taylor in August 1862.

death will be felt and feared no more. Where we will meet our dear ones who have gone before and behold the New Jerusalem with its streets paved with gold and above all and over all we shall behold our blessed Savior face to face and live and reghn with him forevermore. Oh! what a prospect is this to contemplate and to feel that one day they will be ours. Oh then dearest Malinda why should we complain. But poor human nature will give way sometimes and become despondent. But cheer up dearest wife. Let us live as we may wish we had done when we come to die and hope for better days.

I have written to you every week since I left. I am willing for Davis to sell those negroes.[72]

I hardly know what to say to you about coming to see me. Times look like they will be squally before long. I understand that we have orders to be in readiness to meet the foe at any hour, but that has been the talk so long that I do not know what to believe about it. I do not believe the Yankees will make an attack here before the rivers rise. If you are ready to come when you get this maybe you had as well come on immediately and trust to God for the consequence.

You can find out at Macon [MS] whether they have made the attack or not. I have no doubt but what this is the best time you will ever have to come and it looks quite gloomy. But I want to see you mighty bad and I know you do me. Try to get Pap to come with you. If you come you had better go to Macon and then there will be no change of cars unless the roads get bad. In that case you had better come to Gainsville to get on the cars.

When you get to Mobile you can hire [a] cab or buggy to bring you out to camps. If you get there in the night you had better get conveyance to the Roper [Hotel][---------] and stay all night. You will find those cabs or carriages (they are all the same) all along by the cars when they stop at the depot. Or you can go down the street that runs up on the right hand of the depot called Royal St, untill you come to St. Francis Street and get on the horse [street] cars and come out to the 4 Mile Station where the 18th Reg is camped and then get off the cars and turn square to the left and come that

---

[72] This reference is to the slaves in the estate of his father Archelaus Taylor.

direction a short distance and you will see our camps about a half or 3/4 of a mile ahead of you. I think you had better come by hiring a carriage although it will cost 2 or 3 dollars the most. It will save you from walking any.

If you hear nothing more from here by the time this comes to hand come to the Railroad and then you can find out more about it. You need not put any dependence in the rumors that we have left here. I have no idea that we will leave here.

Ide is in fine health and sends his best respects to you. He wrote to Betty yesterday.[73]

53

Oct the 19th [29] 1862

Kinde and beloved husband,

Through the mercies of God I am permitted to pen you a few lines once more. We are not all well. I have had a sever attact of toothache and jawache evrry since last Friday. The rest is well and all the connection[s] as fare [far] as I know. I hope these scrawls will finde you in the same good health.

I recieved 2 letters from you last Monday. One Dated the 12 of Oct the other the 24 of Sept. You sent it to Cushing and I never got it before I moved. It was rebacked [readdressed] and sent to Pleasant Grove. The other one had been written 2 weeks before I got it. This makes the 4th letter I have written since I moved here. I sent one by Stevens last week.

Grant, you donte know how it made my heart ache when you said how mutch more pleasant it would bee if you could have some of the Children on your knees and the rest around you instead of standing around a little smoky fire and then crall [crawl] into your tent and streach your w[e]ary limbs on your harde pallet. But it revived me up when you said you had an unshaken

---

[73] This letter is not signed in the usual way. However, the last paragraph was written in the margin as though he had finished.

confidence that thare is happy days for us on Earth yet. Little Mary says you have gon and left her again.

I wrote to you before that Davis wants to know if you are willing for the negrows to bee solde this winter. They are all willing but dully I believe.[74]

I am going to Lucretas [estate] sail [sale] today.[75]

Grant you said for me to know about that land and let you know. Pap wrote to you 3 weeks ago what he thought of the place. I hope you have got it before now.

Oct 30th 1862

I went to the sail. The things went very low.

Dick Russel has got his furlow extended until the 12 of next month.[76] I will send your gloves by him. You said you would write when for me to come. I am afraid you wont write atall.

Grant I am not half so lonesum as I was at our old place. I enjoy myself very well here. I can get corn delivard here from the Perrarays [Perry's] at one dollar and 30 cents per bushel. I expect to get one hundred bushels. The man that has the corn to sell is sending his waggons by here evry day or too [two] withe corn. He is halling now for Ves and Minard.[77] The way I will have to do [it] is to write a letter and send it by the negro to his master and he will send me the corn.

I heard today that Pap was gon to Tennessee. Watt and Bud was left at Noxvell. They ware sick but they got better. They got wose again and sent for Pap to go thare so he started last sunday.

Grant, Jack was taken a prisner. Mr Mitchell saw him. He sent word to the c[h]urch to pray for him publickly, that he had been backward and cold, that he now felt the kneed of prayer. So they praid for him at the big meeting.

Leonard wants me to write to you that he can spin [a top] a little. Tell Ide I saw Betty yesterday. She was well but Mary was

---

[74] Dulcena "Dully" Taylor Teer, Grant's sister.

[75] Lucretia Taylor Mullins, widow of William Mullins, is having a sale to pay debts. Later, she will move to Texas.

[76] Richard M. Russell (Co G 40th AL).

[77] Probably John Ves Peebles. Minard (Maynard?) is unidentified.

passing blood through her. Grant maybee you and Ide can get to come home when the sail is.[78] Begin to beg your Capt now and mabe he will let you come.

Goodby loved one. So I remain your lonely wife until death.

Malinda Taylor

When this you see remember mee tho many miles apart we bee.

54

Camp Forney

November 2nd 1862

Beloved wife and children,

I seat myself this rainy Sabbath day to pen you a few lines. Thank the Lord I have got about well one time more though I am quite weak. I am not able to do anything yet and my mouth has not got fairly well from being salivated, though the salivation was slight. Last Tuesday I came very near having an attack of pneumonia but working against it in time that dreaded disease was staid.

I hope and humbly pray that these lines may reach you and our dear children enjoying the best of health. Although I hope to see you before you see this as I wrote to you yesterday was a week ago and also last Monday to come on if you were ready as I thought this would probably be the best time you would ever get. Although it does not look exactly safe for we are ordered to hold ourselves in readiness to meet the enemy at any hour. I believe it is the general belief among the big men that Mobile will be attacked before long.[79] But I hardly think we will be attacked before the rivers rise.

---

[78] The sale is for the estate of Grant's father, Archelaus Taylor.

[79] In late October, Alabama Governor John G. Shorter wrote President Jefferson Davis that Mobile was the "only Gulf port of any importance

I wrote to you full directions how to reach our camps in both those letters and which is unnecessary now. [———] From Saturday evening until Tuesday morning last I do not think I ever suffered worse with cold. I was quite sick and the weather was very windy and cold and I had nothing but 2 blankets under me and 3 over me. Since then I bought a blanket considerably worn and paid seven dollars for it and fixed me a good pine straw bed and I am much more comfortable. I and Ide sleep together.

I have heard that they are making preparations to build cabbins for our winter quarters which will be much more comfortable.[80] But even in our present circumstances we ought to be very thankful that we are as well fixed up as we are. For it might be a great deal worse with us than it is in General [Sterling] Price's army where Jack is, not more than one third of the men have even one blanket and no tents. I do not see how they can stand [it].[81] And I heard Old Moses Hammond say the other day that he saw fifteen hundred convalescents that is men who have been sick and discharged from hospitals without a shoe to their feet and half of them half naked and the snow was six inches deep.[82] This was last Sunday in Knoxville Tenn. Then how thankful ought we to be.

Dearest Malinda, let your grateful thanks be raised to an ever merciful God that I even I a poor sinful being should be as highly favored as I am and let your prayers rise as incense to a throne of Grace that He may continue his great mercy to me and that I may live an humble and contrite life.

There are several cases of Pneumonia in the Reg. Two lieutenants died with it this week. One was taken on Sunday and

---

which is left to us and one of the most important lines of communication in the Confederacy." See Arthur W. Bergeron, *Confederate Mobile* (Jackson MS: University Press of Mississippi, 1991) 58.

[80] Actual construction of these winter cabins did not begin until November 23, 1862. See Willett, *History of Company B*, 12.

[81] General Price's army spent the winter of 1862 near Springfield, Missouri. See William Watson, *Life in the Confederate Army: Being the Observations and Experiences of an Alien in the South During the American Civil War* (Baton Rouge LA: Louisiana State University Press edition, 1995) 267.

[82] Moses Hammond is unidentified.

died Tuesday.[83] George McDaniel of our company has been very sick with it but is getting better.[84] John Boon is getting well. Hammond said he saw Jake and John yesterday was a week ago in Knoxville Tenn. They were both well. He knew nothing of Bud and Wat but was under the impression that Wat died in Charleston Tenn but I think this is the same old tale we heard when I was up thare. The army with Jake and John left Knoxville for Murfreesboro Tenn and Hammon left there on Sunday.[85] He says that Talbert['s] Reg was not in the fight at Perryville [KY] an account of which I sent you. They did not come up with [General Braxton] Bragg until after the fight. Jack is paroled but is held at Holley Springs [MS] by our forces to be exchanged.

Monday morning I have nothing to add only I am still on the mend. I think I shall be able to go on duty in a few days. I saw Mr Porter, Jo Leavell and all those boys Saturday evening. They were all well except Porter. He was quite poorly with jaundice. There was a slow rain here nearly all day yesterday and this morning the wind blows like it is going to be cold again. Continue to pray for me. Kiss the children for me and believe me your loving husband as ever,

To Mrs M J Taylor [from] Grant Taylor

55

Camp Forney

Nov. 9th 1862

Beloved wife and children,

I seat myself this beautiful Sabbath evening to pen you a few lines to inform you that my health has got pretty good again. I was

---

[83] One was possibly Lt. D. R. Rudolph of Co I.
[84] George McDaniel (Co B 40th AL).
[85] Confederate troops began the march to Murfreesboro after General Bragg ordered it on October 23, 1862. See Thomas L. Connelly, *Autumn of Glory: The Army of Tennessee, 1862-1865* (Baton Rouge: Louisiana State University Press, 1971) 15.

returned to duty yesterday morning. And I do hope and pray that these lines may reach you all in the best of health. I received your letter of October 31st on last Tuesday. I was glad to hear from you and that the children were well but sorry to hear of your own suffering.

I have been looking for you for 3 or 4 days for I wrote to you 2 letters two weeks ago for you to come on if you were coming. I think surely you received one if not both of those letters in each of which I gave you full directions how to come. I do not see why it is that you do not get my letters regularly. I get yours every Tuesday after they are mailed on Friday.

I wrote to you some 3 weeks ago how me and Frank Parker traded about his land and gave you full directions how to proceed about getting titles to it. I also wrote to Pap at the same time telling him the same things. I want you to be sure to write whether you ever got that letter if you do not come to see me. I have also written twice that I am willing for Davis to sell those Negroes. If you intend to come, you had better come along as every day you stay away makes it more dangerous for you to come. I have no idea there is any danger yet. At any rate I think this [is] as good and probably the best time you will ever have to come and see me.

I read a letter from Jack yesterday stating that he was taken prisoner at Corinth and paroled and had got back to old Mr Boon's safe and sound. He was in 3 battles. The Yanks were very kind to him during the 9 days they had him a prisoner.

There is a good deal of sickness here mostly pneumonia and it is tolerably fatal. A D Crimm, a brother of old John Crim's, died in the hospital here last night and there are 2 other men from our company very dangerous.[86] One of them has the choking quinsy.[87]

I have just returned from Col. Smith's Reg. where I saw Mr Porter, Jo Leavell and the other boys. They were all well except Jasper. He has had the Jaundice but is nearly well. I also saw Rickard Smith today. He and all the boys in their Reg. were well except Brantley Garner and he is gone home on sick furlough of 25 days. Tom Salmon is in bad health yet. He has been in the hospital

---

[86] Private Allen D. Crimm (Co G 40th AL).
[87] Quinsy was an inflamation of the throat.

nearly ever since he came back but is back in camps now. The boys told me that Jack Leatherwood was dead. He died in Clinton Teen. Neither his wife nor father got to go see him. The boys had got letters from home stating the fact. Old Ingram is dead also. He belonged to Tolbirts Reg. I hope it not prove true about Jack's death. For with all his failings, I could not help but like him.

What a number of widows and orphans are being left by this cruel war. I feel sorry truly for Sally. One of our men got word yesterday that his wife died a few days ago up there in Pickens [County]. She had been sick a long time but he could not get to go to see her. They say he takes it very hard, and well he may, to be dragged away from her and her sick and not be allowed to go to see her on her dying bed. May God forgive those that are the cause of all this distress.

If you have money enough to answer your purpose in buying all you have to buy and paying for that land and can spare Betty ten dollars, I want you to let her have it. Ide has the money here to pay me or to send to her but he is afraid to send it by mail and he has no other way of sending it and Betty needs it to buy something to eat, but I hope to see you down here before you get this and if so you can take it home for him. The drum is beating for dress parade and I must quit. Continue to pray for me and may God bless you all is the prayer of your loving husband.

Mrs. M J Taylor [from] Grant Taylor
& children

Monday morning There is a powerful frost this morning and I feel first rate. I have to go on guard in a few minutes. Ide has a very bad cold. He sends his best respects to you. Your piece of hair look very natural and sweet. It made me think of how many times I had rubed my hands over that dear head. O shall I ever see it again and be permitted to dwell with you in peace.

[Between these two letters Malinda visited Grant in Mobile for a week about Nov 16-27.]

56

Camp Forney

Nov 28th 1862

Dearest Malinda,

As Lafayett leaves this morning for home, I will pen you a few lines. I am not very well. You know I had the headache when you left me Saturday evening. Well that continued 3 days when I took the Dysentery which makes me feel right bad though I have kept on duty all the time and I feel better this morning. I hope this may find you and the dear children in the best of health. I want to hear how you got along on your way home very badly.

I have no news to write. The health of our company is getting pretty good again. No prospect as yet of an immediate attack on Mobile.

Ide's health has improved some but he is not able to go on duty yet. I clear forgot to get any rice for you to carry home. I am very sorry for it. I will send you some as soon as I can. I would send some by Lafayett but he does not know how he will get home from the railroad.

I saw that you took parting from me very hard. But do try dearest wife to bear your troubles with patience for although we may never meet on earth again yet God doeth all things right. I hope you will not despair and become disheartened but be constant and fervent in prayer.

We have more very cold weather here now and I am writing out of doors by the fire. I must close and write the more next time. Kiss the children for me. Give my best respects to all enquiring friends if any think enough of me to enquire after me. And believe me your ever loving husband,

To Mrs M J Taylor   [from] Grant Taylor
& children

P.S. I send my old socks. If you have thread, you can foot them and have them ready for me.

57

Camp Forney

Nov. 30th 1862

Dearest wife & children,

I seat myself this holy Sabbath day to pen you a few lines. I wrote a few lines to you last Friday and sent it by Henry Jones stating to you that I was not very well that I had the Dysentery. I have got about well of that but I have got a very bad cold which makes me feel pretty badly. I hope and pray that you and our dear little ones are enjoying the best of health.

I have nothing of importance to write more than to let you hear from me. It is said that 2 or 3 cases of smallpox have occurred in this Reg. But others assert that none have had it in any of the Regiments about here. So I do not know what to believe about it, but if there is any virtue in vaccination I have nothing to fear from it, for it took finely on me. I had a sore arm for 3 or 4 days.

I do not think you need to be uneasy about me as I am not about myself. I feel that I am in God's hands and the Lord of all the earth will do right. It is true that it is my greatest earthly desire to be permitted to come home and live with you a little while longer in peace and when I close my eyes in death be laid at dear old Forest Church. Where the first Gospel sermon I ever heard was prech[ed] among my deares[t] kin.

How dear to my heart are the scenes of my childhood
When fond recolection presents them to view
The orchard, the meadow, the deep tangled wild-wood
And every loved spot which my infancy knew.
But dearer than any of these are those dear ones that I call wife and children. Oh the happy days we have seen together. Will they ever return? I believe they will. But not my will but the Lord's be done.

Malinda, what were you doing last night from five to seven o'clock? Were you thinking of me as I was of you. I was on guard during those hours of the night near to the 36[th] and 38[th] Regiments after which I was released and sent to my tent because I was not well. During those two hours I was in hearing of a perfect babel. First dress parade with its din of drums and fife and as the night de[e]pened, what a confused sound did I hear. Some were laughing, some hollowing, some profaning the sacred name of God as though they never had to appear at the judgment seat of Christ to be judged according to the deeds done in the body. Some were engaged in auctioning off some kinds of goods. While others were devoutly engaged in singing those blessed old songs of Zion (which we have sung together so often) and in prayer to a merciful God to have mercy on their souls and our distracted country.

It was a befitting time for contimplation to a thinking immortal mind as I walked my solitary post. In hearing of all this noise and yet virtually shut out from the society of men for those two long hours. Yet I feel that I was not shut out from the society and communion of my blessed Savior. I turned from this babel of confusion and thought of home my dear earthly home and the dear ones left behind perhaps never more to behold them again on this side of Eternity. I then cast my eyes upward and beheld the bright twinkling stars and the mild pale-faced moon, which seemed to say to me in all their beauty and loveliness, Vain man why be contemplating earthly happiness. Where all things are confusion and vanity and vexation of spirit! I then let my mind, as I watched those beautiful orbs passing in all their grandeur, contemplate that Glorious home above. That home where my Blessed Savior reigns without a rival! That home where all is peace and quiet and lovely and Glorious! That home where sickness, sorrow, pain and death never come! That home where no cruel wars are waged by more cruel despots to mar its Glorious peace! That home where parting between loveded ones that reach that happy place are known and felt no more. That sweet home where I hope to safely arrive one day, and where I hope to meet you my dearest earthly friend. That home where we will sing the praises of our dear Redeemer through the ceaseless ages of eternity.

Home sweet home, prepare me dear Savior for Glory, my home. Oh, Then dearest Malinda, what a prize is held out to the finally faithful. How vain and sinful are our murmurings when the

God of Glory has prepared all this for us if we but hold out faithful. Then let us persevere and never give over the conflict until the victory is gained. Let us never say that if such and such things are not granted that it is useless to pray but let us pray always without ceasing and leave the result to God, for I feel that he will do right. I feel this more than I ever did in my life and more humble.

I wanted to talk to you more when I was with you about that sweet home, but I was fearful thy [that] my utterance would fail me. But here in my tent this holy days with the most of my messmates asleep arou[n]d me I can let my pen run in unison with my thoughts. While my heart swells with love and gratitude to my heavenly Father that He has shown us so much mercy. I almost long to fly away and be at rest but I know that my Savior wills it otherwise.

Do all you can to raise up our dear children in the nurture and admonition of the Lord. Try to teach them early the worth of their immortal souls. I can look back and see that I have misspent many precious moments through a false delicacy in naming such subjects in the family but do you try to over come that. Be strong! Be courageous. Let your works shine in both words and acts before your children. And rest assured that God will reward your efforts.

All is quiet here so fare as the Yankees are concerned. But there are deep complaints made on the account of the way we are fed and treated about furloughs and being guarded so tight. There are ~~one hundred and twenty~~ guards placed all around these three Regiments and we are not allowed to go out even to get a stick of wood without a pass from the Captain and Col. And then it is a mile to where they will let us cut down a tree to get wood. That is, I have been told that it is that far and they have not hauled us any since you left. I do not see how we are to cook our pittance if wood is not hauled soon. We have commenced building cabbins for winter qarters, but we make slow progress for the want of tools.

Ide's health is improving but he is not stout yet. Give my love to Bettey and the rest of my brothers and sisters and believe me your ever loving husband,

To Mrs M J Taylor [from] Grant Taylor
and children

PS I want to hear how you got along home and the children
made out very badly. Continue to pray for me. Tell Betty and
Lucreta to remember me in their prayers. Give my best love to
pap and mother and all your sisters and if Wat is still alive to him
also. Tell him to put his trust in God. Tell him that I want to see
him one time more in this world if no more. But the chances are
now that we will never see each other in this life but I want him to
meet me in heaven.

CHAPTER 4

THERE IS A HEAP OF SICKNESS IN THE REGIMENT

During the winter of 1862 and into early 1863, Pvt. Taylor was concerned with staying warm, dry, and healthy. The soldiers of the 40th Alabama were cold and sleepless for many nights at a time due to the constant moves of their regiment. Illness again struck the regiment with full force. Pneumonia, "camp fever," dysentery, and smallpox were among the ailments that afflicted the men, and Taylor himself was eventually stricken.

58

Camp Forney

Dec. 2nd 1862

Dearest Malinda

We have just received orders to go to Jackson Miss.[1] We start in one hour. I am in reasonable health and go off in pretty good spirits. Though I may be going to where I may receive a death stroke. Pray for me. I would write more but I have not got time. Ide is not well enough to go with us. May God bless you all,

To Mrs M J Taylor [from] Grant Taylor

---

[1] Colonel Coleman received orders to move the 40th Alabama to Jackson, Mississippi, via Meridian on the Mobile and Ohio Railroad early that day. See J. H. Curry, "A History of Company B, 40th Alabama Infantry, C.S.A." *Alabama Historical Quarterly* 17/4 (Winter 1955) 166.

59

Camp near Jackson Miss

Dec 6th 1862

Dear Wife & Children,

This leaves me in very good health and I hope that you and the children are so too. On the 2nd inst. we were, several of us, out getting timbers to build our houses when orders came about 11 o'clock for us to march at 3 o'clock to Mobile to get on the cars for this place. We did so and landed in Meridian next morning and stayed there till next morning [at] 4 o'clock when we started for this place.[2] We landed here just before night and met orders for us to not to take time to change cars but to hasten on to Grenada Miss which is 100 miles north of here. Accordingly we started at breakneck speed and went 28 miles to Canton where [we] were ordered to return back to this place.[3] We turned back and landed back [here] about 2 o'clock that night.[4]

So here we are in camps with orders to keep 3 days rations cooked on hand and to be ready to march at a minutes warning but to what point we will go next God only knows. We had a very disagreeable time on the cars. There were from 50 to 60 crowded into a box car. We were crowded so that many of us could not sit down and then in [it] rained nearly all the time and the cars leaked dreadfully. We slept but very little from the time we left Mobile until last night which was 3 days and nights and part of the time but little to eat for we did not have time to cook it. I wrote a few lines to you just before we left Mobile stating that Ide was not coming with us but he did and stood the trip very well. I could not bring my pillow and gave it to Mr Porter to keep for me if he could stay there until I returned if I ever should do so. I am

---

2 Jackson, Mississippi.

3 Ibid.

4 The 40th Alabama retraced it steps to Jackson after a clash at Coffeeville with advancing Federal units. See Curry, "A History of Company B," 166.

engaged in cooking our rations and have no time to write any more.

Direct your letters to Jackson Miss. Maybe I will get them some time. Still pray for me and may God bless you. The mail is ready to start, I must close.

To Mrs M J Taylor [from] Grant Taylor

60

Camp near Jackson Miss

Dec. 8th 1862

Beloved wife & children,

I am once more seated to pen you a few lines away down here in Miss. I wrote you a note the day we left Mobile and also one day before yesterday. Just as I had sealed my last to you I received your kind letter of Nov. 27th which had followed me on from Mobile. I was truly glad to get it as it was the first since you left and gladder to hear that you had got home safe and found all well. But I feel indignant at Woodward at the way he treated you after you lay over a day to put a few dollars in his pocket.[5] He is a scoundrel and I never shal have any more use for him. Now if you had claimed your right and have gone on that day and knocked him out carrying those other men then I should not have thought so much of it but even then ten dollars were too much.

This leaves me in good health and spirits and I hope it may find you all enjoying the best of health.

We received orders last Tuesday the 2nd instant about 11 o'clock (while many of us were in the woods a mile from camps cutting timber to build winter cabbins) to march at 3 o'clock to Mobile to take the cars at 5 o'clock. We did so and land[ed] at Meridian the next morning where we staid some of us until Thur[s]day morning 4 o'clock when we took the cars for this place

---

[5] Perhaps James A. Woodward of Tuscaloosa County.

where we arrived the same evening about night and met an order to proceed at once without changing cars to Grenada, Miss some hundred miles north of this place. We started and went 28 miles to Canton where we were ordered back to this place to await further orders. We then turned back and landed here about 2 o'clock at night on thursday night nearly worn out for the want of rest and sleep. It rained the most of the way from Mobile and the cars leaked badly and we were crowded so that many could not sit down much less lie down. All the sleep that I got was about 4 hours at Meridian from Monday night until Friday night 8 o'clock.

We are now encamped 1 mile south of Jackson with orders to keep 3 days rations cooked on hand and to be ready to march at a minutes warning. But to what point we will go no one knows. We have a very nice place to camp at but bad water, nothing but a muddy prairie creek.

I have nev[er] been over in Jackson yet and know nothing but hearsay. They wont give a soldier a drink of water there but offer to sell it to them, and the city council come within 3 votes of not allowing the soldiers to walk on the sidewalks. I suppose water is scarce there but if they have water to sell they have it to give away. From what I can hear they are a den of scoundrels. I had much rather be at Mobile.

Several Tenn. Reg.[s] have arrived and camped here waiting for orders.[6] It is thought that there will be a big fight at Grenada before long and more than likely we will go there or to Vicksburg. There is no doubt but that we are to see stirring times before long, but I do not dread it but very little for I put my trust in God and I want you to continue to pray for my protection.

There was some fighting near Granada last week and it is said that fifteen hundred Yankee's prisoners were brought here day before yesterday but I do not know how true it is.[7]

---

[6] These were the 79th, 80th, and 81st Tennessee Infantry of General John C. Vaughan's Brigade.

[7] Part of General U.S. Grant's advance on Grenada caused a series of actions in the area during the first week of December, 1862. See E.B Long, *The Civil War Day by Day: An Almanac 1861-1865* (Garden City NJ: Doubleday, 1971) 292-293.

I gave my pillow to Mr Porter to keep for me if he got to stay there and I should ever return there. Ide is in bad health yet but he is able to go about. I am cook this week and I have a pretty hard time of it cooking our 3 days rations. I have no time to write much of my feelings. But I still feel that I shall weather the storm and if I do not but fall in the army, I feel that all will be well. Tell all howdy for me and may God b[l]ess you and my dear children is the prayer of your loving husband,

To Mrs M J Taylor [from] Grant Taylor

PS Excuse bad writing as I have a very bad place to write.

61

Camp near Jackson Miss

Dec. 11[th] 1862

Beloved wife & children,

I seat myself this morning to pen you a few lines to let you know that I am in good health and I hope these few lines may reach you all in the enjoyment of the same great blessing.

I have written two hurried letters to you since I came here. I gave you a description of our breaking up from Mobile and landing here. I will say in this (for fear you do'nt get those[)] that we got orders at 11 o'clock AM on the 2nd, got on the cars at five P.M. and landed here about 4 o'clock PM on the fifth and met orders to proceed on to Granada about 100 miles north of this. We started and went 28 miles and were ordered back to this place to await further orders. We landed back here about 2 o'clock on Friday morning nearly worn out for the want of sleep and rest. We were so crowded in the cars that we could not all of us get to sit down. We were in old box cars and it rained nearly all the way from Mobile and the cars leaked badly.

I slept at Camp Forney on Monday night and I did not sleep more than 4 or 5 hours until Friday night. So you see that I had enough to wear me out but I stood it finely and feel as well this morning as I ever did in my life. We are encamped 1 mile South of Jackson. We have a very nice place to camp but very bad water. We have orders to keep 3 days rations cooked on hand and to be ready to march at a minute's notice. But to what point we know not. I wish we may be ordered back to Mobile but I fear that will not be done. There have several Tennessee Regts came here since we did waiting for orders.

Ide's health is improving and he has gone on duty. He sends his best respects to you. You sent some messages to Mrs. Dade and Family but I have never seen them since you left except Mr. Dade.[8] It is said that there are 3 cases of smallpox in our Reg this morning but I do not know how true it is.

I received your letter that you wrote after you got home 2 days after I got here, which I answered in my last. You said that you never would forget that pleasurable week you spent with me at Mobile. Neither shall I, and I hope we will spend many more such together before we die. Dangers thicken around me but I do not feel afraid. My trust is in my blessed Savior and whether I live or die, I believe all will be well.

I know noth[ing] of Jackson but from hearsay and from that I infer that it is a perfect den. I have not been out of camps since we landed here and we are guarded so that I cannot get out without a pass.

The night after we left camps at Mobile Bat Peebles and several others who were left behind whip[p]ed Lieut. [J.H.] Pickens' negro pretty badly and the negro was found dead the next day not far off.[9] They arrested Bat before he got away and have sent on here and have arrested the others and they and the witnesses start for Mobile this morning to stand trial. I cannot say that the whipping killed the negro but it is said that he was badly bruised. His offence was that while we were in the hurry of moving he got hold of some liquor, got drunk, stole and wasted a good deal of lard belonging to Bat and then cursed and sauced him.[10]

---

[8] Mr. and Mrs. Dade are unidentified.

[9] William Battle Peebles (Co G 40th AL).

[10] Private John R. Hicks of Company B was also implicated in the assault. See Curry, "A History of Company B," 166.

I think Woodward treated you doggishly after getting you to stay and all I have got to say is that I think he is a puppy.

Make hast[e] and get your corn. Continue to pray for me and may God bless and save you and my dear children is the prayer of your loving husband,

To Mrs M J Taylor [from] Grant Taylor
& children

PS Direct your letters to Jackson Miss. instead of Mobile Ala.

62

Camp near Jackson Miss.

Dec. 15ᵗʰ 1862

Beloved wife & children,

I seat myself once more to write to you. This leaves me in fine health and spirits or at least as good spirits as could be expected under the circumstances and I hope these lines may reach you all enjoying the best of health. I received your kind letter of the 4ᵗʰ and 5ᵗʰ inst. on the 12th and was very glad to hear from you once more but sorry to hear that Leonard had suffered so much. That one was the second that I have received from you and this is the 4ᵗʰ that I have written to you since I came here. Little did you think when you were writing your letter of the 4ᵗʰ and lamenting our situation that we were at Meridian that night until 4 o'clock A.M. hovering around the fire or trying to sleep under an open shed. That was the case with me and Teer and about 15 others of our company. The rest started that night at 10 o'clock for this place. We staid because the cars were so much crowded but did not better it.

I blistered one of my feet very badly marching to Mobile with my new shoes on and suffered a good deal with them. The night you wrote your letter I could scarcely get about. But they are about well now. Mrs. Stuckey staid until the next Monday week and we left Mrs. Monchet down there waiting on her husband, he being sick.[11] I have never heard from there since. The health of our company is better now than it has been in a long time. There are several cases of jaundice but they are all getting better and one case of verioliod, that is a species of smallpox but not bad enough to be catching. Old Mr Heritage has it.[12] There is no doubt but that the small[pox] is in our Reg. Several cases have occured. One in a company next to us. The company that was next to our table when you were down. But it does not seem to be very dangerous. I do not think anyone has died yet. I do not feel the least uneasy.

A dreadful storm of rain and wind is now rageing and I must quit for this time. We have had a fine rain and it is still raining. I was in Jackson last Saturday and found it a perfect den as I wrote to you I believed it was.

I had been living on short rations before I went over there and went into an eating house and got as sorry a dinner as we eat in Mobile and had to pay one dollar. I then bought a pair of horn pocket combs just such as my old ones and had to pay one dollar for them. Everything that I priced was a heap higher than they are in Mobile. It sprinkled on my paper and blotched it. You must excuse it.

I have no idea how long we will stay here. It is said we are ordered to Vicksburg but I do not believe it. Although it maybe possible. I have got so that I care but little which way they carry me since I cannot come home.

I think if you can get 14 cents per lb. for your cotton you had better sell it. I believe it will either be burnt or fall into the hand of the Yankees before March. I am fearful that they will overrun that country befor spring. I want it burnt rather than for them to have it. I want you to get a place and get corn as soon as you can. Then I will be better satisfied.

I study a great deal more about what is to become of you and the children than I do about myself. I know you see many hardships that you were never used to and that makes me see many an anxious hour. I want to see you all as bad as I ever did in my life, but I know that is impossible. A good many say they are

---

[11] Mrs. Stuckey and Mrs. Monchet are unidentified. Mrs. Monchet might possibly related to either Private H.C. or J.S. Monchet.

[12] Private Henry F. Heritage of Company G.

going home at Christmas whether they have leave or not. Some are very uneasy about the negroes rising at Christmas but I am not.[13] Give my best respects to all enquiring friends and believe me, your loving husband and father, as ever,

    To Mrs M. J. Taylor   [from] Grant Taylor
    & children

P.S. Continue to pray for me. The boys are jowering about my going to cooking and I must quit. Excuse all mistakes and shortness of letter. It looks like I never will have time to write another letter as I wish to.

Dec. 16th I am still well. There is still strong talk of our going to Vicksburg Miss but we know nothing certain. Continue to direct your letters to Jackson Miss. They will follow me. O how I wish I could see Mary with her rings on and also the rest of them. Kiss them for me.

63

Camp near Columbus Miss

Dec. 22nd 1862

Beloved wife and children,

    I seat myself this morning to pen you a few lines to inform you that I am well except cold and have been ever since I left Mobile. I do hope that you and the dear children are enjoying the best of health. I expect that you will hear by J V Peebles before you get this that I am here.[14]

    On the 16th about dark we received orders to be ready by daylight next morning to march to the depot at Jackson with 3 days

---

[13] On January 1, 1863, President Lincoln's Emancipation Proclamation, issued in September 1862, would go into effect. Once effective many feared a rebellion by the slaves. See James McPherson, *Battle Cry of Freedom: A Civil War Era* (New York: Oxford University Press, 1988) 562-563.

[14] John Ves Peebles.

rations cooked. I sat up cooking nearly all night so nigh so that I never slept a wink. Well the next morning we went to Jackson. Five companies got of[f] about 8 o'clock, but my company and 4 others had to stay there until 5 in the evening. We then started (the most of the men crowded on flat cars with no shelter from the piercing cold wind and no fire) for Meridian about 90 miles. I was fortunate enough to get into a box car but nearly froze. We got to Meridian about 4 o'clock in the morning.

We then lay there until 12 when 8 companies left. But our company and Capt Willet's staid until 2 o'clock PM when we got in the passenger cars and had a very pleasant trip to Artesia, 13 miles from here where the Columbus railroad intersects the Mobile and Ohio [Rail]road.[15] We got there about 2 o'clock in the night and had to get out there and stay two hours. We were then crowded on old flat cars again where we were so jamed together that we could scarcely move and ran off to this place where we landed about daybreak on the 19th nearly frozen.

So you see that we were traveling or preparing for it three days and nights with no chance [to] sleep and the most of our traveling was done in the night. I have stood it finely so far much better than I had any thought that I could. And I did not suffer for sleep as bad as you would think although I slept but very little in three days and nights.

Many of our men are on the sick list from exposure. We left John Walker sick at Jackson with camp fever but he was better and another man named James Cuningham very sick with Pneumonia.[16]

I have no idea how long we will stay here for they have got us on the move and I expect they will keep us moving. I hear this morning that our forces have taken Corinth, but I do not believe it. We are beginning to see something of a Soldier's life. When we are ordered to move, it is always done in a hurry and everything is in confusion. We lost a good many of our cooking utensils when we left Mobile. But we have been fortunate enough to keep our tents up and to draw more. My mess has a good wall tent, bran[d] new like the officers had when you were down.

---

15 Capt. E. D. Willett (Co G 40th AL).
16 John J. Walker and James R. Cunningham (both of Co G 40th AL).

We are encamped in sight of Columbus on the northeast side. We [have] splendid Artesian water but wood is scarce.[17] Although I am within 40 miles of home, I feel farther off than I did at Mobile for I never was here befor and we came such a round [about way] to get here. We have traveled about 475 miles since we left Mobile.

Notwithstanding we are so near home there is no chance to come for there is no chance to get a furlough. A good many say they intend to go home anyway but I do not believe they will. James Rogers of our company got a pass to go to Jackson last Saturday was a week ago and has not been heard from since 2 o'clock PM that day.[18] It is believed that he has gone home.

I would have written to you as soon as I got here but it was too late to get a letter in the mail for Pleasant Grove for las[t] Saturday. I expect to write another to you this week and if I do and they both go right you will get them at one time. I will write 2 for fear one may not reach you.

I would like for you to come and see me if it were not for the smallpox and you could bring the children. I will write to you before long if we stay here what I think about it. I sent you the scab off my arm from Jackson to vaccinate you and the children. If you have received it and it has taken on you there is but very little danger of the smallpox. If you have not been vaccinated yet I want you to be as soon as you can.

I wrote to you from Jackson in my last to sell my cotton if you could get 14 cents per lb for it. I still say so for I believe it will either fall into the hands of the Yankees before April or be burned by our own people for I am fearful that the Yankees will be all over that country before that time.

I had rather be here than any place I have been at yet for we are now between the enemy and those I love and it seems more like defending you here than away down at Mobile or Jackson.

Let your prayers continue to ascend a throne of Grace for peace and for my safe return. Ide is in tolerable health and sends his best

---

[17] The 40th Alabama camped at the fairgrounds outside Columbus. See Willett, *History of Company B*, 167, and War Department, *Official Records*, I, 17, Part I: 797,799.

[18] James W. Rogers (Co G 40th AL).

respects to you. Give my respects to all enquiring friends and believe me your true husband as ever,

To Mrs M J Taylor [from] Grant Taylor
& children

Dec 23^d I am still well except cold. I have to go on guard in a short time. Nothing new has transpired since writing the above. Direct your letters to Columbus Miss. They will follow me. I have not received any that you sent to Jackson. All that I got while there came by the way of Mobile.

64

Camp near Columbus Miss

Dec. 24th 1862

Beloved wife and children,

I seat myself again this morning to pen you a few lines to inform you that I am quite well except a slight cold and I hope these lines may find you all enjoying the best of health.

I am very anxious to hear from you. I have not heard from you since the letter of the 4th and 5th of this month which you sent to Mobile and which reached me a day or two before I left Jackson. I wrote to you day before yesterday and yesterday giving you a detailed account of our trip from Jackson to this place. Suffice it to say that we got orders about dark on the 16 inst. to start to this place the next morning by sunup which we did and landed here on the 19th about daybreak after having suffered a great deal with the cold and for sleep, not having slept but very little in three days and nights.

There is a heap of sickness in the Reg. and some dangerous cases of Pneumonia and camp fever. I do not think there are any bad cases in our company though there are a great many on the sick list. I think about one more such move as we have just made will put nearly all of us on the sick list. John Walker was left at

Jackson very sick with camp fever but was thought to be a little better. Jo Lancaster was left there to nurse some sick in his company and took the Pneumonia and the last I heard from him he was very sick.[19]

Malinda, I would like mighty well for you to come here to see me but I expect your chance is bad at this particular time on the account of your having to move and then there is great uncertainty about how long we will stay here. If we stay here a week or two and you are situated so you can, I want you to come certain. There are a great many writing for their wives and if too many comes at once there will be no chance to stay out of camps with you. For even now there are so many sick that the well ones have to go on guard every two or three days.

I should not be surprised at no time to hear orders for us to march to meet the enemy. Even now we are ordered to hold ourselves in readiness for we may be needed at Vicksburg on the Mississippi River, but that does not signify that we will go there or any other place for certain in some time.

William Colvin, William Goodson, W Stapp and John Sanders have all written for their wives to come next week.[20] I want you to send your likeness by them for fear you do not get to come at all. You can suit yourself about what time you come unless I write to you especially not to come.

God only knows when I will be called to meet the enemy in deadly conflict, but let the time come when it may. I do not feel that I shall dread it but very little. We have been twice situated lately so that the prospect was that we would have to measure arms with the enemy in 2 or 3 days at farthest and it did not excite me in the least. But then I know the reality would put strange feelings on me. One reason why I do not dread it is that I know that I have a loving Christian wife who parys [prays] for me daily and that thought makes me feel strong. I put my trust in my blessed Savior. I have prayed and continue to pray fervently that I

---

[19] E. Joseph Lancaster (1827-1908) of Co B 40th AL. Willett also named Lancaster as being left with the sick.

[20] Wm. A. Colvin (Co B 40th AL); William Newton Goodson (Co G 40th AL); William M. Stapp (Co G 40th AL); John W. Sanders (Co G 40th AL).

may live through this struggle and I feel that our united petitions have been heard. Whether they have or not it gives me hope.

I hear no talk of the smallpox now among us although there may be some cases in the Reg. But I have my doubts of there ever having been any real smallpox among us. If there is it spreads very slow.

Kiss all the children for me and tell them that they are Pa's kisses. I got a few lines from John yesterday in a letter from Enoch Yearby to Jim.[21] It was dated the 9th Dec. John had the mumps and Jake had been sent down into Georgia sick with them. John was at Murphreesborough Tenn.[22]

Give my best respects to all the connexion and enquiring friends and believe me your loving husband and father, as ever,

To Mrs M J Taylor [from] Grant Taylor
& children

PS Direct your letters to Columbus Miss. This is Christmas Eve. How changed is our condition from las[t] Eve. What will it be next?

I have no idea there is a Yankee within 40 miles of this place. I do not think any of you need be afraid to come here on their account.

Christmas morning. I am in very good health this morning. I would wish you a happy Christmas but that I know it would be making a mock of the thing. How many happy Christmas mornings have we seen together, but alas the times have changed and we must spend this one separate. Let [us] bear [it] as well as we can and hope for better days. We [are] certainly ordered to hold ourselves in readiness to march at a minute's notice to Vicksburg.

If you have a good chance to come the first of next week, I want you to come. Maybe you will get here before I have to leave. If you cannot bring all the children bring as many as you can and if you cannot bring any conveniently come without them. I do not

---

[21] Grant received a note to Enoch's brother, James E. Yerby (Co B 40th AL) from John Parker in a letter from Enoch Yerby (Co A 41st AL).
[22] Murfreesboro TN.

want you to make too much sacrifice to come but if you can come conveniently do so. If we start of[f] before you get here you will be apt to hear it in Carrollton. I want you to exercise your own judgement whether your affairs are so you can come.

I got a letter from Hughs last night dated the 17th. It was sent to Mobile first. Him nor his wife were well. The rest were well. I have never heard from Wick yet. I have no idea where he is.

65

Columbus Miss

Dec. 25th 1862

Dear wife,

I sent a letter to the office for you this morning. Orders have just come in for us to go to Vicksburg immediately.[23] We will start this evening or in the morning. Pray for me, Dear wife. God only knows what is before me. Your Loving husband, as ever,

Grant Taylor

2 o'clock. The talk is now that we will not start before Saturday for the want of cars but we will be most certain to go as soon as cars can be procured to carry us off. Direct your letters to Columbus until you hear from me again. I will write to you ever[y] chance and let you hear from me if I cannot hear from you. This is the third letter to you since I have been here. The mail closes now shortly and I must close. This [is] the last chance I will have to start a letter to Pleasant Grove this week. Goodby, dearest wife and children. May God comfort you in your lonesomeness. I have a bad chance to write.

Grant Taylor

---

[23] On December 25, General John C. Pemberton sent a telegram to hurry the 40th Alabama to threatened Vicksburg. See Edwin C. Bearss, *The Campaign for Vicksburg*, 3 vols. (Dayton, Ohio: Morningside Press, 1985-1986), I: 150 and War Department, *Official Records*, I, 17, Part II: 666.

66

Dec the 28th 1862

Dear husband,

I am now seated to drop you a few lines. We are all well hoping you are too. I got two letters from you Friday and 3 yesterday whitch I was glad to get. I was very sorry to hear that you had orders to leave Columbus. I was fixing to start this morning. It was a sad disappointment. Me and Lucy Ann Colvin and Theron Teer was going but I considder it all for the best.[24] That is the way I look at evrything now and I want you to look that way too.

Grant, you allways reque[s]t me to pray for you. Whenever, I com to the requst I dont read any ferther until I restle with God in your behalf. I b[e]lieve if prayers from the heart will save you, you will go through the struggle.

I have not moved yet but will shortely. I sent you a letter by Ivy Ritcherson last Monday but you never said any thing about it in non[e] of your letters, staiting that I had bought Tom Thomas place at $100 but I ante [ain't] pleased with it. I want Martha Taylors place.[25] It suits me the best of any place I have seen. I went all over the land. I think it a better place than we left. I can get it for 8 hundred and 50 dollars and I believe for 8 hundred. She never com down to that until I bought the other. I can pay for both places and have $1 hundred still, that is if I get that school money and if I can get 15 cen[ts] [per lb] for your cotton I will have that mutch more. I have never been to the old place yet. I am going next week.

---

[24] Lucy Ann Colvin is unidentified. Theron S. Teer (1846-1916) was Grant's nephew.

[25] Ivy Richardson (born c1833), son of Rhoda Richardson. Tom Thomas (born c1836), son of William and Jane Thomas. Martha Taylor is probably not a relative and is unidentified.

Rachel left this morning and went to Ataway Davisis and I have to send her things thare.[26] They went on foot. Me and Milt Mullins is going to carry them and come back by the old place and get them Toomstones [tombstones] and the rest of my things.[27] Lucreta is going to hall [haul] them for nothing.[28]

The reason that I have not bought Marthas place is that it is doubtful about making good rites.[29] If I finde she can make rites I expect I will bigh it. I think I can sell the other place for doble what I give for it. It puts me to my studdys to know what to do about my affares but I do the very best I can.

I have had 25 bushels corn hald and it cost me $405. I had to give dollar and quarter per bushel, $12 for halling, one dollar and half ferage.[30] Mrs Goodsen hald for me and will hall another next week that will bee 50 bushels.[31]

Pap is going to give me my bread from the mill. I am going to try to do on 50 bushels. Pap is going to give all the children thare bread. That is a greate accomodation to us now he is to give it. I am now at Lafayettes wrighting these scrawls to you.[32] Excuse these ugly lines. I am writing on my lap and the paper ant [ain't] ruled but I can write a little better I think so I will try.

I staide at Lisheys last Sunday night.[33] Dulceny sendes her love and respects to you and she is grumbling because you donte write to her.[34] Wick is at Kies.[35] He has got a discharge. I have not seen him. Little Mary is so sorry because she did not get to go to see

---

[26] Malinda's hired help, Rachel, decided to leave Malinda's employ and go work for Ataway R. Davis (Co C 43rd AL) of Greene County.

[27] Milton Mullins, Grant's nephew.

[28] Lucretia Taylor Mullins, Grant's sister.

[29] Martha Taylor is unidentified.

[30] Malinda's computation seems incorrect. At $1.25 per bushel for 25 bushels plus $12 for hauling plus $1.50 for ferryage, the total should be $44.75.

[31] Probably Elizabeth Goodson, widow of John Goodson of Pickens County.

[32] Hugh Lafayette Mullins, Grant's nephew.

[33] Elisha Teer, Grant's brother-in-law. Malinda refers to him as "Lishey."

[34] Dulcena Taylor Teer, Grant's sister married to Elisha Teer.

[35] William M. Taylor and Malachi Taylor, Grant's brothers. In this letter Malachi is called "Kie."

you this morning. Sister Mary got your letter. I red it the next day. I had heard that you was at Columbus. Grant, pray for me that I may go through this trial. Pray that God will bring you home safe. That is my greatist disire. Oh that I could know that you ever would get home in peace.

I must quit for the want of paper. May God bless and smile on you is the often prayer of your unworthy wife. I will sende my likeness by W Stap.[36]

Malinda J Taylor

Oh that we could live together in peace one time more in this life. I keep in pretty good spirits with the thoughts that we will one day by and by.

This was the last of Malinda's letters to survive until November 5, 1863. On Sunday, April 19, 1863, Grant wrote that he felt it was no longer a wise practice to keep her letters: "I burnt up all your letters just before I started on this last tramp for fear they would fall into the hands of others than myself." Such destruction was common among Civil War soldiers.

67

Warren County Miss

January 4th 1863

Sunday
Beloved wife and children,

Once more am I permitted to be still long enough to pencil you a few lines. This leaves me in good health and spirits and I hope and pray that these scrawls may reach you and the children all well.

---

36 William M. Stapp (Co G 40th AL).

We landed at Vicksburg last Tuesday night about dark and started here at ten o'clock that night.[37] We are 7 or eight miles north of Vicksburg on the edge of the Miss swamp. We left every thing at Vicksburg except what clothes we have on and one blanket. We lie out at night and take all kinds of weather. It's rained a lots in the last 36 hours and we had to wrapt up in our blankets and take it. Night before last I lay on two rails with a jug for a heading. I slept pretty well although it rained heavily the most of the night. My blanket kept me nearly dry. Our cooking is done at Vicksburg and only get one meal a day. It is pretty rough but we all stand it finely and are in fine spirits.

They fought here for several days before we came. It just ended the day that we got here except the day before yesterday they had a little brush near here. We heard it plainly and were ordered out and marched a short distance but it was over before [we] got far.[38] I did not dread it in the least. I felt that God was my protector and I had a chance to defend you and the dear little ones.

Last Monday they made a charge with 9 or 10 Reg[s] on 3 of our Regts in the breast works. Our boys mowed them down like grass, killed and wounded several hundred and took 400 prisoners. After I came I could see the dead lying all over the field. Our men burried about 50 of their dead and took care of all their wounded that they could get hold of. On Thursday the Yank sent in a flag of truce to burry their dead.[39] They hauled off 30 or 40 waggon loads of dead. Besides they found several wounded that

---

[37] The 40th Alabama left Columbus by rail on December 27th for Vicksburg. They arrived on the evening of December 30th. The bumpy ride combined with continuous rain and cold left the troops, in the words of one, "in a bad humor generally." See Curry, "A History of Company B," 167.

[38] On December 29, 1862, Union soldiers under General William T. Sherman attacked Confederate positions north of Vicksburg at Chickasaw Bayou. This advance failed with more than 1700 Federal casualties against 207 Confederate losses. See Long, *Civil War Day by Day*, 301, and Bearss, *Campaign For Vicksburg*, I: 225.

[39] At noon on January 1, 1863, Union burial details worked under a flag of truce. Approximately two hundred Yankees were buried in a gully near the 40th Alabama's position. See Curry, "A History of Company B," 169.

had lain there from Monday. I mean Yankee wounded. We took one Colonel prisoner the next day after the fight and he says their loss must have been 1000 or 1500, maybe more. Our loss was very slight not being over 100 in all the engagements.

On last Friday they went on board their boats and left and we do not know where they have gone.[40] There is no prospect of another fight here again soon. Our men took lots of arms, amunition, and a good deal of provisions from them.

Jan. 5th After writing the above we moved about half mile from the swamp out in the hills.[41]

Our company is in better health than it has been in a long time. Ide is in pretty good health and sends his best respects to you. There are a great many soldiers here. God only knows how long we will stay here.

This is certainly the most hilly country I ever saw. Many places are so steep that a man cannot go up them. I do not believe there is any chance for the Yanks to take the place.

Continue to pray for me and excuse my pencil writing and short letter as my writing materials are all in Vicksburg and I had to borrow these.

You must do the best you can with your affairs. I am too far off to give advice. Surely Pap will advize you. I think if you can you had better get more than 50 bu of corn.

Give my best respects to all the connexion and enquiring friends. Kiss the children for me and believe your true one, as ever,

To Mrs M J Taylor   [from] Grant Taylor

I received your ambrotype.[42] How sweet and natural it looks.

---

[40] January 2, 1863.
[41] The 40th Alabama moved to Synder's Bluff about eight miles above Vicksburg on the Yazoo River. See Willett, *History of Company B*, 18-19.
[42] An ambrotype was an early type of photograph.

68

Near Vicksburg

Jan. 8th 1863

Camp of 40th Reg. Ala Vols

Beloved wife and Children,

Thank God I am permitted to pen you a few more lines in good health and I hope and pray that these few lines may reach you and our dear children in the best of health.

I started you a few lines the other day Giving you an account of the fighting here which ended the day that we came here. Suffice it here to state that after several days skirmishing the enemy charged our works and got one of the worst little whippings that a set of rascals ever got. In the charge they left between 400 and 500 dead on the field and we took 400 Prisoners. It is not known exactly how many they did lose but we know they lost as many as the above. Our loss did not exceed 20 in killed. The Yanks are all gone, we do not know where.

After we got here I could see the dead Yanks were lying all over the ground. I was not nearer than three hundred yards yet I could see many of them. 3 days after the battle the wounded Yanks could be seen crawling about over the ground. I[t] was a horrid sight.

2 days after we got here there was a little fight in the swamp not far off, we could hear it plainly. 3 or 4 Regts. made a charge on the Yanks as they were leaving. My Regt was ordered into line and marched 3 or 400 yards towards the fight but it ended and we were marched back.[43] I was not the least excited or scared although I believed we would be in a fight in less than one hour. My prayer to God was (as we marched along) for him to cover my head in the

---

[43] On January 2nd, the 40th Alabama supported an attack on the retreating Union forces led by General H. Dabney Maury. See Willett, *History of Company B*, 18.

hour of battle and I believe he would have done it. I believed it so strong that I was not afraid.

We have moved nearly ever day since we came here and we are now encamped on a portion of the battlefield 5 or 6 miles from Vicksburg. Yankee bullets, cannon balls and bomb shells are plenty. I picked up a handful of bullets this morning in a few minutes. The trees are shattered and scarred dreadfully, where there are any trees. This is the most disagreeable place I have ever been in. It is the most hilly I ever saw, many places nearly perpendicular for 150 to 200 feet and when it rains the roads are so muddy that one can scarcely get about. The hills are very rich. Cane grows 15 feet high all over them and the bottom lands are just as rich as they can be.

I have not got but 2 letters from you by mail since I left Mobile and they were sent there. I got a letter and your ambrotype by Wm Stapp. It looks very natural only a shade of sadness about it. It makes me feel very lonesome to look on the likeness of one I love so dearly and knowing that I am so far away from her. God bless you, maybe we will see each other some day. I would request you to pray for me but that I know you do it and the request would be useless.

Direct your letters to Vicksburg, Miss. Farewell,

To Mrs M J Taylor [from] Grant Taylor
& children

P.S. You had better buy more than 50 bu corn. Let it cost what it may. It is cheaper now than it ever will be again.

Be sure you get good titles to Martha Taylors land before you buy it. Will not Pap assist you with his advice how to manage your affairs.

Last night is the first time I have slept in a tent since we got here.

69

Camp of the 40th Ala Regt

Jan 14th 1863

near Vicksburg Miss

Beloved Wife & Children,

By the goodness of God I am permitted to pen you a few lines. This leaves me in fine health and spirits and I hope it may find you and the dear children in the best of health. I received your kind and welcomed letter of the 8th and 9th inst. yesterday evening. You don't know how glad I was, for with the exception of the one by Wm Stapp I have got but 2 from you before this last since I left Mobile and they were both sent to Mobile. I never heard of the sickness of the children before I got this letter. Thank God that He raised them again. Oh, how could I stand it for them to be buried and me away off here[?] I asked Collier about the Negro you have got.[44] He says she is a hard bargain for her victuals and clothes. That none ever can get much out of her. I think you had better give her up if you can and get another one. I have written two letters to you since I came here before this one. Be sure you got good titles to that land before you pay out your money.

Our forces did gain a complete victory here on Monday before we got to Vicksburg on Tuesday night. An account of which I gave you in both my other letters. Everything is quiet here now, no sign of the enemy. I hear that they are fighting at Port Hudson 60 or 70 miles below here on the river. If they force a passage by that place it is likely that we will have hot work here, but we have no fears of the result.[45] This is the strongest natural position that I ever saw and then it is well fortified. I do not believe there is any

---

[44] Lt. John N. Collier (Co G 40th AL). Obviously, Malinda has hired another black helper once Rachel left service.

[45] Taylor may be confusing Port Hudson with Arkansas Post (Fort Hindman) which fell to Union forces on January 11th. See Long, *Civil War Day by Day*, 310-311.

chance for the Yanks to get it. The Regt that James Smith and George Roebuck belong to is some where here but I do not know exactly where.[46] I was in sight of their fires one night but could not get to them without wading and they have moved since then. We have got all our tents and baggage with us at last and we are doing finely, but I tell you the first 8 days after we got here saw sights for we left everything in Vicksburg but one blanket each and 2 nights it rained heavily. Our cooking was done in Vicksburg and we only had enough sent out for one meal a day. But now we get tolerably plentiful of beef and bread.

While we were in Jackson on our way here Miles Walker went to the hospital to see his brother, John, and we came off and left him.[47] A day or two after, he started after us and the engine ran off the track and broke his thigh. I do not know where he is now. There is a heap of diarrhea among us but I do not think there are many dangerous cases of sickness in the Regt. I think you might have got more for your cotton but perhaps you did well. Old Mrs Jones treated you just as I thought she would.[48] I thought from her looks she was a great rascal.

Those people need not be so particular about what Township money there is coming to them for it has all been paid and credited on their accounts, as anyone can see, except for the last month that I taught. Surely they cannot object to paying what was due last winter on the three months school, whether the Township ever pays anything on the last month. That month's schooling has nothing to do whatsoever with the first three months. I will send a few lines to Mr Phillips in this letter and if he still holds the accounts you can send it to him by mail.[49] But if you have them, you need not send it. If they do not pay up for the first 3 months tho I will sue the last one of them if I ever get back. You said you got all that was owing to you over there. Did you get what John Holley was owing me?[50]

---

[46] James Smith and George N. Roebuck did not belong to Grant's regiment. They are both unidentified.

[47] Miles W. Walker and John J. Walker (Co B 40th AL).

[48] "Old Mrs. Jones" is not identified.

[49] Mr. Phillips of Phillips' Mill.

[50] John Holley of Tuscaloosa County.

Ide is in very good health and sends his best respects to you. He and I sent Betty and you the scabs off our arms while we were at Jackson for you all to be vaccinated with, did you get them?

You asked me if I remembered that letter. I do very well and have wondered since if you ever got it. I shall never forget that letter and my feelings. Oh, how often am I cheered with the thought that it is not all of life to live, nor all of death to die. That, though I may fall in a foreign land far, far away from those I love most dearly on earth yet it will only release me from this world of bloodshed, sin and death and usher me into that happy world above. Where all is peace and joy. Yet I firmly believe that we will meet again in this world. I have strong faith in my blessed Savior that he has heard our united prayers on this point. But when I contemplate the possibility of being disappointed in this thing, there is a sweet serenity in my mind from the fact that if we fail to meet on earth there is yet another chance for us to meet and that is in heaven. Oh, I hope there is no chance to be disappointed on that.

Malinda, I have strange feelings when I contemplate your likeness. How natural you look. How I yearn to press those silent lips to mine and hear those sweet words of love fall from them once more. How strange it seems to be, apparently in your presence and to think how many weary miles intervene between us.

Malinda, watch over those sweet buds, our dear children, as the apple of your eye. Strive to train them up in the nurture and admonition of the Lord. So that when it pleases the Lord to remove us from this world of trouble we may be a family united in Heaven.

We are having a good deal of rain. It is raining now heavily. Give my best respects to all the connections and enquiring friends, also to Mr Mitchell. Tell Brother Ashcraft to remember me in his prayers that although we are strangers now, I trust we are of the same fold and will one day meet in that upper and better world.

Kiss the children for me. Tell them that Pa often thinks of them and wants to see them so badly.

I gave you a history of this country in my other letters and deem it unnecessary here.

Everything is very high here. Tobacco is one dollar per plug. Continue to pray for me and believe me, your own true loving husband, as ever,

To Mrs M J Taylor [from] Grant Taylor
& Children

70

[Vicksburg, MS]

Jan 23 1863

Dear wife,

I sent you a long letter by John Baily giving you full direction about that school money and also about my being taken sick on the 14th.[51] I am still sick. I have fevers every day. Not severe, but enough to keep me growing weaker. I am not able to sit up but very little. Writing this is a great effort. I send your likeness back to you. It is too mournful a pleasure for me to enjoy and then I stand a very good chance of loseing it if it stays here. I received your letter of the 16th yesterday, but I am not able to answer it now. The doctor has not got a bit of medicine and he has orders not to send any more to the hospital. But God can take care of me still. I must quit. Kiss the children for me. Farewell,

To Mrs M. J. Taylor [from] Grant Taylor

Dont be uneasy about me.

Jan 26th 1863

Malinda, I am still down sick tho I [feel] a little like the fever is broken this morning. I am not able to sit more than a half hour at a

---

51 John Bailey (born c1822) of Pickens County.

time, in fact, I scarcely ever sit up any. But I hope for a better time. I have tried to get them to send me to the hospital but they would [not]. I do not know the reason. I must quit as I am feeling quite faint.

Farewell, farewell,

G T To M J Taylor

Being too ill to write, the next letter was composed by Malinda's brother Jack Slaughter with a postscript by Grant Taylor.

71

Vicksburg Miss

Jany 29ᵗʰ 1863

Dear Sister,

I am again seated to drop you a few lines which leaves me suffering some with cold but hope these may come to hand & find you & your dear little ones in perfect health. I arrived here last Tuesday & found all of our company well.

We have a rough time here. We have to eat cornbread and Beef only & very scanty that. We are camping in an old field just 4 miles from Town & on the ground where the Battle was fought 4 or 5 weeks ago. We are now all exchanged but none of the Paroled Boys have got in except myself. I received a letter from Wat yesterday. He wrote that Mary had 2 sick children, Milton and Pony. Milton was thought dangerous. It also contained a History of the death and sufferings of Bud which was truly affecting for me to read but we should be consoled to know that he is now happy & free from all of our present troubles.[52]

Liney, I have been to see Grant 4 times since I have been here.[53] He is camping next to our Rigiment. You have no doubt heard before this time that he is and has been sick. Although he is

---

52 Malinda and Jack's brother Atlas Slaughter has died.
53 "Liney" and "Linny" are nicknames for Malinda.

pronounced better he is very desirous of being moved to the Hospitle, but the Hospittle in Town is broken up. He is lying in his tent. He has plenty of Bed clothing to keep him warm. Ide waits upon him. He was taken with heavy headache which lasted 3 or 4 days. Since that time he says nothing has hurt him. He does not wish you to try to come to see him for this is no place for a woman. He is better I assure you than he was when I came here & I think if no back set he will be up in a few days. His disease is disposed to run into Typhoid. He says he will write to you in a few days. He was able yesterday to go out to the fire & sit awhile.

Liney, I do not think we will ever have a fight here. It does appear to me that God has blessed us here with natural Fortifications for their defeat. 40,000 men can hold this place against 200,000 Yanks. Another evidince that we will not have them to fight is they have landed a force six miles from Town in the bend of the river where it is thought they have resumed their old Canal work, which if be true they have abandoned the idea of trying us any more on this side.[54] If we are successful here I do not think the war can last much longer.

I have given you all I know, I believe. Pray for me. Pray that I may make a firm soldier of the cross & that I may live to the end of this war & that I may once more return to the dear ones of earth. I want you to write to me immediatily. Give me all the news of the country & be not uneasy about Grant for there is yet no cause for Alarm. Nothing more.

I remain your Brother, as ever,
A[ndrew] J[ackson] Slaughter

Direct to A. J. S., Vicksburg Miss, Care Capt Wells, Co B, 42nd Ala Vol.

PS I have light fevers every evening but as my strength comes to me they will wear off. Your affectionate husband until death.

---

[54] Union forces had begun an abortive project to dig a canal as a bypass from the Vicksburg batteries in the summer of 1862. See Samuel Carter III, *The Final Fortress: The Campaign for Vicksburg 1862-1863* (New York: St. Martin's Press, 1980) 110.

Grant Taylor
per A J S

I received yours 21 & 22nd inst.

The next letter was written for Grant Taylor by his brother-in-law,
Andrew Jackson Slaughter.

72

Vicksburg Miss

Feb 4th 1863

Dear Malinda,

I have been confined now twenty one days but am now better.
The fever is broke on me and if I take no back set will be up again
in a short while. My Mess has been verry kind to me all the while.

If you should get this letter in time I want you to send me two
shirts if you have them done. The weather is verry cold & wet.
Today it is sleeting here. I have received your letters regular all
the while. I have a great [d]eal to write to you and will be able to
write in a few days. I wished when I was so sick the Doctors to
send me to the Hospitle but they would not. If they had, I intended
to send for you. If you can send me by John Boon who I want the
shirts sent by, some Butter that is if he is to start in 3 or 4 days but
if he should not come in 2 or 3 weeks you need not send the
Butter. This is a bad place for a sick man to get any thing to eat.
Do not be uneasy about me but continue in prayr for me.

Kiss the children for me. Your loving husband,

Grant Taylor

73

Camp Timmon near Vicksburg[55]

Feb 8th 1863

Beloved wife and children,

I will try to write you a few lines at last. I am very weak yet. This is 25 days since I was taken sick and yet I am not able to sit up but very little yet. I had The Typhoid fever for 18 days. I have had no fever for 7 days and yet I mend very slowly. But I hope if I get no backset I will get well now. I hope and pray that these few lines may reach you and the dear children in the best of health. I would not attempt to write to you now but I reckon you will be glad to get another letter by me. I received your letter of the 29 and 30th Jan. last Wednesday. You appear to be very uneasy about me but do not be so. God will still take care of me. I am not able to write much.

Some think there will be an attack here by the Yankee gun boats but I do not believe there ever will be another land attack made here. A gun boat ran by our batteries the other morning and went on down the river.[56]

Gilbert Taylor has just left here.[57] He belongs to the 31st Lousiana Reg and is encamped 3 or 4 miles from here and has been there ever since before we came here. But I did not know any thing about him until he stepped into my tent and called me uncle Grant. He has been sick a long time but has got able to go on duty. Sally is in Union Parish Lousiana.[58]

Malinda, I have a heap to write to you but must wait until I get stronger. Jack has come to camps. He wrote to you the other day and also wrote a letter for me to you which I sent to Olney by Mr

---

[55] The camp was named for Lieutenant Colonel Barnard Timmons of Waul's Texas Legion who was fatally wounded in action on December 28, 1862. See Clement A. Evans, ed., *Confederate Military History* 13 vols. (Atlanta: Blue and Grey Press, 1899) 11:164.

[56] On February 2, 1863, the Union ship *Queen of the West* sped past the Vicksburg batteries unharmed. See Ivan Musicant, *Divided Waters: The Naval History of the Civil War* (New York: Harper Collins, 1995), 272.

[57] Gilbert Taylor, Grant's nephew.

[58] Sarah Stewart Taylor, Gilbert Taylor's wife.

Miller which I hope you will get to-day.[59] Jack has been to see me every day since he came and has been a brother to me indeed. The next day after he came he turned out and got me some milk and found out where I could send and get it myself. I have to pay one dollar per gallon for it. It is all that I can get that I can eat to do any good. Some days I cannot get it and then I almost starve.

Several in our com[pany] are sick. Dock Boon is very sick.[60] If I could have got off to a hospital I intended to send for you but here in camps there is no place for you to stay and there is not a private house that I know of in 2 miles of this place.

The letter that you got from me with Phillips letter in it was the one I sent by John Baily. Malinda, I have had some mighty sweet thoughts of heaven since I have been sick. Oh I felt like that if it had not been for you and the children I would have been perfectly willing to die. I felt that death would release me from the troubles of this world and introduce me to the joys of heaven. I felt that there was not a cloud between me and the upper sky but "all was well, all was well." O such sweet thoughts they were.

There is no chance to get a furlough. I have tried and failed so I will have to be patient and tough it out. I did not send your likeness back because I thought I would die for I did not think so. But as I said I had no way to keep it and it made me feel too sad to look at it. I want it and mine kept for our children when we are laid under the clods.

I must close and lie down for strength is exhausted. Read this if you can. It is the best I can do now. Give my best respects to all enquiring friends and connexion. Kiss the dear children for me and believe me your loving husband, as ever,

To Mrs M J Taylor [from] Grant Taylor
& children

My messmates has been very kind to me and Ide has waited on me most kindly. May God bless him and them for their kindness.

---

[59] Mr. Miller is unidentified.

[60] The only Boones in Grant's company were John M. Boone and R. N. Boone. Both surnames were sometimes spelled as Boon.

Ide sends his best respects to you. Continue in prayer for me my dearest wife.

74

Camp Timmons near Vicksburg

Feb. 13th 1863

Beloved wife & children,

With thankfulness I seat myself this evening to pen you a few lines to inform you that my health is improving thoug[h] I am quite feble yet. I am not able to sit up more than half my time. Tomorrow it will be one month since I was taken sick.

If I could get any thing fit for a sick man to eat I could get my strength faster. I succeeded in getting 1 1/2 gallons milk at one dollar per gallon but that resource has failed me and there is nothing to buy. Sometimes pies are brought into camps but a pie a little larger than my hand sells for one dollar. Once in awhile I can hear of a little butter in Vicksburg but it is $1.75 per lb, flour 60 cts per pound and lard $1.25 and I cannot afford to pay such prices as I am nearly out of money and God knows when we will be paid any more. We only draw a little sugar and Molasses and corn meal and the poorest kind of beef and my stomach do'nt seem to want such diet. Although I have it to eat or eat nothing. We have only drown one days rations of hog meat since we have been here.[61]

I have just received your affection[ate] letter of Feb. 6th and 7 and am truly glad to hear that you are all well and that you have moved and are so well satisfied. I hope if ever I get home I will be as well satisfied. I am glad you have your meat and corn for this year. Thoug[h] you have a small supply I feel thankful and hope you will not suffer. It seems your hogs were very small for 2 years old. How much did Pap charge you for fattening them. I want you

---

[61] A veteran of the 40th Alabama remembered that at this time "rations were scanty, beef very poor and meal very coarse, and the other rations inferior in quality and scanty in quantity." See Willett, *History of Company B*, 27.

to pay him the interest on that not[e] if you have the money to spare. I am fearful you will run very short of money as you will have to pay cash for every thing you buy and very high at that.

I want you to put in your claim for your share of the public money for you are as much entitled to it as any of them and if I have to stay away this year you will have to depend on yourself for a living for it is impossible for me to save any money to send to you unless I suffer for many little things that I need here. And if you go over about the old place soon see Mr Leatherwood and get him to try to get what you ought to have got last year from the public.

If you have no shelter for your waggon you had better hire one put up and if you need money sell it. Do'nt take less than $75 for it. Try to get more if you can. I think you had better plant a few acres of your best land in corn. Let you get either Negro woman you may. I think as your provisions are scarce you had better take the woman without children unless the children are very small. But I suppose the trade will be closed before you get this. If not you can exercise your own judgment about it as you have to do in most cases.

I do not like Nan Herndon for a teacher but I want the boys to go to school and you might try her with half a schollar with the understanding that you send more if you wish to and pay for what you send.[62]

I got Jack to write you last week requesting you to send me 2 shirts and some butter by John Boon and sent it by a Mr Miller to Olney. I expect you got it last Sunday or Monday. I also wrote to you myself last Sunday and sent it by mail which I hope you will get in due time. In that letter I gave you an account of Gilbert coming to see me that day. He is encamped 3 or 4 miles from here and belongs to the 31st La. Reg. Sally is in Union Parish La.

There is a good deal of sickness in camps. I cannot give an oppinion whether there will be fighting here soon or not. The enemy have a large force 4 or 5 miles from Vicksburg on the opposite side of the river but if they stay there all the time there never will be any more fighting here. Gen. [John C.] Pemberton

---

[62] Nancy M. Herndon (born c1838), daughter of John and Nancy Herndon.

seems to think there is danger of their bombarding the city as he has ordered the women and children out of the city.[63]

Jack is encamped next to us and was well night before last. He has been very kind to me. Ide is well and sends his best respects to you. He cooked for me and waited on [me] most kindly in my sickness. Also all my messmates were very kind to me. May God bless them all. I tried to get a furlough but failed. None can get furloughs here now.

Malinda, I had mighty sweet thoughts of heaven when I was sick. I felt that if the Lord called me off all would be well and I was perfectly resigned to his will only I regretted to leave you and the children. Continue in prayer for me for I feel that your prayers will avail much.

I would like to correspond with Dulcena but paper and every thing is so high I cannout afford [it]. I scarcely ever write a letter to any one but you. When you see her give her my best love also Elisha and the children. I got a letter from Richard Smith at Mobile the other day. He was sick in the hospital. Also, Lifus Leatherwood.[64] The rest of the boys were well. He said Mat passed through there a few days before on his way home on a sick furlough.[65] The Doctors said he had the consumption.

I would be mighty glad to come home and see you in your new home but God only knows when I will get to come home whether ever or not. I hope I will be permitted to come home some day to stay.

I see some of the papers are pretty confi[dent] that peace will be mad[e] some time this year and some think it will be as early as the first of June. They say the Northern states are splitting all to pieces. But I do not believe but very little I see in the papers. Deserters from the Yanks come over the river to Vicksburg nearly every day. Some on rafts some in skifs and one came across on a log. They say they are heartily tired of the war and would not fight if they could help themselves and that hundreds would come

---

[63] Many civilians opted to ignore this advice and stay. See McPherson, *Battle Cry of Freedom*, 626; and Peter F. Walker, *Vicksburg: A People at War 1860-1865* (Chapel Hill: University of North Carolina Press, 1960) 151-152.

[64] James Lifus Leatherwood, son of James and Mary Leatherwood.

[65] Mat is unidentified.

if they had any way to get across the river and could make their escape through their lines. As soon as they come they are paroled and sent home. Give my best respects to all the connexion. Tell them to remember me in their prayers. Kiss the dear children for me and believe me your loving husband and father, as ever,

To Mrs M J Taylor   [from] Grant Taylor
& children

PS Excuse bad writing as I can scarcely write since I was sick. I do not need any pants yet.

75

Camp of the 40th Reg

Feb. 20th 1863

Beloved wife & children,

I am once more seated through the kind mercies of God to pen you a few lines. I am still improving. I am able to walk about a right smart [bit] but I am far from being stout yet. I hope and pray these lines may find you all well and doing well.

We have moved again, 2 miles farther from Vicksburg and an awful move it was. It had been raining 4 or five days and the order came in just before night for all the well men to pack up and start except the cooks. They did so and start[ed] about dark in the rain and found the road from 6 inches to 2 feet of soft mud and it was so dark that they could shun no place but had to take the mud as it came. They tumbled and fell. Some lost their shoes, some the mud pulled off their shoes and they took it in their sock feet and it raining all the time.[66]

I and the rest of the sick came the next day. They had to haul me. I never saw as much foolishness in all my life as is practiced in the army or it looks to me to be foolishness and this move in the night top[p]ed the climax of foolishness.

---

[66] A member of the 40th Alabama stated that this mud march to the new camp near Chickasaw Bridge took four hours to cover the three miles. See Curry, "A History of Company B," 172.

The Yanks shelled Vicksburg yesterday and day before but I have heard of no damage except they killed one horse and broke one mans arm. I do not know of any prospect of a general engagement coming on soon. It is reported in the papers of today that our forces captured the Gunboat that ran by here a week or two ago down on Red River. I doubt the report, yet it may be true. I hope it may be so.[67]

I started a letter to you last week giving you directions about several things. I hope you will get it. I wrote to you that I did not like Nan Herndon as a teacher but you might sign 1/2 schollar with the understanding that if you sent any more you would pay for what time you sent. I want Leonard and Jimmy to go all they can. If she gets the school and you don'nt like her as a teacher stop the children whether you have sent all your time or not. I hope she wont get the school.

I received my shirt and was glad to get it but sadly disappointed in not getting any butter. I was in hopes that you had some checked shirts ready for me. You need not send the other one until I write for it. And if you can, try to make me two colered ones of some kind. I am very thankful for the one you sent me, but white shirts are mighty hard to keep clean especially when we have no soap. I have not drawn enough soap since I left Columbus to wash one shirt. I can do without any more shirts for some time. But if you get white cloth and make the shirt before you get this send it on. If you can send me three or four pounds of hard soap I would be very thankful but I know of no chance to send it now for none of our reg is there any where near you.

Jack was well day before yesterday, the day I came up here. I am very sorry that we are separated so soon for although we are only 2 miles apart yet we may never see each other again. For we know not when we will get orders to go away off to some different place. Or he may get the same order and before to-morrow night we may be going in entirely different directions. A soldier never knows one minute what orders he may receive the next.

Ide keeps well. I have heard of but 2 deaths in the Reg. since we came here, though there are a good many complaining, and I

---

[67] The *Queen of the West* ran aground engaging Confederate batteries on the Red River and was captured. See Musicant, *Divided Waters*, 274.

think many more such marches as they took the other night will slay a many an one.

We are faring worse in the eating line now than we ever have before and there is nothing to sell. Some of our mess went out yesterday and begged a man out of 9 1/2 pounds of poor middling pork at 50 cents per pou[n]d. Our beef is so poor that there is not an eye of grease on the water that it is boiled in. We got hold of some corn yesterday and made a fine pot of ley hominy for breakfast which was a great treat as we had a little grease to put on it. We only get meal enough for breakfast and dinner and sometimes we have none from one morning till the next. Then we eat our beef by itself or with pease if we have them. But generaly we have two meals a day and sometimes we boil grits for supper when we can get enough out of our meal to do any good. We get more sugar and molasses than we did at Mobile. Yet we do pretty well and keep in good spirits.

Tell Pap and Mother and all your sister[s] and Wat howdy for me. Tell them to remember me in their prayers and not to quit writing to me because you have moved over there. A letter from any of them would be thankfully received at any time.

I am more determined to try to hold out faithful to the end than I ever did before. I feel that the Lord has been most merciful to us and I feel very thankful. Continue to pray for me. When you see Betty give her my best love. Tell her that I often remember her in my poor petitions to a throne of grace and I want her to do the same. That I often think of her and her three sweet little children and the happy days we spent to-gether in our you[n]g days and immediately after I was married.

Tell my sweet children that Pa has not forgotten them but thinks of them many times a day and wants to be with [them] again. That he tried to get to come home when he was sick to see them but they would not let me come.

Malinda if I ever get sick again and can get anywhere that you can stay with me I intend to send for you. I would have sent for you this time but as I wrote to you, the doctors would not send me to the hospital and there was no chance for you to stay in camps. I often thought in my sickness how much pleasure it would be to have you to wait on me, but the Lord willed it otherwise and I feel that what he does is all right. May God bless you and all yours and bring a speedy peace so that I may return to you again to live together is the prayer of your loving distant husband.

To Mrs M J Taylor [from] Grant Taylor
& children

Jack wrote that letter that the backing frightened you so. I was not able to write then.

PS Capt. Lofton told me that his wife and you staid all night with Betty and after discussing the merits of your old men you sagely came to the conclusion that you had 3 of the best men in the Confederacy. I reckon most women think so.

Febry 24th Beloved wife & children I am again seated to pen you a few more lines in addition to the foregoing letter. I would have sent it off when I wrote it but while I was writing it I understood that the mail from the east had stopped on account of some rail road bridges being broken down. I am still on the mend so that if I get no backset I shall be able to go on duty in one more week if I can get enough to eat.

Last Saturday evening 17 of us bought one bushel of meal and one half bushel of corn to make ley hominy at 2 dollars per bushel. This is Tuesday and by to-night we shall have eaten it all except a little corn besides what meal we have drawn from government. So you see how we fare for bread. And the cattle that they have for beef are dying up with poverty in the lots. That is I have heard that they are. But I understand that the General has condemned them and [they] are going to stop our allowance of beef and give us molasses in its stead.[68] So I do not know when we will get any more meat after to-day. If they will give us plenty of molasses the loss of the beef will not be much for a man had to have a mighty good stomach to eat it. I eat it but it is because I have nothing else to fill up on. I hope the times will be better some day. I can put up

---

[68] The 40th Alabama's brigade commander was General John C. Moore. See War Department, *Official Records*, I, 24, Part III: 612.

with almost any thing as long as I know you and the children have meat and bread to eat.

Our company are all gone, except two well men and 12 of us puny ones, down in the swamp about 3 miles from here on picket to stay 7 days. They started last Sunday and will stay until next Saturday. They took cooking utensils with them and do their cooking down there. They have good houses to stay in when they are not on post.

It is said here in camps that the Yanks have left the vicinity of Vicksburg and gone up the river again. I am not certain that the report is true.[69] If they have, they have not gone very far for we can hear their cannons sometimes to where we are. But I rather believe they have moved some farther off. I am still of the opinion that there will be no land figh[t]ing here soon if ever. They may cannonade the city from their gun boats but they cannot affect much that way or I do not believe they can, though I may be deceived.

I heard from Jack yesterday. He was well. Ide was well when he started off on picket. Give my best respects to all enquiring friends if any and also to the connection generally.

Continue to pray for me. Cheer up and do'nt become disheartened for God will certainly hear us if we faint not. I hope there is yet a bright future before us in this life, though everything looks dark at present. Yet the darkest time of the night is just before day. I feel certain that although our pleasures may be done in this life that we will have pleasures unbounded in that life which is to come. Where we shall bask in the smiles of our blessed Savior and drink in pleasures forever more. Then dear Malinda why should we who have such a bright future before us become sad and dishearted at anything in this life.

Farewell for the present,

To Mrs M J Taylor [from] Grant Taylor
& children

---

[69] A Federal expedition through Yazoo Pass north of Vicksburg was underway at this time. See Carter, *Final Fortress*, 135-136.

March 2nd I am in tolerable good health this morning. I hope you are too. My knapsack and clothes came up last night but as I wrote those few lines I will send it to show you what soldiers have to put up with sometimes.

I expect we will start in a day or too to Greenville some 60 miles north of this on or near the Miss[issippi] River.

We are faring finely now. We get plenty of bread and the finest of beef and pork and if we chance to get scarce of meat we go out in the woods and kill a beef or hog. The cattle stay fat here all the time.

The Yanks carried off a great many negroes and burnt several houses and destroyed a heap of other property on this creek last weeke and the week before. The buildings and corn were still burning when we came up here. I do not suppose that two hundred thousand dollars would cover the damage they did on this creek in one short week.

Ide is well this morning and sends his best respects to you. I received 3 letters from you 5 or 6 days before I started up here which I answered. Hope you got it. This is the first I have written in nearly 3 weeks. Continue to send your letters to Vicksburg. I want to see you all very badly but it is uncertain when I will get to do so. A great many here think that peace will be made this spring. God grant it may come. I am heartily tired of the fun. Tell the boys to make haste and learn to write and send me a letter.

May God bless you all is the prayer of your loving husband and father,

To Mrs M J Taylor [from] Grant Taylor
& children

CHAPTER 5

OH THAT THIS CRUEL WAR
MAY SOON CEASE

After a full-year of experience, Taylor became impressed with the seriousness of war. In the following letters he uses the phrase "this cruel war" twice. Moving through Mississippi, the regiment arrives at Vicksburg during the Grant's seige. There are no letters from the Taylors during the final months of the seige.
76

Camp of 40th Regt

March 17th 1863

near Vicksburg Miss
Beloved wife & children,

Through the mercies of God I am permitted to pen you a few lines. I am in good health and I hope these few lines may find you and the children in the best of health. I have nothing of interest to write more than to let you know how I am. For if you have not heard from me since I got a letter from you, you are getting very anxious to hear from me. I have not received a letter from you since the one by Can Baily. But Wiley Horton told me when he came that you were all well. I will send this letter in one of Ides to Betty as the mail is more certain to go from Bridgeville [AL] to Olney than to Pleasant Grove as [the] Sipsey [River] has stopped the mail by there for a season.

Ides health has not been good for several days but he is better now. He had the diarrhea. Jack left here last Thursday the 12th inst for Yazoo City some 70 miles up the Yazoo River his Regt having been ordered up there.[1] He was well when he left. I was very sorry that he had to leave for it was a great pleasure to me to be with him. And now it is uncertain whether we ever meet again. But let us hope for the best.

The Yankees ran a gun boat up the Yazoo River within 2 miles of our camp last Friday and shelled our pickets off the river but returned without doing any damage. And now the smoke of one of their boats can be seen near the same place.[2]

Malinda after writing the above I laid down my pen and went out to drill when the mail came in and brought me 3 letters from you and one from Dick Smith. Your letters were dated from Feb 15th to March 6th. Oh how glad I was. I could hardly obey the commands for thinking of my letters as I had not then read them. How glad I am that you are so well satisfied and that you are sending the boys to school. God bless sweet little Mary. How I do wish I could hear her sweet prattle once more.

I think you had better get a Negro if you can and make a crop if possible. I do not need any more clothes yet and I shall not need my pants this spring. Dick Smith has been discharged on the account of his lungs and is at home. Tell Leonard and Jimmy to be good boys and make haste and learn to write and write me a letter. Lieutenant [John T.] Terry starts to Pickens [County] in the morning and I must close in order to get it in his bundle.[3] May God bless you all. I will write to Mary in a day or two. Your loving husband, as ever,

To Mrs M. J. Taylor [from] Grant Taylor

PS Give my best respects to all the connexion and enquiring friends if any. I still think there will be no more fighting here soon on land.

---

[1] Andrew Jackson Slaughter, Malinda's brother.

[2] Union gunboats were also active on the Yalobusha River near Confederate Fort Pemberton. See E.B. Long, *The Civil War Day by Day: An Almanac 1861-1865* (Garden City NJ: Doubleday, 1971) 328.

[3] Lieutenant Terry received a sick furlough and left for Alabama. He never returned to the 40th Alabama. See John H. Curry. "A History of Company B, 40th Alabama Infantry, C.S.A.," *Alabama Historical Quarterly* 17/4 (Winter 1955) 4:175.

77

Deer Creek Miss

April 1st [18]63

Beloved wife and children,

I seat myself to pen you a few lines on this scrap of paper. I am in good health and I hope you and the dear children are the same.

We took a boat on the Yazoo River on the 21st March bringing nothing with us but the clothes we had on and one blanket each and came up the Yazoo some distance then up the Sunflower [River] and landed near the head of little Sunflower on Sunday morning the 22nd. Then marched 8 miles and came up with the Yankees with several gun boats and a considerable land force.[4] There was some skirmishing between some Missippi troops and their land force about half a mile from us about the same time our artillery opened on their boats and pass[ed] a few rounds.[5]

Our Regt. was stationed near our artillery behind a little rise in the ground near the creek. There were several [cannon] balls and bombs passed directly over our heads. I tell you it made me feel very curious but we lay down behind the rising ground and were comparatively safe. That night the Yanks retreated down the creek. We followed on the next day and overtook them on Wednesday when another skirmish took place between two of our companies in this Regt and their pickets in which we lost one man

---

[4] Union Admiral David D. Porter led five gunboats in support of Federal troops under Sherman moving up Steele's Bayou through Black Bayou to Deer Creek in hopes of finding another way around Vicksburg's defenses. U.S. War Department, *War of the Rebellion: A Compilation of the Official Records of the Union and Confederate Armies* 128 vols. (Washington, D.C.: Government Printing Office, 1880-1901) I, 24, Part I:461-463; Charles Royster, ed., *Memories of General W. T. Sherman* (New York: Library of America, 1990) 330-332; and Samuel Carter, *The Final Fortress: The Campaign for Vicksburg 1862-1865* (New York: St. Martin's Press, 1980) 141.

[5] The 22nd and 33rd Mississippi Infantry regiments were engaged in the area. See *Official Records*, I, 24, Part I:457-460.

killed and 3 shot through their clothes.[6] The man killed was a stranger to me. That night they left entirely and we turned back to this place where we have been 3 days.[7]

We are on Deer Creek between the Miss and Yazoo Rivers about 50 miles above Vicksburg.

[This unsigned note was written with pencil on a ragged scrap of paper.]

78

Deer Creek Miss

April 7th 1863

Beloved wife and children,

With pleasure I embrace the present moment to pen you a few lines. This leaves me in fine health & I hope you and the dear children are enjoying the best of health. I received a letter from you day before yesterday dated March 26th containing one from mother. I was truly glad to get it and to hear that most of you were well but Sorry to hear of little Buddy's sickness. I hope he is well now.

You said you were waiting for a chance to send me some soap and something to eat. I need the soap but I do not want you to send me any provisions. We are getting plenty of bread and the best of beef now. And if we were not I do not want you to send anything for it would be a mere chance if I ever got it. I have got so far from Vicksburg and then I know you have nothing to spare.

---

[6] Companies B and C of the 40th Alabama clashed with the Union rearguard as it retreated down Black Bayou toward the mouth of the Yazoo. See Elbert D. Willett, *History of Company B, 40th Alabama Regiment, Confederate States Army 1862 to 1865* (Montgomery, AL: Viewpoint Publications, 1963) 30.

[7] Private James Yarborough of Company C was one of the two battle deaths reported after this engagement. See *Official Records*, I, 24, Part I: 459-460; and Curry, "A History of Company B, 40th Alabama Infantry, C.S.A.," 173.

I wrote to you on the 1st inst. and started it by Tom Winburn, but I understand he is still at the steamboat landing 8 miles from here waiting for a boat.[8] I expect to send this to-morrow to him to carry also. That letter contains some of my hair and a full description of our ups and downs up to that time.

Since then our company and one other have been lying still. Eight companies of our Regt has gone north of us some distance.[9] We are kept here to guard different places. Lieutenant [J.N.] Collier and Ide and 5 others from our company started this evening on a scouting expedition some 20 or 30 miles off. I do not know how long they will stay. A dispatch came in last night stating that the Yanks were coming down on us from the Miss River north of us, ten thousand strong. I hear cannons firing in that direction while I am writing. I expect they are fighting up there to-day.[10]

I wrote to you sometime ago [a]bout Jack's being sent with his Regt above Yazoo City. That was about one month ago. Since that time I have heard nothing from him.

I stood guard the other night over 2 Yankee prisoners. They said the north was determined to conquer the south and restore the Union if there were men enough in the north to do it. But they had been in the army 18 months and knew nothing of the sentiment of the north. They lived in Iowa.

I never saw a finer farming country than this. But there will be but very little raised here this year. For between the Yanks and our own men a great many negroes have been carried off and what are left are doing nothing towards making a crop or but little. The people don't think it worth while to try to make a crop believing it will be destroyed. Some are making a little preparation for farming, but there are large fields of the best of land lying idle. I hope there will be a plenty made to live on.

---

[8] Thomas Lee Winborne (1837-1911) of Co G 42nd AL.

[9] Six companies of the 40th Alabama were sent 60 miles north along Deer Creek to block an expected Union advance. See Willett, *History of Company B*, 30.

[10] Union General Frederick Steele reportedly led 13 Yankee regiments southward for Greenville. See Willett, *History of Company B*, 30.

I have lost Gilbert.[11] I have never seen nor heard from him since he came to see me when I was sick. I will write a few lines to Mother but as I commenced on the wrong side of my paper I will have to write on the inside of this. The man that carries the letters off are going to start in a few minutes and I must close. I will write to her in my next. James Yearby died in Vicksburg 4 or 5 weeks ago.[12]

Give my best respects to all the connexion and enquiring friends. Continue to pray for me and believe your loving husband and father, as ever,

To Mrs M J Taylor [from] Grant Taylor
& children

Read this to Mother. I intended to write to her when I commenced writing not knowing the mail man would start so quick. Excuse mistakes for I have not got time to correct mistakes.

Sunday 19th

Dear wife, this leaves me in fine health and I hope it may reach you and the dear children well and doing well. I failed to get this letter to Winburn before he left. I then put it in the hands of Capt Lofton as he expected to get off home, but he has not gone yet. So the letter is here yet.

The 8th of this month we started up Deer Creek and went up it 50 miles after the Yanks and just got back day before yesterday. We marched up there and back. It nearly wore us all out. You never saw so many blistered feet. The Yanks came in there as I wrote in the first part of this letter and drove what few men we had up there 30 miles until our men met reinforcements when they turned on them and they started back. There was no fighting done except a little cannonading. No one hurt on our side. They burnt up nearly all the houses, corn & steam mills for thirty miles & carried of[f] lots of negroes. I never saw such destruction of property. It was worse than on the lower part of the creek that I

---

11 Gilbert Taylor, Grant's nephew.
12 James E. Yearby (Co B 40th AL).

wrote to you about by Winburn. I cant believe God will prosper any people that act so.

Ide is not very well. He has the diarrhea nearly all the time. I heard yesterday that Jack was in the hospital in Yazoo city waiting on the sick. His regt. has gone back to Vicksburg.

Thire has been a heap of rain here of late and last night there was an awful storm. It blew down many of our tents. I burnt up all your letters just before I started on this last tramp for fear they would fall into the hands of others than myself. Paper is from 2 to 4 dollars per quire in Vicksburg and I am out of money and only have one sheet of paper left. I will have to make my letters short until I can get some more paper.

May God bless you all and hasten the time when I may be permitted to come home. It is now a little over 12 long, long, months since I left home. Is it possible that it will be 12 more before this cruel war shall close. God forbid. Spring has opened finely and every thing is putting on the clothing of green and would look cheerful under other circumstances, but nothing looks cheerful to me. But the pretty bright weather makes me feel lonesome and sad and a long ways from home. Home sweet home! Will I ever enjoy the sweets of home again. Oh!

Continue to pray fervently that I may come home and may God bless and prosper you and all the other dear ones at home is my prayer.

To Mrs M J Taylor [from] Grant Taylor

I expect we will start in a day or too on a land march of 50 or 60 miles north of this. 2 of our companies have already gone.[13] I received 2 letters from you to-day in one dated the 12th and 19th of March which made me glad. I have not seen Ide but twice since we come over here. He is detailed for cook and is kept in our rear. He is not very well. We have a hard time over here taking all kinds of weather, marching sometimes day and night, and some of the time from shoe mouth to half leg deep in mud, yet the men are in

---

[13] This portion of the letter was written on a ragged scrap of paper which was a printed notice for tax payers.

better health than usual. We get plenty of meat and bread to eat. This is the finest country I ever saw.

You must excuse this scrappy letter as I can get no other paper not having seen my knapsack since we came over here. But I expect it will come up tomorrow.

God bless little Mary. How I want to see her and the rest of you but God only knows whether I ever will see you or not. I hope so. I do not know when I will get to write to you again. Continue to write to me and pray for me. Give my best love to all connexion and friends and believe me yours as ever,

G Taylor

I forgot to send a lock of my hair in my last, I will send it in this.

79

Issaquena County
on Deer Creek Miss

Apr. 22nd [18]63

Beloved wife & children,

I am well this morning except cold and I hope you and the dear children are too. I received your welcome letter yesterday dated the 9th. I was truly glad to hear from you once more. I know you are anxious to hear from me. I would have sent one by mail before now but Capt Lofton has been expecting to get off home for some time and I have been waiting to send by him. The mails are so uncertain and paper is so high that I do'nt like to send by mail if I can help it. We are fifty or sixty miles north of Vicksburg and that is our post office. The Regt. has a mail carrier between here and there that carries the mail once or twice a week.

We have never been to Yazoo City. The Regt that Bob Wells is in was sent there a few days before we were sent here.[14] We are 35 miles west of Yazoo City between the Yazoo River and the Miss. This Regt hung two noted Negroes within the last 15 days. I do not know their particular crime but it was enough to cause them to be hung.

I am sorry that you cannot draw anything from the public. I think there is no justice in it just because you happened to have a little money to buy provisions with to refuse to let you draw when other families that have Negroes to work for them drew corn and I have heard Captain Willets wife drew. There is no justice in any such doings. If I could see Mr Peebles I would tell him so.[15]

How much money have you on hand now[?] I am trying to quit using tobacco in order to save some money but I do not believe I can do it. But I will try. We will be paid 2 months wages to-day.[16] They will then be behind nearly 4 months but I suppose they cannot get any more to pay us now. I gave 1 dollar for 2 or three pounds soap the other day and the same for a pair of socks.

I am truly sorry to hear of Johns death.[17] A better man never lived according to my judgement but we have the assurance that our loss is his eternal gain. Wm Colvin was sent to the hospital in Vicksburg some 3 weeks ago and the last I heard from him he was very low.[18]

You say your are laying plans for me to carry out when I get home. I hope I will get there some time, but the chance looks slim now, for it does look like that praying does no good in such cases for no man ever craved more to get home than Bud and John and yet both poor fellows had to die in a strange land among strangers far! far away from their loved ones. Yet I still believe I will come

---

14 Robert Wells (Co B 42nd AL).

15 The entire Confederacy was experiencing a grain shortage in the spring of 1863. Soldiers' families could often draw corn at public expense. See Emory Thomas, *The Confederate Nation 1861-1865* (New York: Harper and Row, 1979) 199-201.

16 Infantry privates earned 11 Confederate dollars per month in 1863. See Bell I. Wiley, *The Life of Johnny Reb: The Common Soldier of the Confederacy* (Baton Rouge LA: Louisiana State University Press, 1978) 136.

17 John Parker, Grant's brother-in-law.

18 William A. Colvin (Co G 40th AL).

home some day. Continue fervently in prayer for me. Tell all howdy for me and kiss the dear children for me and believe me your ever true and loving husband,

To Mrs M J Taylor [from] Grant Taylor
& children

PS. If I get sick and can send for you I will be sure to do it. But I am in such an out of the way place I might sicken and die before a letter could get started. I want you to be with me when I am sick as bad as you possibly can want to.

80

Issaquena County
on Deer Creek Miss

Apr. 27th 1863
Beloved wife & children,

I embrace the present hour to pen you a few lines. I am in reasonable health though I have not felt right well since I took that long march up Deer Creek. I have not stopped from duty. I do not know of anything in particular that ails me. I hope and pray that these lines may reach you and find you all in the enjoyment of the best of health. I started a letter to you 4 or 5 days ago by a Mr Harper, Mrs Craig's father that lives near R Peebles'.[19] It was written at different times from the 7th up to 22nd inst. It will explain itself why I did not send it sooner.

I received a most welcome letter from you yesterday dated the 16th. Oh! how glad I was. It was sunday evening. I had just finished reading a very interesting novel. My mind wandered back to by gone days when happiness shone upon us. I was thinking of Brother Leonard's death and our engagement and the happays Sabbath days of our weded life, gone gone forever, and

---

[19] Mr. Harper is unidentified. Mrs. Craig is probably the wife of William E. Craig (Co C 40th AL). Orren Robert Peebles (1821-1887).

was feeling as lonesome as it was possible for me to feel.[20] I even (as I lay on my pallet) had to rais[e] up and gasp for breath. Just then I received your letter. Oh how it revived me. It seemed for an instant that all former happiness had returned. Oh if I could only see you as plainly as I saw you last night in my dream, but I was only with you for a very short time. I thought I had to leave you and go to my hated duties as a soldier. But I hope things will change for the better some day.

You say when you think of Bud and Mary you are almost out of heart about my coming home.[21] Now our cases are somewhat different for if I mistake not neither one of them believed that they would ever see their loved ones again. Now here was a want of faith but in our case we both believe that we will meet again on earth. Although we may be disappointed yet my faith is pretty strong. Oh that it may be stronger and I fully believe that you have strong faith.

I think you have come to a right conclusion when you say you feel like this war will be a long one. That has been my oppinion for a long time and I think we had just as well look the worst in the face and steel ourselves to bear still greater trials, then if peace should happen to come the surprise would be so sweet.

You say that Mary wants to see me so bad. Well I want to see her too but I would be but a poor comforter, for I feel that I need comforting myself for I loved John as a brother indeed. I hope God will be a hus[band] to her and bind up her broken heart and that many happy days are in store for her.

By the by, how does Nealy get along.[22] I sent a few lines in my other letter to Mother and Mary. Ide is gone again on a scouting expedition on lake Washington which is some 25 miles west of here. 100 went off, 27 from our company. I have no idea how long they will be gone.

April 28 While writing the above the remainder of our company received orders to move 7 miles on a bayou call[ed]

---

[20] Leonard Taylor (1826-1852), Grant's brother.

[21] Grant is refering to the fact that John Parker died and that John and his wife Mary Slaughter had been apart because of the war.

[22] Cornelia Shirley Slaughter, widow of Malinda's brother Atlas J. Slaughter (died Oct. 1862).

Rolling Fork, which move we made and landed here last night about dark. We are put here for picket and other guard duties.[23]

As to war news I hear but little that is reliable. Several gunboats have passed Vicksburg lately. The Yanks are going to make a strong effort to take Vicksburg.[24]

There have been lice among us ever since we came to Vicksburg. Some have been very lousy. I have had a few on me but I think I am clear of them now. But I do not know how long I will be so. They paid us $22 the other day, which paid us up to first of January last.

This is a very rich country but it is now nearly all overflowed. The banks of the creeks and lakes are higher than the other parts of the bottom lands and those banks are all but what is overflowed now. The dry land is from 1 quarter to 2 miles wide. In dry weather the roads are splendid but when it rains they are nearly as muddy as the prairies. We are encamped on a ridge about 3 feet above the water and 100 yards wide. This country presents a desolate aspect. Nearly all the farms are lying idle. The citizens and the Yankees between them having taken the most of the Negroes off. And now the citizens are moving their property out of here every day for fear of the Yanks. There will be scarcely any thing raised in here this year. It is a great pity that so much rich land should lie idle. Would to God that this cruel war might close.

Give my best respects to all enquiring friends and tell the connexion howdy for me. Kiss the dear children for me.

Continue to pray for me and believe me your ever true and loving husband,

To Mrs M J Taylor [from] Grant Taylor
& children

---

[23] On April 28th, Major T. O. Stone took three companies of the 40th Alabama to the mouth of Rolling Fork with orders to head to the Little Sunflower River. See Curry, "A History of Company B," 175.

[24] On April 16th and 22nd, Union gunboats and transport ships ran past the Vicksburg batteries at night as part of General Grant's new plan to move down and then across the Mississippi to attack Vicksburg from the south. See Long, *Civil War Day by Day*, 338, 340.

81

Vicksburg Miss

May 9th [18]63

Beloved wife and children,

I embrace the present moment to pen you a few line. I am tolerable well. I have the diarrhea some but not enough to stop me from duty. I hope these lines may reach you all well. I received a letter from you day before yesterday dated 23^d and one yesterday with 2 in it dated 26 and 30th of April. I was glad to get them but sorry to hear of the boys' sickness. I do hope they have got well.

William Graham died at Lauderdale Springs the 13th of April.[25] I do not know anything about Mary's filly. You can do just what you think is best or rather what Pap thinks best if he will advize you anything about it.

I do not need any clothes of any sort yet and if I can draw from the government I shall not draw any more from home. But you can save the cloth until I write to you about it. I have had to leave my overcoat and one blanket behind. I do not expect ever to see them any more. I would have written to you oftener but Capt. Lofton has been trying to get off home for 4 weeks and I thought constantly that he would leave and kept waiting to send by him. He will start home to-day. He has resigned his office on the account of rheumatism. He has got one letter for you but I expect to send this by mail as he has as many letters as he can carry.

We have left the Deer Creek country and are now in Vicksburg.[26] They have been fighting heavily at Grand Gulf and Port Gibson some 25 miles down the river. The Yanks have taken those two places and are moving on up trying to get in the rear of Vicksburg. Our line of battle extends 30 miles. I expect we will

---

[25] There was a W.D.H. Graham in Co G 40th AL and a William L. Graham in Co E 40th AL.

[26] The 40th Alabama was ordered to Vicksburg on May 5, 1863. See Curry, "A History of Company B," 175.

move on down there to-day.[27] And more than probable before you get this, I may be in a bloody battle. May God protect me.

It is a little after sunrise and I must close and eat my breakfast and get ready to march. We got here yesterday. I feel very sore from marching.[28]

Continue in prayer for me. I am determined to send for you if I ever get where you can come to see me. Give my best respects to all the connexion. Kiss the children for me and believe me your true one as ever,

To Mrs M J Taylor [from] Grant Taylor

PS. Ide went out on a scout 2 weeks ago and has not caught up yet. He was tolerable well when I heard from him.

This was Grant Taylor's last letter before the surrender of Vicksburg on July 4, 1863.[29]

---

[27] Union forces crossed the Mississippi on April 30th and clashed with Confederates at Port Gibson, Mississippi, on May 1st. Nearby Grand Gulf fell to the Federals the next day. See Bruce Catton, *Grant Moves South* (Boston: Little, Brown, 1960) 426-429.

[28] On May 8, 1862, the 40th Alabama marched 15 miles to its new position. On the 9th, it moved another 10 miles to Warrenton south of Vicksburg. See Willett, *History of Company B*, 33.

[29] For the operations of the 40th Alabama during the siege of Vicksburg, see Willett, *History of Company B*, 33-40; and Curry, "A History of Company B," 176-180; and *Official Records*, I, 24, Part II:380-383.

CHAPTER 6

WE ARE FARING BADLY FOR SOMETHING TO EAT

After Grant Taylor's unit surrendered and was paroled at Vicksburg in July 1863, he returned home to Pickens County. However, his regiment was ordered to report to parole camp to await exchange on August 23, 1863. Another month passed before the officers and enlisted men began reporting reluctantly in Demopolis. Taylor did not join his company until October 5th and his letters from there reveal deep frustration. Unlike eighteen months ago the men now knew the true story of war and the conditions under which they will be serving.

82

Camp near Demopolis Ala

Oct 12th 1863

Dear wife and children,

It has come to this again. I take my pen this morning to pen you a few lines. This leaves me well and I do hope these lines may reach you all well and doing well.

I landed here on Monday the 5th and would have written to you last week but I put it off until it was too late for it to reach you by that mail. The health of the company is good. John Sanders has the chills.[1] He had them at home and went to Carrollton to get a certificate fixed to stay at home awhile and the cavalry took him and sent him here without any clothes. We are here nearly out of doors having three flies for the company. The Capt. has a tent but lets the men stay in it. The company has only 3 ovens besides

---

[1] John W. Sanders (Co G 40th AL).

what they brought from home. We get plenty of beef and cornbread, a little flour, bacon and rice.

The general impresion here is that we are not exchanged but the officers hold out the idea that we are. We have drawn arms and are drilling every day. The men are afraid to resist. I do not [know] what they will [do] with us for staying away so long. I expect from General [William J.] Hardee's orders, they will knock us out of our wages from the 23^d of August up to the time the men came in. That is all that came in after the 4th of Oct.[2]

There is a great revival going on here and has been for several week[s]. There is preaching every night and from 50 to 100 mourners. They say that 190 have joined the different denominations. 9 were baptized into the Baptist denomination yesterday. Oh how touching it is to see strong men come up with tears streaming down their manly cheeks and tell that they have found the Lord precious to their souls. May the good Lord carry on his good work until every soldier shal be converted.

I have nothing more to write that will interest you. Yes I found your little knife in my pocket the evening I left home and gave it to James Goodson and told him to give it to Martha Mullins for you.[3] I want you to send that little kettle but not the skillet by E Teer if he comes this way as he goes to the salt works.[4] Give my

---

[2] General Grant ordered the 29,000 Confederates who surrendered at Vicksburg to be paroled on the promise that they would not take up arms until properly exchanged with Union prisoners. Pemberton granted the parolees a thirty-day furlough beginning July 19, 1863. The Confederate government later cut the Alabama troops's leave to 15 days ordering them to report to Demopolis by August 23rd. General Hardee had the difficult task of forming these reluctant troops into fighting units again during the month of September. See U.S. War Department, *War of the Rebellion: A Compilation of the Official Records of the Union and Confederate Armies* 128 vols. (Washington, D.C.: Government Printing Office, 1880-1901) II, 6:299; Michael B. Pollard, *Pemberton: A Biography* (Jackson: University Press of Mississippi, 1991) 181-182; and Nathaniel C. Hughes, Jr., *General William J. Hardee: Old Reliable* (Baton Rouge LA: Louisiana State University Press, 1965) 160-161.

[3] James Goodson of Co I 3rd AL. Martha Mullins, wife of Hugh Lafayette Mullins, Grant's nephew.

[4] Elisha Teer.

love to all the connexion and friends and believe me your loving husband and father as ever,

To Mrs M J Taylor [from] Grant Taylor
& children

PS. I received your 2 letters that you sent while I was in Vicksburg since I came here. Also, one from Mary and one from Hughs sent during the seige.

83

Camp near Demopolis Ala.

Oct 18th 1863

Dear wife & children,

I embrace the present hour to drop you a few lines. This leaves me well except cold which makes me have a severe head-ache. I do hope these lines may reach you and the dear children all well. I thought I would have got a letter from you before now but I have not.

We have just got marching orders but I do not know when we will leave nor to what point, but it is said we will go to Missippi again. Lafayette got here yesterday and is quite sick to-day. I will send my old hat and cotton pants by Jake Goodson.[5] Your little knife is at Lafayette's. I wrote to you how I found it in my pocket the evening I left home. I have drawn a new hat and a splendid pair of pants but if you can get my new hat made keep it until I call for it if I ever do. I heard last night that they caught Wat last Wednesday night with dogs.[6] If so poor fellow. I tremble for his fate.

---

[5] Jacob Goodson of Co A 19th AL.
[6] Walter Slaughter, Malinda's brother, deserted on August 26, 1863.

I saw General[s] [Joseph E.] Johns[t]on and Hardee and President Jeff Davis. He does not look to be anything extra, similar to a smoked dried herring.[7]

The meeting that I wrote to you about is still going on. Eight are being baptized in the river now. I have been to preaching nearly every night since I got here but I feel very cold and distant most of the time. I sometimes feel almost crazy. I feel like I have sacrifized everything for a phantom. O Malinda pray for me, pray that I may be enabled to drag my weary limbs through this struggl. Sometimes I feel nearly out of heart of ever living to see you again. But may be God will lengthen out my poor life to see that happy day once more. He is my only dependence.

The health of our Regt is very good but many are absent. I miss many familiar faces. Many have gone to the bar of God since we left Vicksburg and many are at home or some where else.[8] Five have died out of our own company since we started home.

Tell all the kinfo[l]k howdy for me. Tell them to pray for me and may God bless us all is the prayer of your ever loving husband,

To Mrs M. J. Taylor [from] Grant Taylor
& children

---

[7] President Davis met with Generals Hardee and Johnston at Demopolis on October 18th during an inspection tour and troop review. See Elbert D. Willett, *History of Company B, 40th Alabama Regiment, Confederate States Army 1862 to 1865* (Montgomery, AL: Viewpoint Publications, 1963) 43, and Hughes, *Hardee*, 162.

[8] The 40th Alabama's losses at Vicksburg were 18 killed in action and 39 wounded. See *Official Records*, I, 24, Part II:369.

84

Camp near Demopolis   October 28th 1863
Beloved wife and children,

Once more I seat myself to pen you a few lines. This leaves me in reasonable health and I hope you and the dear children are in the best of health.

I wrote to you in my last that we were going to Meridian but that order was countermanded and we are now ordered to Chattanooga Tenn and are to start tomorrow at daylight. Our waggon train leaves this morning. One brigade are now leaving.[9]

O how I want to see you and my sweet children before I go away probably never to return. I can almost hear the shrieks of you and the children and especially Leonard's the morning I left home. When he said he never would see Pa any more. But there is no chance for me to come now.

I have never received any letter from you yet. What is the matter[?] I have a very bad bile [boil] on my right arm so that I can hardly write. I received a letter from Hughs yesterday. All were well. Lucreta is married to a man named McAdora.[10]

They have not paid us any money yet. You will have to do the best you can without my help for it will take all my wages to keep me along here. We only get beef enough for 2 meals per day. The other meal we have to eat musty bread unless we buy potatoes at 3 and 4 dollars per bushel. We get one third of a pound of bacon for 7 days and one pound flour. God only knows what we are coming to.

My arm hurts me so that I must quit. Kiss the dear children and tell all my friends howdy for me. Continue to pray for me and believe me, you[r] ever loving,

To Mrs M J Taylor [from] Grant
& children

---

[9] Moore's Brigade, including the 40th Alabama, left for Chattanooga via Selma, Montgomery, Atlanta, and Chickamauga Station on October 29, 1863. See Willett, *History of Company B*, 44.

[10] Lucretia Taylor Mullins, Grant's widowed sister.

85

West Point Georgia, Sunday Morning

Nov. 1st/63

Beloved wife & children,

These few lines leave me in good health though considerably jaded for the want of sleep not having lain down in the last 2 nights to sleep. I wrote you a few lines last Wednesday [28 Oct] stating that we should start for Chattanooga Tenn. the next day. We did so. Took the cars at 12 o'clock M [meridian] and arrived in Selma that evening. Staid there till 12 the next day. Took steamboat there and landed in Montgomery yesterday morning at daylight.[11] Staid there until last night 12 o'clock. Took the cars and landed here one hour ago. Where we will stay til this evening. Then we will take cars for Atlanta.

The question of our being exchanged is about settled and our Regt is in fine health and pretty good spirits.[12] James Rogers and Rabe Parker ran away the day before we left Demopolis.[13] They did not go off together. I saw Drate Leavell last night at Montgomery.[14] He was well and sent his best respects to you. He is working in a gunsmith shop for the government at $90 per month. Griff was killed at Chickamauga.[15] Jo and Mr Porter passed through the fight unhurt.[16]

---

[11] The steamer *R. B. Taney* landed the 40th Alabama in Montgomery. See Willett, *History of Company B*, 44.

[12] The 40th Alabama was officially declared exchanged on September 12, 1863. See *Official Records*,II, 6:280.

[13] James W. Rogers of Co G 40th AL. Rogers ran away previously in Dec 1862. Perhaps C. R. Parker of Co G 40th AL.

[14] Richard Drayton Leavell (c1832-1896).

[15] Probably Griffin J. Leavell of Co F 41st AL. Union and Confederate armies fought at Chickamauga Creek on September 19-20, 1863. Though Federal troops suffered a defeat and heavy losses, General Braxton Bragg failed to follow it up. Both armies suffered a 28% casualty rate. See E.B. Long, *The Civil War Day by Day: An Almanac 1861-1865* (Garden City NJ: Doubleday, 1971) 441, and Peter Cozzens, *This Terrible Sound: The Battle of Chickamauga* (Urbana: University of Illinois Press, 1992).

[16] Probably Joe Leavell and either John H. Porter or William Jasper Porter of 36th AL.

I gave $5 per quire for paper in Selma. Steel pens are generally 25 cent apiece. In Montgomery pork is $1.50, beef $1.00, butter $3.50 and honey $2 and flour 50 cents per pound. Common pocket knives are $15. What are we coming to[?] Potatoes are about $8 per bushel.

Malinda, a broad strip of country is lengthening out between us. Oh shall I ever see my sweet home and family again? I hope so. If not, I hope we will meet in that happy home above. Continue to pray for me. Tell the connexion howdy for me and tell them to pray for me. I am very much disappointed at not hearing from you since I left home.

Your ever loving,

To Mrs M J Taylor [from] Grant
  & children

Direct your letters to Chattanooga Tenn. in care of Capt. J H Pickens Co (G) 40th Regt Ala Vols.

86

Atlanta Ga.

Nov. 3d 1863

Beloved wife and children,

This leaves me well and I hope that you and the dear children are so too. I wrote to you on the 1st from West Point Ga. stating that we would leave there that evening but we did not start until yesterday morning and landed here yesterday evening at 3 o'clock P.M. I do not know when we will leave here but presume we will start shortly.

I saw Dave Drummond yesterday.[17] He was slightly wounded in the head at the battle of Chickamauga or we called it the battle

---

[17] David T. Drummond (c1831-1896) of Co B 36th AL.

of C[h]attanooga. He has got well again. Jo Leavelle's wife died about the 1st Sept.[18]

Atlanta is 173 miles from Montgomery and 127 miles still to travel over to reach Chattanooga. O how far it seems that I am from home. David Cobb Died a few weeks ago at home.[19] Thomas got his feet frozen off last winter in Tenn and cannot walk without crutches.[20] James Smith left here with his Regt this morning for Chattanooga.[21] They are fighting some up there nearly every day.[22] I expect we will be in it before many days. May God in whom I trust cover my head in the day of battle.

This is the place where poor John breathed away his last.[23] It makes me feel sad and lonesome to think of my many wanderings and at last have arrived so near his earthly remains. If I knew where to find his grave I would visit it. But I hope to meet him some day where sin and trouble will not mar our happiness.

Everything is very high here. Such paper as this is worth $6 per quire. Oh that this cruel war may soon cease and that I may come home to spend the remainder of my days in peace.

Kiss the dear children for me and believe me your ever loving,

To Mrs M J Taylor [from] Grant
& children

PS Direct your letters to Grant Taylor in care of Capt J H Pickens 40th Regt Ala Vols Chattanooga Tenn.

---

[18] Joseph M. Leavell's wife was Agnes Henderson. They had married in Greene County on April 14, 1860.

[19] David Cobb (1845-1863) was buried at Beulah Cemetery.

[20] Thomas W. Cobb (1844-1911) probably of Co G 5th AL Cav.

[21] James Smith is unidentified.

[22] On October 27th, General Grant started operations that would open the "Cracker Line" that would relieve the Army of the Cumberland in Chattanooga. See Peter Cozzens, *The Shipwreck of Their Hopes: The Battles for Chattanooga* (Urbana: University of Illinois Press, 1994) 48-65.

[23] Grant is referring to the death of his brother-in-law John Parker who died April 1863 in Atlanta.

87

Ala

November the 5 1863

Dear husband,

With pleasure I am seated to pen you a few lines. We are all well hoping you are in good health. I supose you have left Demopolous and gon to Chattanuga. I heard yesterday they ware fighting thare. I am very sorry you are gon thare but maybee all for the [best]. I have not got but the 2 letter from you yet. Wat is going to his Company tomarrow.[24] Jake is at home very sick with pneuralga.[25] He will go back when he gets able. Reports say that Ely Going is dead.[26] John Powel was wounded at the Chattanuga fight in the thigh, had it taken off and died the 9 of Oct.[27] I havent mutch news to write as I wrote 4 pages to you last week. I am going to Betties tomarrow but I wont bee happy as I was when I was thare before you and Ide not beeing thare.[28]

I have the childrens winter clothes ready for the loom, 25 yds. It is now daylight. I have been w[r]iting by firelight. I must quit and get breakfast. I keep in good spirits yet and I want you to do the same. Hastletine is up yet.[29] George, Jasper, and Milton Mullens is going off to Demopalous in the boy company.[30]

---

[24] Walter Slaughter, Malinda's brother.

[25] Jacob Parker, Malinda's brother-in-law.

[26] Eli T. Going (c1816-1889) was not dead.

[27] John Powell is unidentified.

[28] Malinda is referring to Elizabeth Taylor Teer and her husband Iredell Teer.

[29] Hasseltine Lindsey Taylor, married to Grant's brother Malachi Taylor. Malinda most likely refers to Hasseltine giving birth to daughter Jerusha Taylor.

[30] George Taylor (born c1845) and Jasper Taylor (born c1847), sons of Malachi Taylor; Milton Mullins (born c1848), son of William Mullins and Lucretia Taylor. All of these boys were Grant's nephews. In 1863, the Confederate government called on the states to raise local defense troops from men not conscripted. Boys of seventeen served in the Junior Reserves. See Albert B. Moore, *Conscription and Conflict in the Confederacy* (New York: MacMillan, 1924) 239-240.

Grant, I have been very lonesum since you went off but am getting over that now. I expect to send this by James Williams as he is here now.[31] I believe I have wrote all. Write evry chance you have and I will do so two.

You can write on the other side of this leaf. Nothing more, only I remain yours, as ever,

Malinda J. Taylor[32]

88

Near the foot of Look-out Mountain Tenn

Nov. 6th '63

Beloved wife & children,

This leaves me in good health and I hope that you and the dear children are in the best of health. I wrote to you on the 1st from West Point and on the 3[d] from Atlanta GA. We left Atlanta on the 4th and landed at Chickamauga station 11 miles from Chattanooga that night at 1 o'clock. We staid until 1 o'clock in the evening and started on foot for the mountain in the rain. We marched until after dark and stopped in an old field, made fires and lay down in the rain and slept soundly. This morning we took up the line of march and came about 2 miles to this place. We have merely stopped to rest I think befor crossing over or around the mountain.[33] The mountain is a grand sight. It is said to be nearly one mile high. A short distance from here we can see a part of the Yankee

---

[31] Probably James G. Williams of Tuscaloosa Co in 1860, later married Mrs. Mary Tate Wells in 1886.

[32] This letter was written on the back of Grant's letter dated Nov. 15, 1863. The next extant letter in the collection from Malinda is dated Sept. 28, 1864. Some of Malinda's letters throughout the war were destroyed or lost in Grant's regimental moves. However, their two-way conversations for the next ten months can be inferred from Grant's letters.

[33] The 40th Alabama camped at the foot of Lookout Mountain until November 10th and did picket duty along Chattanooga Creek. See Curry. "A History of Company B, 40th Alabama Infantry, C.S.A.," 185.

encampments, and once in awhile we can hear the sound of a distant cannon. We have a tremendous Army here. More than I ever saw before and they are generally in fine spirits and confident of victory should the[y] have to fight again.

I saw Amaziah Teer, Dock Edds, Tom Herrald and John Goodson yesterday and John Elledge.[34] They were all well. Albert Teer was sick with chills in camp.[35] I did not see him. They never punished the boys for coming home with Watt.[36] Wiseman Cook was of[f] in the hospital sick.[37] I saw Jo Leavelle this morning.[38] He was well and all of our acquaintance was well. John Henderson died at Tulahoma Tenn some time last summer.[39] I wrote to you in my last how to direct your letters but I will write it again. Mr Grant Taylor in care of Capt J H Pickens 40th Regt. Ala. Vols. John Powell got his thigh broke in the battle and had to have it cut off from the effects of which he died.[40]

Read this letter to your folks and it will do instead of writing to them, but I want them to write to me. Contin[u]e to pray for me. I feel that I am in a dangerous position and that my life may be snatched away at any time but I put my trust in my blessed Saviour believing that he will do all things right.

Some of the boys got letters yesterday among them Ide got one. But none for me. To-day is five weeks since I left home and not one word have I heard from you since then.[41] I am getting very anxious to hear. I will close farewell for the present from your devoted,

To Mrs M J Taylor [from] Grant

---

[34] Amaziah Teer (1841-1863); perhaps John A. Eeds; perhaps Tom N. Harrell of Co F 41st AL; John Goodson is unidentified; probably John H. Elledge (c1830-1901).

[35] Albert Teer (1844-1889), Grant's nephew.

[36] Walter Slaughter deserted August 26, 1863, but returned to his regiment November 17, 1863.

[37] Sergeant Wiseman Cook (Co F 41st AL).

[38] Joseph M. Leavell (Co B 36th AL).

[39] John Henderson is unidentified.

[40] John Powell is unidentified.

[41] Grant left home on September 25 to report to the unit in Demopolis by October 5.

& children

To the children. Pa is away up here among the mountains of Tenn. and I may never see you any more. But I want you to be good children. Mind and do all that your ma tells you to do. Oh how often I think of you and how badly I want to see you and hear your sweet talk and sweet little Mary. God bless her. O dear children be good and meet me in Heaven where we will never part anymore.

89

On the side of Look-out Mountain Tenn.

Nov. 15th 1863

Beloved wife and children,

Withe pleasure I avail myself of one more opportunity of writing to you. This leaves me in good health except cold and I hope and pray that you and the dear children are enjoying the best of health.

I received your letter of Oct. 29th three days ago and was truly glad to get it for I was beginning to think long of the time sure enough but was blaming the mail instead of you for I was sure that you had written before you did. I Received this one yesterday evening and was glad enough to get it as indeed I always am. I wrote to you the day before we left Demopolis and from West Point, Ga. One from Atlanta GA and one after we got here or rather on the other side of the mountain. Which was on the 6th inst. I hope you will get all those letters as they contain much information that I can not write in this as to our traveling, etc.

We are encamped now on the west side of the mountain 700 or 800 feet above the valley. We are over here on picket. Our camps are on the other side of the mountain some 3 miles back where our cooking is done. We have been over here now 5 days and how much longer we will stay here I do not know. I saw plenty of Yanks yesterday in the valley where we were on picket. The

Picket lines are not more than 40 or 50 yards apart but they are not allowed to fire on each other which is a very good arrangement. The Yanks and us all get water out of the same creek not more than 20 s[t]eps wide and could talk to each other if we were allowed but we have strict orders not to speak to them.[42]

We are faring badly for something to eat. I had no meat for 5 days until last night. We drew 2 days rations of beef and I could have eaten it all at 2 meals and not have had enough. And we do not get near bread enough. I hear of desertions daily and in fact I do not see how men can expect to keep an army together on such fare for we all know they could give us bread plenty.[43]

I saw Mr Porter, Sellers, Pearson, Jo Leavell, Dob Knox and Brantley Garner last Monday the most of them were tolerably well but they look as poor and starved as we did when we come from Vicksburg.[44] Sellers and Pearson had just come from the hospital where they had been for several days sick. Wat's Regt is camped about 4 miles from ours but I have not had the chance to go there yet. I hope to do so soon. Mr Porter got that letter I sent him from home.

There is no fighting going on here except occasionally a shell from one side or the other. I have not seen a hog nor cow since I came to Tenn. except some that came from Ga. on the cars and there is no chance to buy anything to eat.

What is the reason that Ki will not let you have any leather.[45] Tell him that he must let me have enough to make me a pair of shoes with that upper leather that I let him have if he possibly can. If he does not I always shall think he ought to for if he had not promised it to me I should have tried to make some other arrangement. The rocks here are very severe on shoes. I do not

---

[42] On November 13th, the 40th Alabama went on picket duty along Lookout Creek west of Lookout Mountain. See Willett, *History of Company B*, 45.

[43] The newly arrived Alabama men suffered from poor and scanty rations. See Cozzens, *Shipwreck of Their Hopes*, 118.

[44] Probably all of these men were in the 36th AL: John H. Porter, or William Jasper Porter (Co B), Elijah Sellers, Pearson is unidentified, Joseph Leavell (Co B), and Dobson Knox. Brantley Garner served in Co F 41st AL but may have also been in the 36th AL.

[45] Malachi "Ki" Taylor, Grant's brother.

believe these I have will last longer than Christmas. If he will let you have the leather, I want you to have me a pair of Large number nines made and have them ready for me for there is not much chance to draw shoes here. Many are nearly or quite barefooted now.

If there is any chance for you to do it I think you had better have a crop made next year for this reason, maybe this war will close sometime next year and then we would have something to go on but you and Buster can exercise your own judgements on it.[46]

I saw Amaziah Teer once since I came up here. He was well. Lab was at our camps last Monday, but I was away and did not see him.[47] Tell all of the connexion howdy for me and continue to pray for me do the best you can.

I was well pleased to get those few lines from Leonard. I want Jimmy to try his hand in the next. Dear Malinda, I dream of you often and oh, what pleasure it is to be with you but when I awake find its all a dream, how sad I feel.

I hope some day to see you in the flesh and if I am dissappointed in this I have strong hopes of meet[ing] you in that bright world above where there will be no more cruel war to separate us. I try to keep that happy home in view so that when my savior call[s] I may be ready to go. Farewell for the present, my dearest,

To Mrs M J Taylor [from] Grant Taylor[48]
& children

I have writen to you two or 3 times how to direct your letters. I will now say Direct to me Co G 40 Regt Ala Vols. Chattanooga Tenn.

---

46 Josiah "Buster" Archibald.
47 Albert "Lab" Iredell Teer, Grant's nephew.
48 This letter was written on the back of Malinda's letter dated November 5, 1863 as she directed.

Camp on the side of Look-out Mountain Tenn

Nov. 22nd 1863

Beloved wife and children,

Through the mercies of a kind Providence I am permitted to write you a few lines this bright Sabbath morning. I am in good health and I do hope that you and the dear children are in the best of health. I wrote to you last sabbath from the west side of the mountain, but that evening we came around on this side on picket. We have now been on this mountain nearly 13 days on picket and throwing up breastworks. We have to go on duty every second or third day. I have had to work two nights this week until midnight. Our duties are very heavy for it is great labor to climb up and down this mountain. We sent men this morning to work on breastworks, but the Yanks have shelled them away. There was a little skirmish some 8 or ten miles from here two or three days ago but with what success I do not know.[49] There is considerable cannonading this morning. This evening was two weeks ago there was a detail of men from our Regt and the 42nd Ala sent on picket. When they got near enough the Yanks threw a shell among them and wounded 11 from the effects of which one died that night and another had his leg cut off. They were all from the 42nd and four of the wounded were from the Lane Guards, but none that you knew. We are faring much better now than at the time of my last writing but we do not get near enough to eat yet of the coarsest quality.

I saw Amaziah day before yesterday. He was well. Jake and Jim Goodson have got here.[50] I saw them both. Albert Teer was well.

We have had beautiful weather most of the time since we got here. Some pretty cold weather, plenty of ice but it does not seem

---

[49] On November 18, there was a skirmish at Trenton, Georgia, involving approaching Union reinforcements for Chattanooga under General William T. Sherman. See Long, *Civil War Day by Day*, 434.

[50] Jacob Goodson and James A. Goodson served in the Pickens County "Ruff and Readies" in 19th AL.

to hurt me like cold used to. Night before last it commenced raining about midnight and continued until yesterday 12 o'clock M which was pretty tight considering we had no shelter except our blankets, our tents all being in the valey about a mile from here. Not withstanding the rain, we stretched part of our blankets over a pole and fa[s]tened them down on each side and wrapt up in the remaining blankets and slept finely. Last night it cleared off and this morning is clear cool and quite bracing.

According to an order of Gen. [Braxton] Bragg our company is entitled to send one man home on furlough. But Pickens would not let any have a chance that did not report at Demopolis by the 27th of Sept, so I was cut out of the chance of drawing for it.[51] I told him if he intended to punish me for staying at home, I wanted him to do it and be done with it and not be always about it. He said if I did not like it I might rip. I think it a very unfair piece of business. The General has ordered that none should be paid from the 23[d] of August up to the time they reported, that is those that did not report there by that time. I hear of our men deserting almost every day.

There is a cave in the point of this mountain about a mile from here in which there is the dead body of a woman. Awhile before we came up here one of our officers found two small children in there alive but the supposed mother was dead and her body is said to be in there yet. Who she is or how she died none can tell. Probably the wife of some poor soldier who may be alive and who may never know how she died. May God shield you from such a fate.

According to another order of Bragg's I expect John Walker will go home on furlough.[52] If he does I want you to have me a pair of shoes made out of that leather I let Ki have if you can get the sole leather. If he does not let me have enough to make me a pair I will always think he ought to. Have them made large nines with 3 soles. These rocks are very bad on shoes. The soles of these I have on are wearing out very fast. I do not think they will last me

---

[51] Grant reported for duty on October 5th, considerably past the deadline of August 23 [see note 41].

[52] John J. Walker of Co B 40th AL.

longer than Christmas. I see several soldiers crimpleing over the stones barefooted.

Continue in prayer for me. Give my best respects to all the connexion and friends and believe me, your ever loving husband and father,

To Mrs M J Taylor [from] Grant Taylor
& children

PS I received your letter sent to Demopolis and the one by James Williams.

91

Marietta Ga

Nov 28th 1863

Dear Malinda,

I hasten to drop you a few lines. I am well except a sprained ankle. I am in the Academy Hospital at this place.[53] I came here yesterday evening.

Well, Malinda the great battle of Chattanooga has been fought and lost. The fighting commenced on Monday evening about 5 miles from us. On Tuesday, they attacked the Lookout Mountain where [we] were. We fought them several hours but they were so much stronger than we that we had to leave the mountain that night about 2 o'clock.[54]

As we started I slipped and sprained my ankle badly. The Regt was engaged the next day on Missionary Ridge and were driven

---

[53] The Academy Hospital had moved from Chattanooga to Marietta after that city's fall to Union forces in September, 1863. See Glenna R. Schroeder-Lein, *Confederate Hospitals on the Move: Samuel H. Stout and the Army of Tennessee* (Columbia SC: University of South Carolina Press, 1994) 122-123.

[54] On November 24th, three Union divisions under General Joseph Hooker drove Confederate defenders from the mountain. For the 40th Alabama's role in the battle, see *Official Records*, I, 31, Part II: 704-705.

back again.[55] I have not heard from the army since Thursday morning. It was then falling back to Ringold some 25 or 30 miles from Chattanooga.

On Tuesday our company lost one man killed John Turnupseed and 3 wounded and 8 prisoners and one missing. James McCulley and Dave Lynch were among the prisoners and John Stuckey is missing. On Wednesday Dallis Clayton was killed and two others were wounded.[56] In all our loss our company lost 16 in kill[ed], wounded, missing and prisoners.

The last I heard from Ide he was safe. Thank God for his protecting care during the hours of struggle that I was engaged in.

This is now Saturday evening. Our army was badly demoralized and I think our loss pretty heavy especially in cannon.[57]

Dear Malinda, continue to pray for me. Direct your letters as I have directed you before. I think I shall be able to go back to my Regt in a week. It is nearly dark I must quit. May God bless you all. I will write more next time.

From your loving

To Mrs M J Taylor [from] Grant

---

[55] The Army of Tennessee suffered a distastrous defeat at Missionary Ridge on November 25th. Then it retreated back into Georgia in confusion. For the best account of this battle, see Cozzens, *Shipwreck of Their Hopes*.

[56] John A. Turnipseed, James A. McCulley, David Lynch, John J. Stuckey, and William Dallas Clayton, all of Co G 40th AL.

[57] The Army of Tennessee lost some 40 cannons in the retreat from Missionary Ridge. See Cozzens, *Shipwreck of Their Hopes*, 389.

92

Marietta Ga

Dec. 2nd 1863

Beloved wife and children,

Once more I take an opportunity to pen you a few lines. I am well except a sprained ankle and I hope you and the dear children are in the best of health. I wrote a few lines to you the other day since I came here and I will send you a letter I wrote a few days before the battle but have had no chance to send it off.

Well to begin. On Monday evening the 23^d of November the enemy made an attack on our lines about 5 miles to our right but did not make much.[58] Then on Tuesday Morning they attacked Look-out Mountain on the west side about forty thousand strong where we had but one brigade to oppose them. They soon scattered that brigade and here they came like wild beasts to attack us. Our brigade held them in check several hours for the ground was so broken that they could not bring all their forces to bear on us at once. But we fought at least 5 to one several hours until reenforcements came when we fell back a short distance. But they then attacked our reinforcements and my brigade had very little more fighting to do that day and night.

Tuesday night about 2 o'clock We left the mountain and retreated 5 or 6 miles to Missionary Ridge. Where our brigade fought them again next day and were driven back again after a hard strugle. We got badly whipped on the left of our army but the right whipped the enemy equally as bad but then we lost our position which was very strong. So upon the whole I think in the 2 days fighting we were badly worsted. I understand that our whole army fell back as far as Tunell Hill Ga fighting as they came until Friday when they turned on them and dressed them out nicely. The last reports are that Bragg was driving them back towards

---

[58] Sherman's attempt to turn the Confederate right flank ground to a halt on November 25th at Tunnel Hill. See Cozzens, *Shipwreck of Their Hopes*, 241.

We are Faring Badly for Something to Eat   201

Chattanooga but I do not how true that is.[59] I think we killed a great many more of them than they did of us. We claim to have killed and wounded twenty thousand of them and they claim to have taken the same number of prisoners from us but either estimate is mere guess work.[60] Part of our army was badly disorganized.

My company lost up to Wednesday night 2 killed dead, five wounded, 2 severely, one missing and 8 prisoners. The killed were John Turnipseed and Dallis Clayton. Among the prisoners were Dave Lynch, Jack Hunt and James McCulley.[61] The prisoners were on picket at the time of the attack and John Stuckey is missing. I fear he was killed. Ide was safe on Wednesday night. I do not know how the Wells company came out.

On Tuesday night as we were leaving the mountain I fell and sprained my ankle severely. I hobbled along the best I could to the railroad about 12 miles distant. Got there on Thursday morning before day took the cars and landed here on Friday evening and am now in the Academy Hospital in Ward no 6. I am mending slowly. Am able to get about by the help of a stick. We have plenty of warm bed clothes and a plenty to eat such as it is. I fear it will be some time before I am able to go back to my Regt. I had rather be there than here. Still direct your letters to Chattanooga Tenn. for before you get this and return an answer I hope to be with my company.

Oh Malinda how thankful we ought to be to God for preserving my life During the fight when the bullets were flying thick as hail and the shells bursting all around. I did not feel afraid for I felt that I had trusted my all in the hands of my blessed Savior. I felt like I would not be killed and if I did that it would be merely a release from trouble and an entrance into the joys of my blessed Savior.

---

[59] Bragg pulled his battered command together and the Federals halted their pursuit on November 26th. See Long, *Civil War Day by Day*, 439.

[60] Union losses around Chattanooga were 5,824 men and Bragg's army lost 6,667 soldiers killed, wounded, missing or captured. See Long, *Civil War Day by Day*, 428.

[61] One additional man is mentioned in this letter: John J. Hunt of Co G 40th AL.

Continue to pray for me. Give my best love to the connexion and friends and b[e]lieve me, your truly devoted husband.

To Mrs M J Taylor [from] Grant Taylor
& children

Be sure to attend to my shoes and send them the first safe opportunity.

This is the finest watered country I ever saw. Close together all around the sides of the mountain are springs of the finest water and even on the top of the mountain are some very fine springs.

The above was written on the mountain. Marietta is a nice place 20 miles north of Atlanta and in good times it has the appearance of being a right business place.

93

Academy Hospital Marietta Ga

Dec 6[th] 1863

Beloved wife & children,

Once more I avail myself of an opportunity of writing to you. This leaves me in good health e[x]cept my ankle which is mending slowly. I do hope these few lines may reach you that lie so near my heart in good health and spirits. I saw a letter from John Sanders yesterday written to W Stapp who is a nurse here.[62] Sanders stated that he had seen James Goodson since the battle on Missionary Ridge and that Goodson said that Amaziah Teer and Steve Garvin were both killed in the battle.[63] Poor Amaziah the last time I saw him he looked fine and hearty. And to think how many bloody battles he has passed through and at last to be killed in the bloom of his manhood. It almost puts me out of heart.

---

[62] John W. Sanders and William M. Stapp of Co G 40th AL.

[63] James Goodson and Amaziah Teer of 19th AL. Amaziah Teer was Grant's nephew. Steve H. Garvin of Co A 19th AL.

I have written 2 letters to you before this one, telling you what I knew of the battle and how I came to be here and I deem it unnecessary to go over the same ground again. This is one of the most beautiful Sabbath evenings I ever saw but it's very loveliness depresses my spirits to the lowest ebb. The main reason of my writting to-day is to unburthen my mind to one I know can sympathize with me. Here I am shut up in this town not able to go about much and if I were I am not allowed to go off far from the house or the guards will take me up. Plenty of men and women too are here but with the exception of a few of my own company all are strange faces. Those that like myself are exiles from their dear ones at home and care not for my little sorrow.

Oh Malinda how lonesome I feel, how memory carries me back to the happy Sabbath days we have passed together hardly knowing that we were happy. I feel a long, long way from home and friends but I feel that you are one that cares for me, and this is a great pleasure to be allowed to write to each other although I have never recieved but two from you since I left home. Malinda sometimes my hope almost fails me of ever seeing betters days but then I recount the many mercies of God towards me that I still hope against hope. When I says betters days I mean on earth but I do hope to see better days in that happy world to come, and you may think me selfish but sometimes I feel that if it were not for you and the children I would not care how soon my blessed Savior would call for me. But then I know it is wrong to complain and I try to hold up the best way I can. Oh dearest and best of earthly friends pray to God earnestly that my spirits fail me not.

I fear I have written too much already in this melancholy way but I cannot help it this evening. If you can, keep in good spirits for I tell you that the spirit is nearly all in holding us up. For when we become low spirited we are almost sure to begin to feel unwell. But I cannot help low spirits getting the mastery of me sometimes. Maybe there is a better time coming and if not I hope to meet you where parting will be no more. May God guide and direct us in the path of duty is the prayer of your unhappy husband. I intend to go to my Regt as soon as they will let me go, for I had rather be there to share their hardships and dangers than here.

I saw a letter from Capt Pickens to Wm Stapp. He puts the loss of our Co in both days fighting at 18 in all. 2 killed and the rest wounded, prisoners and missing. I expect those that are prisoners are gone during the war for Lincoln says he will not exchange any more prisoners unless the Confederates will exchange negroes for white men which I am sure they will never do. I send you a letter written by a newspaper correspondent giving the best general account of the 2 days around Chattanooga that I have seen. Also a piece concerning [General James] Longstreet about Knoxville.[64] He was sent there from Chattanooga about the time we got there to harrass the enemy and to prevent reenforcements from reaching Chattanooga. If that tale is true you will see what luck he had. Moore's brigade is the one we are in.

There are men here from nearly every southern state and I have talked with many. They are generally low spirited and think our cause is gone. And indeed I think that is one grand cause of our failures now. The men do not think it worth while to fight in so hopeless a cause. They feel like they are sacrificing their lives and their all for nothing. May God soon hasten the time when peace shall shine once more on our distracted country.

My Brigade is 2 miles south of Dalton Ga. They have received orders to build winter quarters. Gen Bragg has been relieved from command by his own request. General Hardee is temporarially in command.[65]

Yesterday there was a poor woman from Ga. came here to see her husband who was wounded but when she got here he had been dead 2 days and was buried.

Tell your folks and mine howdy for me and e[x]cuse this printed up letter I picked it up and wrote on it for it stands me in hand to save all I can. Kiss the dear children for me.

---

[64] Longstreet's corps had been detached from the Army of Tennessee on November 3rd to try to recapture Knoxville, Tennessee, from Union forces. See Cozzens, *Shipwreck of Their Hopes*, 103-104. The letter by the correspondent and the piece about Longstreet are no longer in this collection.

[65] Hardee officially replaced Bragg on December 2, 1863. See Hughes, *Hardee*, 179.

Where is Wat.[66] I do not think his Regt was in the fight. I heard it was sent up the Tenn. river a few days before the fight. I never got to go and see the boys in that Regt. I saw Ki's George on Wednesday evening of the fight.[67] He was well, was with the wagons, was not in the fight.

Your true husband,

Grant Taylor[68]

---

[66] Walter Slaughter, Malinda's brother (Co A 41st AL).

[67] George Taylor (born c1845), son of Malachi Taylor. In early November, Malinda wrote that George was joining the "boy company," but at age 18, he was certainly old enough to join as a man.

[68] A portion of this letter was written on a printed medical prescription form for William Alston, MD, Druggist, Marietta, Ga.

Chapter 7

In Camp Near Dalton

Grant Taylor and his comrades in the 40th Alabama spent the cold, hungry winter of 1863-1864 quartered near Dalton, Georgia. Short rations and the beginning signs of illness plagued him as well as a longing for home and family. Meanwhile the Army of Tennessee endured and grew strong again under its new commander Joseph E. Johnston. Spring brought better weather and the hard realization that active campaigning would soon follow.

94

In camp near Dalton, Ga.[1]

Dec 24th 1863

Dear wife & children,

I [--- ---] the present hour to write you a few lines. I am well except a bad cold. My ankle is nearly well and I hope you and the children are in the best of health.

I arrived here Monday morning and found the boys generally well and going ahead building the winter quarters. The most of the Regt are about done building. They have put up big cabbins large enough to contain about 8 to 10 men and are much more comfortable than tents. Inde[ed] we have no tents for they had to throw them all away on the retreat from Chattanooga and a good many of our cooking utensils. I found the boys in low spirits and generally out of heart. They only draw enough beef and bread for

---

[1] The 40th Alabama, now part of General Benjamin F. Cheatham's division, was camped two miles east of the Western and Atlantic Railroad line and three miles south of Dalton. See Willett, *History of Company B*, 52.

two light meals each day. I do not see how a government can expect to keep an army together fed as we are.

I do not know where Wat's Regt is. Some say they are in east Tennessee. Charley Taylor was here a few days ago.[2] He was well. Ide says he is the same Charley yet. It is reported here that the last that was seen of Amaziah was the Yanks had him prisoner and one of his arms was shot off above the elbow. A man got away from them and brought this news back. I hope he is still alive and may return some day.

We have very cold weather here now but clear.

The last letter I got from you was dated the 2[nd] Dec which I answered from Marietta. I believe I have written about all the news that would interest you.

We are camped 25 mil[e]s nearly east of Dalton. I have no war news to write.

Malinda continue in prayer for me though I know you do that without requesting you to do it. Tell Pap Mother Mary Elizah howdy for me. Also Nealy and Serene.[3] Tell them to Remember me in their prayers. Tell them to pray that I may live to come home and that I may live an humble Christian on earth. Give Elisha and family my best respects.[4] Also David Hood and family and Mrs Powell and all enquiring friends if any.[5]

Kiss the children for me and May God bless us all with every needful blessing and finally save us in heaven is the prayer of your loving husband and father.

To Mrs M J Taylor [from] Grant Taylor
& children

Dec 25th A mery Christmas to you. I am nearly sick this morning with cold. I hope you are well.

---

[2] Charles McCartney Taylor, Grant's cousin, who was married to Grant's niece, Martha Washington Taylor, a daughter of James Hughes Taylor.

[3] Wiley Slaughter (Pap), Lucy Ussery Slaughter (Mother), Mary Slaughter Parker, Eliza Slaughter Parker, Cornelia "Nealy" Shirley Slaughter, and Serena Webb Slaughter.

[4] Elisha Teer, married to Grant's sister.

[5] David Hood (c1826-1880). Mrs. Powell is unidentified.

Jesse McCracken starts this morning for Franconia [Alabama] after clothing for our company.[6] If you have not sent my shoes by John Walker, I want you to send them to Sam Hood's at Franconia by the 12th of Jan and if you have to send the shoes there I want you to send my hat also if it is made.[7] But if you have sent the shoes you need not take the trouble to send the hat alone. The hat I drew is ~~nearly worn out~~ but little account. If you send anything be sure to mark it to me. The shoes had better be marked with pen and ink on the bottoms. I do not want you to take the trouble to go yourself, but try to get some one to go for you. Be sure to get them to Hood's by the 12th of Jan.

They are talking about paying us money for our clothing. If they do I will send it to you but I think it doubtful whether they pay us soon. I have just spent all the money I have for pork enough for my dinner at $1.50 per pound. We are suffering badly for something to eat but if I draw any money for clothing I consider it belongs to you and I will send it to you by the first chance.

95

Camp of the 40th Regt near Dalton Ga

Dec. 28th 1863

Beloved wife & children,

Once more I write you a few lines. I am well except cold and sore throat. I hope you and the children are well and in good spirits.

Our company is in fine health. Gen. Hardee has issued an order that one man out of every thirty well men can have a

---

[6] Jesse McCracken (Co G 40th AL). Wintering in Georgia, the company searched for its own clothing to keep warm.

[7] Samuel W. Hood (1840-1922). Franconia is located in T22S R15W near what is now Aliceville, Pickens County.

furlough for 20 days.[8] Our company drew for it and Ide got it. I expect he will start in a day or two. I was on the sick list and the Capt would not let any of the sick draw. May be it will come my turn some time.

I started a letter to you on Christmas day by McCracken of Franconia. In that letter I wrot for you to send my shoes by him if you had not sent them before. But if you have not sent them to him, you can take them to Ide's and he can bring them. I also wrote for my new hat but I have concluded not to have it sent yet. So if it is made you can hold on to it. I will write in this if Ide does not get off and if he does not, you can send the shoes to Franconia. Provided you can get them there by the 12th of Jan.

Well Malinda I did not think I ever would send to you for something to eat. But if you can spare some 15 or 20 pounds of meat and have a plenty left to do you and the children, I want you to send it by Ide. Also a good pone of light cornbread. Tell Mother to send me a few of her big potatoes if they are not all gone. Send me some some Sausage if you have them to spare and some butter but do not send anything if you think you will be scarce. I had rather suffer on than for you and the children to lack for meat and bread.

We drew 4 days rations of beef and we can eat it up at 2 meals and we only draw meal enough for 2 small meals a day but we can make out to buy a little, sometimes. On Christmas day 7 of us paid $13.50 for pork enough for 2 small meals. So you see we are living bully. On Christmas morning they gave us a small dram apiece, but I sold mine for one dollar and bought meat with it.[9]

I do pray that this war would close. The men are the worst out of heart that I ever saw.

It is reported that the Yank have put all the Vicksburg prisoners to death that were captured at Chattanooga, but I do not believe a word of it. The Yanks dare not do it for if they should do it, our government would kill as many of theirs byt that would not do our poor fellows any good after they were dead.

---

[8] Hardee issued this order to attempt to rebuild the morale of the battered Army of Tennessee. See Hughes, *Hardee*, 182.

[9] Each company received one gallon of whiskey for the holiday. See Willett, *History of Company B*, 53.

I believe I have written all that would interest you. I saw Ki's George yesterday. He was well. Continue in prayer for me and for peace. Give my best respects to all enquiring friends and the connexion. Tell Pap that I fell under many obligations to him for what he has done and is doing for you. Maybe I will get home some day to repay him. I pray God's richest blessings on him. My poor prayers is all I can give him now. Goodbye for the present,

To Mrs M J Taylor [from] Grant Taylor
& children

Dec 29 I received your letter of Dec 16th and 18th yesterday. I was so glad to hear that you and the children were all well. Tell Math[hew] to eat just as much as he wants and to think of Pa when he is doing it. Have you got your sack of salt yet[?] If so, how much did it cost you[?] I only want 3 or 4 of Mothers potatoes. They are too heavy to send many.

Dec 30th. Ide has just got his furlough and will start in a few minutes. I am well as common. I say again if you think you will be scarce of meat [do] not send any. But I would like to have some very well. Yours lovingly,

G Taylor

96

Camps near Dalton Ga.

Dec. 31st 1863

Beloved wife and children,

I am in pretty good health this morning and I hope you and the children are the same. There is a heap of rain here. There has not been but one clear day since Christmas eve. It rained nearly all night last night and is raining this morning. The roads are in awful condition. This is very mudy country. Very little sand here.

There is a report here this morning that they have been fighting again about Tunnel Hill. I do not know how true it is. I hope it is not so.[10] Since I have to stay in the army I want to stay here till spring. Our cabbins are much more comfortable than tents and if we have to leave here we will not have even them.

Ide Teer started home yesterday evening on a twenty days furlough. I sent a letter by him and wrote for something to eat. Columbus Wells starts home this evening or to-morrow.[11] I will send this by him. You will be apt to get this before you will that and if so send immediately for that for directions what to send and how to send it. If Ide can not bring the things, Wells says he will bring them for me. But I had rather Ide would bring them for he will bring them directly to me. I wrote for 15 or 20 pounds of meat some butter sausage a pone of light cornbread if you can spare it but don't stint yourself on my account.

I started a letter on Christmas day by Jesse McCracken of Franconia requesting you to send my shoes and hat by him but you can send the shoes by Lum or Ide and not send the hat. If it is made keep it. I have heard that old man Robinson is dead.[12] If he is and has not made the hat you had better go and get the wool away.

I wrote for Mother to send me three or 4 of her big potatoes if they are not all gone. Tell all the connexion howdy for me. Continue to pray for me and for peace for Blessed are they that hold out faithful.

I got acquainted with a nephew of old man Miles Leatherwood in the hospital. Poor fellow he was shot through the elbow and suffered a great deal. He was from Arkansas.

May God bless you all is the prayer of your loving husband and father,

To Mrs M J Taylor [from] Grant Taylor

PS Direct your letters to Dalton Ga.

---

[10] No serious action was reported on December 31st. See Long, *Civil War Day by Day*, 450.

[11] Columbus Wells (Co B 42nd AL).

[12] Probably John Robinson (born c1797) of Pickens County.

97

Camp of the 40th Regt near Dalton Ga

Jan 10th 1864

Dear wife and children,

I take this opportunity to pen you a few line. I am not very well. I have the Diarrhea and have been sick at my stomach for a week.[13] I still keep on duty but I am realy not able. I tell you it is pretty bad doing for a man to be always sick at his stomach and have but little to eat except corn bread. But I hope it will not always be so. I hope you and the dear little ones are well and doing well. I have nothing of interest to write.

We have much cold weather now. The ground has not been thoroughly thawed in many days. It is now as hard as a brick. It turns a little warm some time and rains a cold rain and then freezes hard again. It has been as cold here for the last three weeks except a few days as the coldest days you ever saw in Pickens [County]. We make out pretty well in our cabbins but if we were out of doors it does seem to me that we would freeze to death. There is a good deal of Diarrhea in camps caused I think from bad diet and having to drink ice water. For we have to use water out of the branch.

I hear that the Yanks thrashed our cavalry out near Charleston Tenn. the other day. It is reported that our men ran like pretty fellows.[14] I am glad the Yanks ran us off of Lookout Mountain for it does seem to me that we would have been bound to have frozen if we had staid up there without shelter as we were.

I heard from Lafayette and Lab yesterday. They were well. Jake Goodson was sick with fever.[15]

---

[13] Diarrhea and dysentery were common ailments in the ranks of the Army of Tennessee at this time. See Larry J. Daniel, *Soldiering in the Army of Tennessee: A Portrait of Life in a Confederate Army* (Chapel Hill: University of North Carolina Press, 1991) 73.

[14] A skirmish took place at Charleston, Tennessee, on December 28th. See Long, *Civil War Day by Day*, 449.

[15] Hugh Lafayette Mullins and Albert Teer, Grant's nephews. Jacob Goodson (Co A 19th AL).

They knocked us out of our money sure enough for not reporting at Demopolis. I lost $14.66. All that I have to say is that whoever caused it would steal a quarter off a dead niggers eyes. I believe the devil has a bill of sale for him now and that he is sure of hell.

I have heard there is a company of cavalry camped near Mrs Jane Bailey's.[16] Is it so and if so how do they treat the people.

John Walker's time has been out 4 days but he has not come yet.[17] They have got old Rabe Parker under guard yet for coming by home.[18] Little Jo Lancaster and 3 more of Willett's men started home some time ago.[19] They got a good distance but they were caught and brought back and are now under trial.[20] I expect it will go pretty tight with them.

Write all you know about Wat. I do not know where his Regt is. There is a heap of dissatisfaction among the troops here. I hear that the citizens are generally out of heart off from the army. The most of them say they will take the oath if the Yanks ever come through here. My God when will this thing end. Will I ever live to

---

16 Mrs. Jane Bailey is unidentified.

17 John J. Walker (Co G 40th AL).

18 Perhaps C. R. Parker (Co G 40th AL).

19 Eli Joseph Lancaster, John T. Elmore, Jordan J. Elmore, and James L. Elmore, all of Co B, deserted on November 30. See Willett, *History of Company B*, 51.

20 On January 2, 1864, Willett wrote in his diary, "Courtmartial continues. The four deserters of Co B to wit: L., E., E., and E., were captured in Cherokee County AL and brought back. Charges and specifications were preferred, and they were tried by the Corps Court and sentenced, the three E.'s to be marked with letter D on left hip and wear barrel shirt. L. to have his head half shaved, wear barrel shirt ten days and marched through the Brigade with music and a guard at charge bayonet. So much for deserting the service!" Several weeks later on January 19, Willett added, "John T. E[lmore] died today. His sickness was measles. He was under sentence of court martial for desertion to be branded by marking on left hip with letter "D." He died before the sentence was executed. He resided in Pickens County AL and left a wife and one child. An unfortunate man!" Probably Joseph Lancaster's punishment was greater because he was a corporal and the others were privates. See Willett, *History of Company B*, 54-55, and Bessie Martin, *Desertion of Alabama Troops from the Confederate Army: A Study of Sectionalism* (1932; reprinted New York: AMS Press, 1966) 130-131.

see the end. The prospect is very gloomy now but may be all will come out as we wish in the end. Continue in fervent prayer for me. Give my best respects to all the connexion and enquiring friends. Kiss the children for me and believe me your ever true and loving husband.

To Mrs M J Taylor [from] Grant Taylor

98

Camps near Dalton Ga.

Jan. 19th 1864

Beloved wife and children,

Thank God I am permitted to pen you a [few] lines again leaving me in very good health hoping you and the dear children are enjoying the best of health. I received your most welcome letter dated from the 20th Dec. to Jan. 1st yesterday. Which made me glad to hear that you were well and doing well.

As to your request about those names. I have picked out some very common ones that will suit me if they will you. If a boy name it Atlas Grant or Wiley Grant, but probably Atlas would do better as he is dead. I have no choice only that. Bud is dead. If a girl Elizah Elizabeth after our sisters will do. I am not choice in names only you request it so earnestly that I could not refuse you.

John Walker got here 3 or 4 days ago and they have him under guard for staying over his time. He brought my shoes to me. I do not think they will hurt him. I wrote to you in my last about little Jo Lancaster and 3 others of Willett's men being under trial for desertion. Lancaster was sentenced to have half his head shaved, to wear a barrel and be marched through the quarters 2 hours each day for ten days with music and a guard. His sentence is now being executed. The others were sentenced to be branded with the letter D on the left hip with indelible ink and were [wear] a barrel

2 hours each day for 10 days but they are too sick with measels to be punished yet. They are none disgraced with the privates.[21]

Ide landed here safe and sound yesterday evening but lost all our provisions at the Gainesville [Mississippi] junction. They had five boxes with them. Lieut [John N.] Collier got transportation for six and when the conductor found the mistake he threw the boxes off at the ju[n]ction without their knowledge and they did not find it out until they got to Meridian. Collier sent his negro back next morning to see about them but he has not come yet. I have some hope that he will get them and bring them through. There was fifteen hundred or two thousand dollars worth of things in the five boxes at the rates things sell up here. Pies the size of a man's hand sells for $1 to $1.25, sweet cakes not so large for the same, goobers $1.25 per quart, flour 80 cents per pound in Dalton when there is any there, pork from $2 to $2.50 per pound, butter $5.

I will send a receip[t] to you for three hundred dollars. Take it and go to Davis and draw that amount now and pay all that I owe out of it and use the remainder as you choose. You can date the receipt when you get the money.

I think you had better fatten that other sow as soon as you can and if you do not draw a plenty of corn you had better buy plenty as soon as you draw that money while it is cheap and if you can you had better take part of the money and have all your fences put in good order and if there is any chance hire some one to make corn for you. But I will leave that with you, but if there is any chance I think you had better use part of that money to get your fences repaired.

I owe little Jo King's estate, Owen doctor bill, Maynard a little, Cosper a little, Jack and Ves some, I recon buster has that and you owe Snoddy some.[22] I think that is all. Have you ever got that six dollars that Elijah Hood owed me in change for that wheat.[23]

---

[21] Captain Willett's testimony that these men had been good soldiers probably saved them from the firing squad. See Curry, "A History of Company B," 108.

[22] Joseph O. King who died in 1862; Dr. Thomas Sidney Owen (1813-1866); perhaps R. P. Maynard, a blacksmith; James P. Cosper (1821-1886); Andrew J. Slaugther, John Ves Peebles; Josiah Archibald; Dr. Samuel A. Snoddy (1809-1894).

[23] Elijah G. Hood (1822-1904).

I will send Davis [a]uthorty to pay you as much money as you want and for you to receipt for it in my name.[24] When you write tell me all about what Davis is going to do with that money. If you get it all, I do not know what you will do with it unless you can loan it out and that will be a bad chance. I do not recon there will be enough to buy a negro woman worth anything.

I was at the 19th Ala Regt last Saturday and saw Lafayett who was well but did not see Lab as he was gone to Dalton to stay 7 days on guard. He was well. Tell Dully that I got hold of Lab's sausages and pressed in about 4 feet.[25] I tell you we smacked our mouths over them.

One of those prisoners in Willett's Co died last night with measels. His name was Elmore.[26]

I hear nothing from Buck Creek, nor from Wat, only as you write it.[27] I want you to settle up ful[l] with Pap if he will have it. Tell him to take pay for what he has done for you. He has the full gratitude of my heart for his fatherly care of you and my dear children. Tell him if he does not want pay not think hard of me for offering it. May God's blessing rest on him and may his latter days be brighter than they are now is my sincere prayer. I want him to take pay for that note and stop the interest on it.

Night before last there fell a light snow here. It then cleared off and froze pretty hard last night but it is quite pleasant. It lacks so much of being as cold as it has been.

I will send a blank receipt and you can fill out the amount and date it. When you get the money Watch Davis and dont let him cheat you.

We drew for 2 more furloughs yesterday. I did not draw one. I drew for it but missed it. Two men drew that you know nothing about. In future Direct your letters to Dalton Ga instead of Chattanooga.

---

[24] William R. Davis, Grant's brother-in-law, who is administering the estate of Grant's deceased father Archelaus Taylor.

[25] Dulcena Taylor Teer, Grant's sister and her son Albert "Lab" Teer. "Pressing" food means taking a share from someone else.

[26] Private John T. Elmore (Co B 40th AL). See previous footnotes.

[27] The community where Grant and Malinda had lived had been called Buck Creek but became Cushing. Later, the name would change to Ralph.

Jan 21st We have just heard Collier's negro got our boxes and they are on the road and will be here in a day or two. It made me right sick when I first heard that they were lost. One of our Co. is with them.

I have written to Wick for him to send you an order on Davis for Davis to pay that note I hold against Wick. If it comes you get it take it and go to Davis and get the money. Have the interest all paid but do not let Davis have neither the order nor note unless he pays the money.

Continue in prayer for me and believe me your ever loving husband and father.

To Mrs M J Taylor [from] Grant Taylor
& children

I want to see you all as bad as I can but there is no chance now. I have no idea that I can get a furlough in the spring for I expect furloughing will all be stopped before that time.

Jan 23d I am still in good health. As to sending to school to Miss Ann, I do not much like the idea but if she is going to teach there any way and no chance to get another, I reckon you had better try her again.[28] But I would not subscribe more than a half schollar and then if you do not like her better than we did last year you can stop the children when you please and not lose much and if she is going to teach anyhow don't subscribe at all but pay for what time you send. I would have started this letter sooner but I have been waiting to send it by hand as far as Pleasant Ridge. We have heard nothing more from our provisions.

---

[28] Probably Nan Herndon (born c1838), daughter of John and Nancy Herndon.

99

Camp in the woods

Jan 28th 1864

Dear wife & children,

Through the kindness of God I am permitted to write these few lines Which leaves me in good health and hope you are all enjoying the same blessing. I have nothing strange to write.

We are incamped 7 miles south of Dalton working on the road. We came here yesterday but I do not know how long we will stay here. If it rains and turns cold we will have a rough time of it not having any shelter whatever.

Our boxes of provisions land[ed] in camps on the 24th but 3 of them had been broken open and nearly all the butter taken out. I and Ide lost all of our butter but nothing else. It hurt me badly to lose it but our meat is splendid. All of my mess got as much or more meat than I did and we are having a greasy time of it. I tell you we enjoy it just as hungry men can. I thought of who fixed up my bundle and thought of how much pleasure it gave you to fix it for me. But then I thought of how much more pleasure it would be if I could be there and let you cook it and set down to the table with our sweet children at [and] eat it.

We are generally in good health. But low spirits. They have stopped giving furloughs to Vicksburg prisoners because we were at home last summer. I do not see how they can expect us to be in good spirits after all our suffering last summer and now to make that distinction between us and others.

Jan 29th Good morning dear Malinda. I am quite well this morning and feel as comfortable as a pig in a peach orchard. I have just finish[ed] a hearty breakfast off those sausages and ham that you sent me. My mess all had a fine mess. You ought to see us eat when we get something to eat. We paid $10 for 10 pounds of flour the other day.

I intended to send you some money but I heard that Davis was going to pay over the estate money and I knew you could use that and I need every dollar that I have here to keep from suffering and then we suffer for we cannot get to buy every time we need it.[29]

I sent a letter to you by hand as far as Pleasant Ridge giving you power to draw money from Davis and giving him authority to pay it over to you. I have never drawn Write to me whether you get it or not. It will be mailed at Pleasant Ridge. I have never drawn any money for clothing yet.

We have had beautiful weather for the last 12 days and if it continues we may expect active operation soon. I fear our rest spell is about done for this winter.

Our colonel got a letter from one of our regt who was taken prisoner in the late fights. They are at Rock Island, Ilanoise. 115 of our regt are there.[30]

The mail starts in a few minutes. I must close. Goodbye dearest for the present,

To Mrs M J Taylor [from] Grant Taylor
& children

100

Camp in the woods of Ga.

Feb. 5th 1864

Beloved wife & children.

I will [avail] myself of one more opportunity to drop you a few lines to inform you that I am in good health hoping you and the dear children are the same.

I wrote you since we came here stating that we are some 7 miles south of Dalton wor[k]ing on the road. We have now been

---

[29] The 40th Alabama received six months pay on January 2, 1864. See Curry, "A History of Company B," 192.

[30] Rock Island Prison was opened in 1863 on an island in the Mississippi near Rock Island, Illinois. In January, 1864, it held 7,149 Confederate prisoners. See Patricia L. Faust, ed., *Historical Times Illustrated Encyclopedia of the Civil War* (New York: Harper Collins, 1986) 639.

here 10 days and I have no idea how long we will stay here. I also wrote some time ago about those names [for the baby] and sent you a blank receipt to enable you to draw money from Davis. Hope you have got them.

Our Regt is in fine health. A rebellion broke out in a portion of this army the other night. The cause was the authorities had tried and shot several men for going home and punished them in various ways until some Tennesseeans would bear it no longer and the[y] released their prisoners and burnts the instruments of punishment.[31] I believe some Alabamans were concerned in it. Nine have been shot in one Brigade of Alabama troops since the battle of Missionary Ridge, the same Brigade that Lab Teer belongs to. Several of our Regt has Reenlisted for the war. 3 out of our co. Ide is one of them or he put his name down as being willing. The conditions are that if a company will reenlist they will grant one furlough to every ten men. I have not reenlisted nor do I intend to do so until I see there is no other chance.

The rebellion is qui[e]ted for the present.

Frank Parker is under guard.[32] I would not be surprised if he is punished pretty severely.

There has been but very little rain up here since Christmas. The weather is very fine now and the roads are getting good very fast. We may expect active operations pretty soon if this weather continues.

I also wrote to you to send to school to Miss Ann again if there were no other chance. Walker brought my shoes through safe. Stealing is carried on to a high extent. Some men can almost steal the sweetening out of a ginger cake. We have to be careful where we put our shoes or any thing else at night or they will be taken.

Continue in prayer for me. Kiss the dear children for me. I dreamed last night of huging and kissing little Mary. I thought my

---

[31] Tennessee troops had been upset since November, 1863, when General Bragg dispersed the Tennessee regiments of General Frank Cheatham's division to other Army of Tennessee commands as a disciplinary action. See Christopher Losson, *Tennessee's Forgotten Warriors: Frank Cheatham and His Confederate Division* (Knoxville: University of Tennessee Press, 1989) 118.

[32] Perhaps Frank E. Parker (Co A 36th AL) or James F. Parker (Co B 40th AL).

mother was present and she [Mary] said, G[r]anny, my Pa has come back again. O how I do want to see her and all the rest of you but there is no chance now. Goodby my own dear one for the present.

Grant Taylor

101

Camps near Dalton Ga

Feb 9th 1864

Beloved wife and children,

I once more pen you a few lines. I received your letter of Jan 28th and 29th night before last announcing the sad intelligence of little Mary's sickness and also yours and Leonard's. Oh how sad it makes me feel to know that those I love so dearly are sick and suffering and I cannot be with them. I would give almost anything that I possess to be with you this morning. I started a letter to you the day before I got yours by one of the Speed's belonging to the 19th Ala.

Gen Johns[t]on issued an order granting one furlough to every 10 men that will re-enlist for the war.[33] I was opposed to it and am still so but I know that I am into it for the war or lifetime and for the chance of getting a furlough now or sometime this spring, I have reenlisted for the war. We drew for furloughs last night and I missed it again but maybe I will come in next time. 30 of our co. has reenlisted. I can see no disadvantage in it and there may be some advantage.

As to where to bury one of our children. That is a sad thing to think about. But as you request it I will state my will if it will suit you, if not suit yourself. I want them buried a little to the left of father's and mother's grave as you stand facing the graves at their

---

[33] Almost 4,000 Army of Tennessee men received leave under this plan. See Daniel, *Soldiering*, 138-139.

heads.[34] So that it will form a line for my grave and yours at their heads. Right at their heads is where I want you and I buried if we should die there and I want the children on our left or next [to] the church.

I got a letter from Hughs the other day. They were all well. I heard from Wick also. He was well. He is stationed near Mobile.

Excuse my short ragget letter as my mind is much discomposed. I will send this by Mr John Goodwin as he starts home this evening.[35] I am in very good health and hope you are all better than when you wrote. Continue in prayer for me. Hug and kiss the children for me. Give my love to all the connexion and enquiring friend[s] and believe me yours affectionately

To Mrs M J Taylor [from] Grant Taylor
& children

102

Camps near Dalton Ga.

Feb. 20th 1864

Dear wife & children,

I am once more seated to pen you a few lines which leaves me in tolerable health and I hope you and the children are in good health. I was sick a few days ago with a pain in my right side and dysentery but have gotten pretty well over it now.

We have moved again. We are some 3 miles from Dalton a northwest course. We swaped places with a Tenn. Brigade.[36] The houses are nothing but huts. We are badly crowded. Six of us are

---

[34] Grant's parents, Archelaus Taylor and Lucy Morris, were buried at Forest Church in Pickens County. There is a cemetery to the left side of the church but these two graves are located in front of the church on the right.

[35] John Goodwin (Co B 40th AL).

[36] Moore's Brigade swapped camps with General Otho Strahl's brigade consisting of the 4th, 5th, 19th, 24th, 31st, and 33rd Tennessee Infantry. See Cozzens, *Shipwreck of Their Hopes*, 412.

crowded into a little house not much larger than a large wagon-body. Everything is quiet up here yet.

James Roe says he called at your house Wednesday was a week ago and said you were all well except Mary and she was mending.[37] Oh how glad I am to hear it. How uneasy I have been ever since I got your letter announcing her sickness. I applied for a furlough but it was disapproved and so I had to content myself the best way I could.

Lum Wells got a letter the other day stating that your kitchen had been burnt up. I do not know what you will do for such things as you need in the kitchen now. They cannot be obtained in that country. You will have to do the best you can. I would willingly come to you but cannot.

May God protect you I do pray from the move the Yanks are making about Meridian. I fear they will soon cut all communications between us and then when we can't even hear from each other, what will we do.[38] Did you get the letter I wrote to you giving you authority to draw money from Davis.

I went yesterday to see Mr Porter, Joe Leavelle and the other boys in the 36th [Alabama]. They were well and the folks were well on Buck Creek. James Hallman got wounded in the battle of Chickamauga and went home and he and Beck Mahaffey got married.[39] Also, the widow Reynolds at our old place married a man from Miss.[40] I do not know his name. Benny Garner was taken prisoner [at] the battle of Missionary Ridge.[41]

I got a letter from Emmaline the other day. They were well but she said that she had to live on bread and water more than half the time and sometimes not enough of that and her children had had no shoes this winter. My God what is to become of the poor.

---

[37] James Calvin Rowe (Co G 40th AL).

[38] On February 3, 1864, General Sherman led 26,000 men on a large raid into central Mississippi to wreck railroads in the general area of Meridian. See Long, *Civil War Day by Day*, 460.

[39] James "Hallman" is unidentified. His name could be Holloman, Holliman, etc. Rebecca was the widow of James M. Mahaffey (Co B 36th AL) who died August 5, 1862.

[40] Widow Reynolds is unidentified.

[41] Benny Garner is unidentified.

Continue in prayer for me. Give my best respects to all the connexion and friends and believe me your as ever,

G Taylor

PS We have had some more very cold weather this week. Ki's George has been in bad health a long time. He has applied for a sick furlough. If he gets it he will start home today or tomorrow and I will send this letter by him. Some how I feel like it will be a long time before I get to come home. It seems that fate is against me as to going home. As to coming home the time you spoke of that will be out of the question. Furloughing will be all stopped before then. I saw Lafayette some 10 days ago. He was well. Ide is in fine health. May God bless you my dearest earthly friend and may we meet in Heaven at last when parting will be no more.

103

Camps near Dalton Ga

Feb 23ᵈ 1864

Dear wife and children,

I am well this morning though I feel drowsy from getting no sleep last night. I was up nearly all night cooking rations. Everything is packed up to move but where to or in what direction I know not. I received your letter sent by Lab last night and glad was I to hear that little Mary was mending but sorry to hear of your bad health.

You said you thought you could get me a recruit. If you can send him on. I have offered two hundred dollars for one but if you can get him for less or if a little more I do not care. But he must be under 18 years of age and healthy. If he comes and I fail to get a furlough on him by the order being countermanded or any other cause except the fault be in him, I will bear his expenses here and back home and pay him a reasonable price for his time. Get him if you can on reasonable terms. If he is under 18 years of age he will get fifty dollars bounty.[42]

I sent a letter by Mr Goodwin. Did you get it. What did your sack of salt cost you[?] Ki's George started home yesterday on a 30 days sick furlough. I sent a letter by him, 19 envelopes and 2 steel pens. I would have sent some paper but could not get it and I sent all the new steel pens I had. I have to write with a pencil because my ink will not write on this paper. John Falls stayed here last night.[43] He was well. His [artillery] battery is camped at Kingston Ga som[e] 40 miles south of this.

If you write again after getting this letter before I write to you, direct your letter to me Co G 40th Regt Ala Vols Moore's Brigade Army of Tenn. without putting any post office on it. I will write as soon as I can again. I expect to send this letter by Reuben Willims who has drawn a furlough and expects to start home in a day or two.[44]

If that recruit comes try to send him with Williams. Have him bound [in writing] so that he cannot recruit for any one else after he gets here for there are men here who will pay almost any price for a recruit. He must bring a written certificate from his parents or guardian that they are willing for him to come. I must close as we are expecting to start every minute. Give my love to all. Continue in prayer for me. Kiss the children for me and believe me yours truly as ever

To Mrs M J Taylor [from] Grant Taylor
& children

PS If you can get someone to go down below Olney you can get corn at $1.00 per bu. I think you had better buy 100 bu. and push [fatten] your pigs. If you do not need it all you can sell it next summer. I think it a poor chance that you cannot draw more than 50 bu. Hold on to all your salt.

---

[42] Soldiers bringing in new recruits were promised a furlough. See Bell I. Wiley, *Life of Johnny Reb: The Common Soldier of the Confederacy* (Baton Rouge LA: Louisiana State University Press, 1978) 139.

[43] John W. Falls (c1843-1867), son of Thomas and Elizabeth Falls.

[44] Reuben Williams is unidentified. He is not listed in the 40th AL.

Feb 28th Dear wife and children Thank God I am back in my cabbin safe and sound once more. Since writing the foregoing we have had stiring times up here. The Yanks made an advance on our front and the same evening I wrote we were marched out in line of battle and staid there until this morning. They attacked the line in two or three places but were repulsed when finding us stronger than they expected. They began to retreat 3 nights ago and night before last they all left and went back in the direction of Chattanooga. We followed them some distance but returned to our old line in a few hours. That was yesterday and this morning we were marched to our quarters.[45]

They did not attack our part of the line so I was not in any fight. Two companies of our regiment was sent out on picket and got into a heavy skirmish and got 3 men wounded. There was no general engagement but some heavy skirmishing and two or 3 considerable charges. Our general loss is small. Theirs supposed to be considerable. They ran off and left their dead and our men had to bury them. The men of the 42nd Ala. buried 10 in one hole. I thank God for his mercies in preserving my life through another critical time.

On their retreat they treated some of the citizens badly. Going into their houses and tearing up their things and rip[p]ing up their beds and scattering the feathers about. In one instance they went into a house took the feather beds out slept on them and when they left cut them to pieces. I have no idea that they will let us be still long.

The weather is very fine and the roads good. Give my best respects to all enquiring friends and relatives and believe me your loving husband, as ever

To Mrs M J Taylor [from] Grant Taylor
& children

---

[45] Union forces under General George H. Thomas probed Confederate positions around Rocky Face Ridge and Crow's Gap on February 23-25. See Albert Castel, *Decision in the West: The Atlanta Campaign* (Lawrence: University Press of Kansas, 1992) 54.

March 2nd Dear Malinda, I am in good health to-day. I have nothing strange to write. We have drawn again for furloughs and I missed again. If there is any chance send that recruit. Have him sworn in as my recruit at Carrollton and if he is sound all will be right I think when he gets here. Secure him as soon as possible for many will be after him.

Congress [CSA] has taxed Confederate money one third. If you have any on hand get advice what to do with it. It must be funded for bonds by the first of Apr. or there will be a heavier tax on it still. See D Hood or some one capable of advising you on it.[46]

The late movements of the Yanks has stopped furloughing to some extent but I think Williams will get off this evening.

May God bless you all is the prayer of your loving

Grant Taylor

March 4th Williams has not started yet. I am still in tolerable health and I hope you and the dear children are the same.

As to funding this Confederate money all bills over five dollars are to be funded by the first of April next. Be sure to get someone to attend to it for you before that time.

If you can get that recruit you can give him an obligation to pay him as soon as I get the furlough. Or if I fail to get the furlough you can have it understood how much you are to pay him for his time. There are men there that can tell you how to have it fixed up.

How is it you did not write to me about your kitchen being burnt up[?]

Tell all your folks howdy for me and tell them that I would write to them separately but I have nothing more to write than I write to you. Consequently it is no use for me to write to them. But the case is different with them. They can tell me a heap of little things that probably you do not know or do not think to write

---

[46] David G. Hood. The Confederate Congress passed a bill on February 17th requiring the exchange of paper currency for 4% bonds. After April 1, 1864, such unredeemed currency would be reduced one third in value. See Clement Eaton, *A History of the Southern Confederacy* (New York: Free Press, 1954) 229.

which would be interesting to me. So I would like for them to write to me sometimes. The same remarks are applicable to my people. You can still direct your letters as you always have done.

Lab Teer was over to see me yesterday. He is in fine health. Also Joe Leavelle and Bud Henderson were over to see me the other day. They were all well in their Regt.

I do not know that I can write any more now that will interest you so, I will close. Continue to pray for me, Your loving husband as ever

To Mrs M J Taylor [from] Grant Taylor

PS. Gen Johns[t]on is having the men shot and hung by the Dozen for Deserting. Some deserted and went home, some went to the Yanks and afterwards caught.

104

Camps near Dalton Ga.

March 9[th] 1864

Beloved wife & children,

I[n] much pain I attempt to write these lines. I was attacked last Saturday night with pain in my right breast just underneath the nipple attended with fever. I could not lye down any more that night. I have suffered a great deal since. My side is rather worse this morning that [than] it was yesterday. I am better I think than I have been because the fever is checked. The Doctor put a big blister plaster on my side a little while ago which I think will relieve me when it draws well. Ever since the first night I have been enabled [unable] to lie with some ease on my back and right side. Do not be uneasy about me for God can take care of me here as well as anywhere and whether I live or die I feel all will be well. I am not uneasy about myself for I do not think I am dangerous.

I should not have attempted to write this morning but Jimmy Martin has drawn a furlough and will be apt to start about to-morrow evening and I wish to write every chance I get.[47] I hope you are all well and doing [well]. Hope you got the letter, Envelopes and 2 pens I sent by George. Also the letter sent by Rube Williams on the 5th inst. giving you direction what to do about a recruit.

The Brigade is gone off on a review to day and I am in my little hut alone, no not alone, for God is with me.[48] Tell little Mary that I dreamed of huging and kissing either that night or near about it. I believe as well as I can recolect it was that very night. We were all lying in line of battle on a hill some 3/4 of a mile from these camps.

I have nothing to eat but a little dry bread and sometimes a little poor beef or fat bacon during my sickness. It is true we have a little rice on hand but I cannot eat it. Mr Hudson who is cooking for the Col. brought me a biscuit and enough but[ter] for my supper and breakfast and just now he brought another biscuit some butter and a nice piece of fried ham.[49] But I have not suffered for anything to eat because I have had not appetite to eat. Sometime though I cannot help studying about the good milk and butter you have and wish I had as much of it as I could eat. Excuse this childish letter for I feel very childish this morning.

You have never written a word whether your turnips did you any good and also your shallotes. If you have any of them to eat this spring just think of me while you are eating them and lay in a good supply for me. Now do'nt turn chicken hearted and think of me so you can not eat any of them.

I know one thing Pap shall have for his kindness to you and that is the everlasting love and gratitude of my poor heart. I will bestow that on him whether he is willing. And I pray the father of Mercies to bless him and his both spiritual and temporal and at last give him a crown of glory outshinning the noonday sun.

---

[47] Jimmy Martin is unidentified.

[48] Army of Tennessee reviews were held at the last base of Taylor's Ridge. See Daniel, *Soldiering*, 2.

[49] Mr. Hudson is unidentified.

I have no war news to write. But the the weather is very fine and pleasant and we will be apt to have stiring times again soon and then Reviews have got to be almost a daily thing and when that is the case some big movement is generally anticipated.

It looks this morning like that we ought to be planting corn. O how I wish I could be at home to put the corn in the mellow ground once more. I think if you wish to make any potatoes you had better have you[r] [fence] rails moved down nearer the branch and fence in some of that flat ~~just~~ [land] below the old patch. Turn the old one all out into the pasture part.

M[a]y God bless you all. I must close. I have sat up too long now. I fear for the best. Goodby my dear ones

Grant Taylor

March 10th My side is a little better to-day though I had some fever last night and today. I got your letter of Feb 25th and 6. I was glad you had all got well.

105

Camps near Dalton Ga.

March 13th/ [64]

Beloved wife and children,

I embrace the present to pen you a few lines. I wrote to you the 9th and 10th and sent it by Jimmy Martin Stating that I was sick. I am still quite sick and feeble but I am mending a little. I received your kind letter of March the 4th. I was glad to hear from you again, but sorry to hear of your helplessness. I have a heap of uneasiness about your situation. You ought to stop the children from school until you get more able to do your business. Situated as you are you had better have paid $130 for a woman even if you had made no crop.

Why have you never written me any word about your kitchen being burned. I would like to know all the particulars whether you saved anything and how much. How is your wheat doing[?]

Don't look too hard for me home this spring. They have stopped us from drawing furloughs but leave it [to] the commanders of co. to say who shall go. Those that act the most meritorious are the ones to be selected. That is done in order that the commanders m[a]y furlough their pets and there are some such in every company. As I have my doubts about standing very high on my Capt's list I think it doubtful about my coming home soon. But yet I do not know how Capt Pickens views my past conduct. I hope favorably for I have always done my duty as faithfully as any.

Malinda if we could all die at once I would welcome the hour. Then there would be a whole family of us in Heaven. Oh glorious thought. But to think of my dying and leaving you and the children in your forlorn condition, the the thought is horrible. But as for my own safety, I have no do[u]bts when I get sick. I must close

Grant Taylor

PS I would write more but I feel to feeble. I will send this by Jesse Carver who lives near Ki.[50] He will start home this evening. I wrote this letter myself.

---

[50] Jesse Carver is unidentified. Malachi "Ki" Taylor, Grant's brother.

CHAPTER 8

I HAVE HAD THE PNEUMONIA

Pvt. Grant Taylor suffered through a serious bout of pneumonia and scurvy from early March 1864 through late May. He spent time in two Confederate hospitals in Georgia and recovered. During this time, his letters show his struggle to heal and his concern with getting proper nutrition. His letters during this time are different as he mentions fewer people. Instead Grant's letters take a philosophical and fatalistic bend.

106

Camps near Dalton

March 27th 1864

Dear wife & children,

This leaves me very feeble indeed. I have been very sick since I wrote last but am a little better now. The fever has left me again but has left me very much reduced indeed. The Doctor says he is going to send me to the hospital today. I will will will write to you as soon as I get the chance after I get to the hospital. I think without a back set I am out of danger now. Do not be uneasy about me. I received your kind letter of the 18th inst. to-day and was glad to hear from you once more. I was in hopes you would have got that recruit for me.

R Williams got back to camps last night.[1] Also G Taylor.[2]

I must quit. Goodby my own Malinda

---

[1] Reuben Williams.

[2] George Taylor.

To Mrs M J Taylor [from] G Taylor

I am not able to answer Leonard's letter now.

107

Newsom Hospital Ward No. 2 Ga[3]

Mar. 31st 1864

Dear Malinda,

Through the kind mercies of God I am permitted to pen you a
few more lines. This leaves me alive and mending slowly. I do not
see any improvement except in my appetite. I am very weak yet. I
am not able to sit up but very little. The Doctor says I lack nothing
now but something good to eat. I get a plenty. I get beef, pork,
rice, potatoes, corn bread, wheat bread both loaf and biscuit, milk
and genuine coffee. Not all these things at one meal, but that is the
variety I get and a splendid bunk to sleep on. I believe if I had
been sent off from the camps when I was first taken I would now
have been well. But the plaguey Doctors kept me there until I was
so reduced that it will be some time before I get stout. The Doctors
here say that I have had the Pneumonia. My side is very tender
and sore yet and my liver hurts me some to-day.

I left camps last Sunday and got here Monday evening. I would
have written to you sooner but I have felt too feeble and now I am
sitting propped up in my bed. I got a letter from you just before I
left camps dated the 18th inst. and wrote you a few lines
immediately. I hope these lines will reach you and find you all
well and doing well. I was glad to get those few lines from
Leonard. I want him and Jimmy to write to me occasionally. And

---

[3] The Newsom Hospital moved from Chattanooga TN to Cassville GA.
See Glenna R. Schroeder-Lein, *Confederate Hospitals on the Move: Samuel H.
Stout and the Army of Tennessee* (Columbia SC: University of South
Carolina Press, 1994) 122.

when you write put in all your little ups and downs for they are all interesting to me.

Write how you had your money matters arranged. I do not approve of letting Davis have anything to do with the money you had in your hands. Of course that money that he had not paid out he was bound to manage that. I am fearful he will get the upper hand of you yet for I tell you he is a scoundrel and if he can beat you he will do it. If I were there and could do it I certainly should take it all out of his hands and put it in some one elses. I would not care much who.

We have had some very cold weather in this month. Last week it snowed 2 times. The first was about 5 inches deep and 2 nights after it snowed largely but nearly all melted by day.

I am glad you will draw more corn but that wont be enough. I still say if you can you had better buy at least 100 bu[shels] even it cost you 2 dollars per bu[shel] for you will find it no drug on your hands. I had a heap rather have corn on hand than Confederate money.

Malinda I feel to thank my blessed Savior that he is raising me out of sickness once more and I want you to join with me in thanking him. Although I was not afraid to die yet for the sake of you and the dear children I want to live if it be my blessed Savior's will. I must close. Kiss the dear children for me and give my best respects to all the conexion and friends. Read this if you can and believe me yours as ever

To Mrs M J Taylor [from] Grant Taylor

PS Still direct your letters to camps. Ide will send them on to me. I do not think worthwhile to send [them] from home here.

108

Newsom Hospital Cassville Ga

Apr 5th/ [64]

My Dear wife and children,

I once more attempt to write you a few lines. Thank God I am still mending but it is very slowly. I am getting so I can sit up right smart but my side has a dead feeling which I fear will be some time in getting well. I feel very thankful that it is no worse. The patients die up here pretty fast. 3 have died since I came here.

Malinda this sickness will prevent me from getting to come home at the time we both so much desire. I do not think there is any chance for me to get a furlough here and I will not be able to go to the company in time to get one even if I were certain of getting one when I get there but that would be uncertain even if I were there. Oh I want to come home so bad. If I were only there I think I would get well directly.

But I ought not to complain. I have many causes for thankfulness that it is as well with me as it is. The Lord's ways are sometimes very mysterious to us but we are assured that the Lord of all the earth will do right. We have have been more sorely afflicted and tried this spring than we ever have been but it is all for the best and let us kiss the rod and bless the hand that aff[l]icts us. I feel very humble but I do not feel humble enough. My rebellious heart will still rise at times in complaints but I strive to put these things down and resign my will and my all to the will of my blessed Savior.

I sometimes lie on my bed and have very sweet communings with my blessed Savior. And Oh at such times I feel that if it were not that I have such tender ties binding me to earth that I would be glad to be released from this diseased tenement of clay and go to my savior and fill my soul with those joys of which we only get a foretaste here in this sinful world.

I have formed a slight acquaintance with the Lady that attends in the hospital. She is a refugee from Tenn. and her husband is in the army. She is a cultivated lady and above all a true christian. She comes to my bed and talks to me a good deal of religion and the comforts of the same. These conversations are highly refreshing to my soul. She furnished me with a good book to read. I am highly interested in her conversations.[4]

I have not heard from my company since I left. I wrote to you on the 31st March from this place. Dear Malinda Continue to pray for me and Let us exercise faith that all will work out right and that at the right time I will get to come home.

Give best respects to all enquiring friends and relatives. We have a very cold disagreeable spring. I must close. Believe your ever true and loving husband and father

To Mrs M J Taylor [from] Grant Taylor

109

Newsom Hospital Cassville Ga.

Apr. 12th 1864

My Dear wife & children,

I seat myself to pen you a few lines once more and very thankful I feel that I am able to do so. I am quite weak yet and my side has never got entirely well yet. But I am mending a little. I have got so I can sit nearly all day and have a good appetite. I hope you and the dear children are well and doing well.

Dear Malinda You will have to be confined without my being with you this time.[5] As I wrote to you sometime ago it seems that fate is against my getting a furlough. I have felt ever since I left home that it would be a long time before I came home again and I feel so yet. I went before the board of Doctors to-day and tried for a furlough but they are not allowed to furlough for a term of less

---

[4] Kate Cumming was the matron of the Newsom Hospital but she did not have a husband in the Confederate army. See Patricia L. Faust, ed., *Historical Times Illustrated Encyclopedia of the Civil War* (New York: HarperCollins, 1986) 197.

[5] It is nearly time for Malinda to have her baby and Grant is concerned about her.

than sixty days and said I would be able for duty in less time than that. I wish I may. And they have stopped furloughing in the army. Only one for every 25 men.[6] So you see there is no chance for me to get home at the time we both so much desired. I never wanted to come home half so bad in my life. But I have no hope of getting to come home this spring. If you were only able to come and see me I would say for you to come while I am at the hospital, but you are not able to do that and so we have nothing to do but to submit. But I try to feel that it is all for the best. For we know that God has shown us great mercy and let us trust him in the future.

I got a letter from Ide the other day containing two from you. One dated the 9th and the other the 25th March. I got yours of 18th March before I left camps. I was truly glad to hear that you were as well as you were and that you had succeeded in buying a little wheat.

You said to get Ide to speak to Capt Pickens about getting me a furlough but that would be useless even if I were there for he has been willing to furlough me some time but he has not got the power himself. A furlough has to be signed by one Col. and three Generals and one of them refusing kills it. I got a letter this morning from Ide and John Sanders. They were all well and everything seemed quiet in front.

That was a beautiful piece of poetry that you sent me and as you say I read it when we were both happy and did not know it. Oh will those happy days ever return again. I have drawn it off and altered it as to suit my own case. I send both to you so you can see the difference. It expresses the sentiments of my heart. I am pining away in a strangers land. And I want to see my wife again. I am low spirited, but I strive against it all I can. I hope to get to come home some day. You must do the best you can without me.

Malinda, you have one of the best of fathers and I can never cease to love him for what he has done and is doing for you. The spring is very cold and backward and very wet. All of north Georgia is hilly and very poor except in the valleys. I have written to Leonard and Jimmy, but there is sweet little Math[ew] and

---

[6] The furlough order was revoked on April 7, 1864. John H. Curry. "A History of Company B, 40th Alabama Infantry, C.S.A.," *Alabama Historical Quarterly* 17/4 (Winter 1955) 4:193.

Mary. O how I love them and want to see them but all I can do is to pray for them and ask you to hug and kiss them for me. Dear Malinda continue in prayer for your poor afflicted husband. This is 38 days since I was taken sick. May God bless us all is the sincere prayer of your loving husband

To Mrs M J Taylor [from] Grant Taylor

To Leonard. My dear child. I was so glad to get those lines from you and to see that you had improved so much in your writing. I was sorry to hear that you were sick and hope it is nothing serious. I wish I could get to come home and help you eat some of those shallots[7] you had been hoeing out but I fear I will not get to do so. I fear it will be a long time before your loving Pa will see you all. I would like it also if I could come home even next year as you say for us to make some corn. Do you think you would be willing to help me work[?] But next year is a long ways off and me and you may be dead before then. Dear child you are old enough now to know right from wrong and I want you to do what is right. Love God pray to him that he may lead you to do what is good and not do what is bad. Be a good boy. Mind all your kind ma says to you and be kind to your brothers and little sister. Be kind to every body. And when you feel that you have done wrong ask God to forgive you and love you. Do these things my dear child that when you come to die God will take you to heaven. Do these things for your loving Pa's sake whom you may never see any more that you may meet me in heaven. I am not mending much yet. I must close. From your loving Pa

To L F Taylor [from] Grant Taylor

Dear Jimmy. I was truly glad to get your letter and to see that you had improved in your writing. You said that you had just got back from [the] mill with some cake for me. By the time I come home, dear child, you need not save it for me for I will not get to go home soon. I wish I could. You must be a good boy and do as

---

[7] A shallot is an onion-like herb.

your Ma tells you. I want to see you all very badly. You must learn as fast as you can and write to me again. Goodby my dear child.

G Taylor

110

Newsom Hospital Cassville Ga.

Apr 19th [18]64

Beloved wife and children,

Through the mercies of God I am permitted to be able to pen you a few lines again. I am still mending but it is slowly though I have mended faster in the last few days. My side has not got well yet. It does not pain me much but it keeps sore which is the reason I think that I do not mend faster. I think I shall go back to my company before a great while. Though I do not intend to be in too great a hurry. I hope and pray that you and the children are well and doing as well as you can under the circumstances.

I expect before you get this that your confinement will have come on. I pray to God that he may be with you and give you grace to bear your sufferings with patience. I pray that He may spare yours and the child's life and that you may do well.

I think I have got all your letters up to the 25th March except the one written the day after your kitchen was burned. I have been looking for one for three or four days but it has not come. The last I have got was dated 25th March and contained Leonard's & Jimmy's letters which I answered. Nobody knows how badly I want to come home but I and my God. I have never wanted a furlough half so bad in my life. But there is no chance to come now. It may be it is all for the best. That is the way I try to look at it.

I have not heard from Ide since I wrote to you last only through Capt Pickens who wrote that the boys were all well. I wrote to him some week ago to send me 10 or 20 dollars. He immediately sent me 10 which he said was all he could spare then. But said If I want any assistance in any way to let him know and if it was in his power he would do it, and I believe he will, for I have tried him.

I want you to write to me how much money you have drawn from Davis. Whether more than the three hundred dollars you first drew and if so whether he has paid you all and how much there is of it all. Also how much you had bonded and whether you have any $5 bills now to spend. If you have no money you had better sell some of your bonds even if you have to pay a large percent.

The first of May next the government will be owing me $177 dollars then due but I have no idea when it will be paid. If I can get back to camps by the last day of this month I am in hopes I will be paid off some time shortly after. If I am and you are needing money I will send part of that to you.

There is no news of interest. At last accounts every thing was quiet above Dalton. I wish it would stay so and that peace would be made. Some and even a great many think that peace will be made this year sometime but they can give no reason for their belief only they say they feel like it will be so. As for myself I have no hope of peace soon and if the people of the Confederacy has to become humble, as I believe they must become, before peace is made, it looks like that it is farther off if possible than when we first began. For there seems to be more wickedness now of every sort than ever before. But God can humble us mighty quick and bring peace when he sees fit.

Continue to pray for me. Give my respects to Mr D Hood and Mrs Powell and the connexion and friends and believe me your ever loving husband

To Mrs M J Taylor [from] Grant Taylor
& children

PS I was mistaken about a recruit haveing to be under 18 years of age. Any that will come in as a recruit if he is received by the Dr will do. No difference what his age may be. The difference is this. When they are under 18 they must have the consent of their parents or guardian and the others of course have no need of any such consent. I have no idea that you will ever be able to get me one but I write this to let you know how it is, so if you should see any chance you may know how to act. I do not much care how much you give in those bonds. Get someone to write as soon as you are confined.

111

Notes of the moves I made in the army
from Apr 9th 1862 to Apr 22nd 1864

1862 Apr 9th Left home for the army and landed at Demopolis Ala. the 11th. Left there the 19th and landed at Mobile Ala 20th. Left there the 25th and moved to Dog River Factory 5 miles west of Mobile. Left there the 21st July and moved to Camp Marshal Austill 2 miles Southwest of the city. Moved to camp Forney Oct 8th 4 miles Northwest of the city. Left camp Forney Dec. 2nd. Landed at Jackson Miss. Dec. 5th. Left there the 17th Dec. and landed at Columbus Miss. Dec. 19th. Left there Dec. 27th and landed at Vicksburg Dec. 30th.

For several days after we got to Vicksburg we made several moves of 1 or 2 miles. In fact we moved nearly every day and sometimes twice each day. About the 10th of Jan. 1863 we established a camp 5 miles north of Vicksburg.

1863. Moved from Camp Timmons on Feb. 18th to C[hic]kasaw Bayou bridge 7 miles from Vicksburg. Moved from there March 19th to Hains Landing on the Yazoo river. Left there on the 21st and landed on Deer creek the 22nd and was shelled from the Yankee gun boats the same evening. Which was the first time our Regt had ever been under fire. Had a skirmish with the enemy the 24th at Charley Four's place. Turned back about the 26th and Marched some 23 miles that night and the 2 following days and camped on the bank of Deer Creek. Took a trip up Deer Creek of 55 miles about the 9th Apr to near Greenville on the Miss. river. Left there Apr 15th and landed back at our old camps on Deer Creek the 17th late in the evening. Left the Deer Creek country May 7th and landed at Vicksburg the 8th. Left there the 9th and went near

Warrenton the same day 10 miles below Vicksburg. Went into the ditches 2 miles east of Vicksburg the 17th of May and was surrounded on the 18th and continued in them under fire from their cannon and sharp shooters until July 3d when a flag of truce came out and we were surrendered up to the enemy on the 4th [of July] 1863. We were paroled July 9th and left there the 11th and struck out for home, which place I reached July 22nd and stayed there until Oct 2nd when I started for Demopolis again the place appointed for the paroled men of Ala. to meet.

Landed there Oct 5th. Left there October 29th and started for Chattanooga Tenn. Landed in Selma Ala the same evening. Staid there until 12 o'clock M the next day. Took Steamboat and land[ed] in Montomgery Ala at daylight AM the 31st and staid there until 12 o'clock that night. Took the cars and landed in West Point Ga. Sunday at 8 A.M. Nov. 1st. Left there Nov. 2nd 8 o'clock AM and landed in Atlanta Ga at 3 P.M. the same day. Left there the 4th and landed Chickamauga Station Tenn. at 1 o'clock AM. on the 5th. Left there for Look-out mountain the same day. Camped in the valley between Missionary ridge and Look-out that night and arrived near the foot of the mountain on the morning of the 6th. Went around on the west side of the mountain on picket out the 10th of Nov. Came back on the east side of the mountain on the 15th on picket and took up camp on that side on the 16th. Went into the fight on Look-out, Nov 24th. Evacuated the mountain that night. As we were leaving the mountain got my ankle sprained. Got to Chickamauga Station about 4 o'clock AM the 26th. Got on the cars and started to the hospital. Entered the Academy hospital at Marietta Ga Nov 27th in ward No 6. The Regt fought on Missionary Ridge Nov 25th. Left Marietta Dec 22nd and arrived at camps near Dalton Ga the 23d.

Moved 5 miles south of Dalton Jan 27th 1864 to work on the Resica road. Returned to our old cabbins Feb 6th. Moved to the camps of Strahl's Brigade, 2 1/2 miles northwest of Dalton on the 12th Feb. Feb 22nd got orders to march. On Feb 23 we were up by day[light] ready to march. At 12 o'clock M took up the line of march. Went about 1 mile and went into line of battle. The enemy began to retreat from our right on the night of the 25th. On the night of the 26th they retreated from our front. On the 27th we followed them 3 or 4 miles, failing to overtake them, we returned and took our old position in line of battle. Feb 28th returned to our cabbins and the same evening Our Regt went about one mile on picket and returned the next evening. Mar. 5th took the Pneumonia and lay in camps 3 weeks. Mar 27 left camps to go to a hospital. Staid in Dalton that night. Mar. 28th arrived at the Newsom Hospital Cassville Ga where I am at the present writing. Apr 23[d] 1864.

Grant Taylor, Co (G) 40th Regt Ala Inft.

112

Newsom Hospital Cassville Ga

Apr 26th 1864

Beloved wife and Children,

Through the mercies of a kind God I am permitted to pen you a few more lines. I am still mending slowly. My side is still sore and hurts me some. I fear it will never be sound any more. I have fleshed up right smart but I cannot get my strength. I expect though the Dr. will send me to my command next Friday the 29th.

I hope these lines will find you and the children well and doing well although I have no doubt but that you will have been confined before you get this letter. I hope the Lord will be with you and bring you through safe. I pray for you daily. I want to be with you very badly but it is impossible.

I have written to you every week since I have been here and hope you have got all my letters. I got all yours stating how your kitchen was burned up and that you had had that old house moved and put up for another. I was made glad this morning by the reception of a letter from Ide containing 2 from you one dated the last of March and first Apr. and the other the 14 & 15th Apr.

and one from Louisa.[8] They all came to the Regt the morning of the 24th.

I was very sorry when I read the first stating that you were so unwell but was made glad when I read the second and found that you had got well. Although I know in your condition you are never very well. Sometimes when I think on your condition (as I almost always am) I am almost sorry for your sake that I came home last summer. But then you wont agree with me I know and it may be it was all for the best. I hope so at any rate.

It looks like it is useless for you to try to raise anything as you say the sheep are eating up your wheat. I am sorry of that. Try to have your little peach trees worked even if you do plant your potatoes in the bottom. What will you do for a calf pasture now that you have rented out your lot field[?] I am very glad to hear that your prospect is good for getting plenty of milk and butter. How I wish I could be there to help eat it. I have bought some butter and buttermilk since I came here. I paid $4 for a pound of butter and 25 cts per quart for milk and it nearly one third water. We get a plenty to eat here.

I have no good news to write. Only Ide wrote that he and the other boys were well. But they were looking for a big fight in a few days. But they were confident if they were attacked of being victorious. If they have to fight I wish it would come on before I get back to them for to tell the truth I have no stomach for fighting.

Yes there is some good news. I hear of great revivals going on in parts of Johnston's army. Nearly entire companies in some instances have joined the church. May God continue the good work until our entire army shall have been converted.[9]

There has been about 12 poor fellows gone to their long homes since I have been in this hospital. I intend to draw my clothing from the government except socks. I cannot get woolen socks from it. I drew 2 pair of thin cotton some time ago. I expect to have to throw away my overcoat as I cannot get any chance to send it

---

[8] Probably Malinda's sister, Eliza Louisa Slaughter Parker.

[9] Religious revivals touched every unit of the Army of Tennessee by the spring of 1864. See Larry J. Daniel, *Soldiering in the Army of Tennessee: A Portrait of Life in a Confederate Army* (Chapel Hill NC: University of North Carolina Press, 1991) 119-120.

home and I cannot carry it. I have worn it but little. I hate to have to throw it away.

Continue in prayer for me and give my best respects to Pap and Mother and the rest of the connexion and believe your loving husband

To Mrs M J Taylor [from] Grant Taylor

PS. I am glad that Jake has gone back to his command for it wont go near so hard with him as if he had been caught by the cavalry and they would have caught him sometime.[10] Gen Johnston has stopped all furloughs for the present which looks like there is something going to be done. I will write to Wat soon. Where is Jack staying at now[?] I have lost his whereabouts and he has quit writing to me. I dream of seeing you very plainly also frequently. I hope we will meet some day on earth. I send notes of all the moves I have made since I came in the army. Take care of it. I may lose my little books that contains it here.

113

Newsom Hospital Cassville Ga.

May 3ᵈ 1864

Beloved wife & children,

Through mercies of a kind Providence I am permitted to pen you one more letter from this place. I am able to go any where I wish within a mile or two of this place. But I am not strong yet and my side is still sore and hurts me sometimes. I expect the Dr will send me to my command in a few days. I intend to stay here as long as I can. I hope you have been confined and are well again. And I hope the children are well also.

---

10 Jacob L. Parker, Grant's brother-in-law, of Co A 41st AL. Records show that Parker deserted September 26, 1863. He returned to the regiment by Union forces on May 16, 1864.

The Dr says I have a touch of the scurvy in my legs. Now that is a disease I know but little about only it keeps one poor and weak but is not dangerous. It is caused by living without vegetables. Raw mustard is said to be good for it and I got a sp[l]endid mess yesterday. I can get buttermilk almost any day at $1.00 per gallon. I have bought a good deal of it since I got able to go to the kitchen to eat for there they do not furnish us milk.

I received a letter from Ide just now containing one from you dated 21 and 22 Apr. Oh how glad I was to get it and to hear that you were well. I fear that scare from King did damage. I am sorry he has to be killed.

If you cannot buy any more corn what will you do. I know your shoats will be bound to suffer. When your sow has pigs sell her for corn for if anything will bring corn it will be them. I say sell them because you said you were going to do so.

I wrote to you some time since why I could not come home. I hope you have got that letter ere this. The reason was this. The board of Doctors have special orders at the hospitals not to furlough any one that they believe will be able for duty in sixty days nor for a less time. So they thought I would be able in a less time and could not give me one. I could have got one for 30 days if they had been alowed to give such furloughs.

Ide was well the first of May and all the boys. He said that on last Friday the cavalry had a skirmish and he drove the enemy back but they had to march out to the breast-works and stay there a few hours but everything was quiet in front on the 1st. We heard here yesterday that they had been fighting monday but how true it is I know not. We are expecting a big battle every day.[11] God grant it may come off before I go back if it must come off at all.

Last week we had a few days of nice warm spring weather but yesterday it turned cold and this morning there was considerabl frost. It rains here every 2 or 3 days and the prospect for a crop is gloomy indeed. I fear there will be a failure this year. If so it is nothing more than I anticipated and told you so last summer when

---

[11] From May 1st to the 3rd, skirmishes along the area of Rocky Face Ridge foretold the coming Union advance. See Albert Castel, *Decision in the West: The Atlanta Campaign* (Lawrence KS: University Press of Kansas, 1992) 121-124.

I saw the selfishness of those who had plenty. For I did not then nor do I believe now the Almighty will bless us with another good crop when we were so selfish and unthankful for his abundant mercies last year in allowing our farmers to make such abundant crops. Would to God our people would become humble that this cruel war may close.

Dear Malinda I pray earnestly for you and the children. As for my own situation I study but little about it only in consideration of the hardships and privations that you have to undergo by my being away. But there is this consolation. If we ever get to live together again we will know how to appreciates the blessings we enjoy and if we are permitted to enter heaven we know that our troubles will not diminish aught of our happiness in that bright world of bliss. But rather will add to our bliss and this of itself is enough to encourage us to bear our troubles with patience.

I must close. Continue to pray for me. Goodby my dear loved ones.

To Mrs M J Taylor [from] Grant Taylor
& children

114

Newsom Hospital Cassville Ga

May 10th 1864

Beloved wife & children,

Through the mercies of a kind Savior I am permitted to pen you a few lines this rainy evening.

My health is not good yet. My side still hurts me and I am not strong as usual. I cannot see that I have improved any in the last ten days and I have felt right poorly yesterday and to-day with cold. The Dr ordered me sent to my command day before yesterday but then told me to stay and help nurse in case a lot of wounded should be sent here. I was very well pleased with that arrangement for I was not able for the active duties in front. But I do not expect to stay here long. They have sent a good many to Atlanta from here expecting a heap of wounded to be sent here from the great battle expected to be fought near Dalton before long.

They have been fighting some up there. The enemy had advanced far enough 2 days ago for our men to see five lines of battle in front of my Division. It had been fighting some but I do not know whether my Regt was engaged or not. It was thought a general engagement would take place yesterday or to-day. But I have not heard whether there was or not. Every account from there represent[s] the army as in fine spirits and confident of victory. And if the Yanks do not fla[n]k our army there I have no idea that they can drive us away by attacking us in front. I pray God to prevent further bloodshed and bring about and honorable peace.[12]

I do sincerely hope these lines may reach you and find you well and doing well. You said in your last letter that you would give almost anything to have the privalege that the lady had of standing by my bed and talking to me. Oh Malinda what is there that I would not give for you to have that privilege. But God in his wisdom has ordered otherwise and let us try to submit patiently to his will. I am very anxious to hear from you now but I do not expect to now until this struggle is decided at Dalton. Give my best respects to the connexion and friends. Pray for [me]. Kiss the children for me. Goodby for this time.

To Mrs M J Taylor [from] Grant Taylor

May 11th I feel tolerably well to-day. We have no definite news from Dalton only they are fighting considerably on some parts of the line. The enemy got in the rear of the army and got within 2 miles of the Railroad 16 miles this side of Dalton but were met and checked by our men. It is said that our men have a good chance of

---

12 On May 7, 1864, Sherman began the Atlanta campaign with orders to move against the Army of Tennessee in the general vicinity of Dalton. The 40th Alabama was not heavily engaged at its position east of the Western and Atlantic Railroad. See Castel, *Decision in the West*, 128-130 and Curry, "A History of Company B," 194.

capturing a goodly number of them. It is also stated that we captured a whole brigade of Yanks the other day.[13]

It is generally believed in the army that if we whip them severely at Dalton and in Virginia this spring that the hard figh[t]ing will be over and that we will have peace sometime this year. May God grant it.

There was a heavy rain last night and to-day it is cool enough for fire to feel comfortable.

I had a fine mess of polk[weed] and pepper-grass cooked up together for dinner to-day. I can eat anything in the shape of greens. The Dr has got me to eat vegetables to cure the scurvy. Yesterday I paid 25 cts for as much lettuce as I could eat but generally such things as lettuce and mustard has been given to me. But giving I believe has about played out here now.

Grant Taylor

115

Ocmulgee Hospital Macon Ga

May 17th 1864

Beloved wife & children,

Once more I am permitted to write you a few lines. My health is only tolerable. My side is rather worse than it was 10 days ago but I am mending from the scurvy. I am able to go anywhere I wish to in a reasonable distance.

I left Cassville day before yesterday and landed here yesterday evening. Macon is 100 miles from Atlanta and about 180 miles from Resacca where they are fighting. We were sent off from

---

[13] Union General James B. McPherson's Army of the Tennessee moved through Snake Creek Gap on May 9th which threatened the Confederate left flank and the important railroad town of Resaca. See Long, *Civil War Day by Day*, 497.

Cassville to make room for those who are wounded in the battles going on. The last accounts they were fighting heavily.[14]

The Yanks made a flank movement and Johnston had to fall back about 10 miles below Dalton to stop them. I do not know how the fights will terminate. They have been fighting and skirmishing over a week. I have heard nothing certain from my Regt and nothing from my company since the fighting commenced. I did hear too that 7 had been killed out of our Regt up to last Friday night. I have not heard that any of my co was among the number but more than likely there is for the Division has been fighting from the very first. I am very anxious to hear but I do not expect to until it is ended.[15]

Neither have I got a letter from you since the one dated Apr 21st & 22nd but reason is I expect that Ide has had no chance to send it to me even if he has received it and he is still alive. I am very anxious to hear from you. But I hope you have got through with your time safely and is now well.

I am badly cheated in my change of hospitals. There is a great many wounded being sent to Atlanta. We are losing a heap of men from what I can hear. I am fearful that we will get whipped again. I have no idea how long I will stay here not many days if they keep on fighting. For I will either be sent to my co. or to another hospital to make room for the wounded. We traveld through as poor a country all day yesterday as I ever saw. From what I have seen of Georgia it is a very poor state.[16]

---

[14] Fighting at Resaca lasted from May 13th to the 15th. The 40th Alabama was now in General Alpheus C. Baker's brigade of General Alexander P. Stewart's division of General John B. Hood's corps. See U.S. War Department, *War of the Rebellion: A Compilation of the Official Records of the Union and Confederate Armies* 128 vols. (Washington, D.C.: Government Printing Office, 1880-1901) I, 38, Part III: 844-845; and Curry, "A History of Company B," 195-196.

[15] The 40th Alabama from May 7th to May 15th had lost 10 men killed, 39 wounded, and 3 missing. See War Department, *Official Records*, I, 38, Part III: 848-850.

[16] Not the usual ending for Grant's letters. It seems that the remainder of this letter is missing.

CHAPTER 9

I SHALL NOT MAKE STRENOUS EXERTIONS TO GET OUT OF THE ENEMY'S WAY

Once recovered from pneumonia and scurvy Grant returned to his regiment in time for the Atlanta Campaign. He has served over two years and the attitudes of the men have changed considerably. By July 1864, Grant decided that being captured by the enemy might be a way out of the war and the suffering it caused.

At home, Malinda has given birth to their son William Rufus Grant Taylor, on May 10, 1864. Both of Grant and Malinda Taylor are concerned about friends, money, food, and the new baby.

116

In the woods of Ga

May 29th 1864

Dear wife & children,

I am permitted once more to write you a few lines. I am tolerably well this morning and hope you are well and doing well. I left the hospital on the 23rd and overtook the Regt on the 24th. We marched about 5 miles on the 25th, met the Yanks about one hour by sun and had a hard fight which lasted until dark. We had slight breastworks of logs and poles which saved us very much. My company had one man slightly wounded in the head. Several got wounded in the Regt and two killed. We stayed there and and fought and skirmished with them until yesterday morning when fresh troops came and relieved us. We are now lying in the rear ready to move at a minutes notice.[1] Since the fighting commenced at Dalton my co. has had one killed and seven wounded, one of which has since died. The one killed was a brother of John Sanders a splendid young man. John Sanders was ~~badly~~ wounded in the arm. I feel very thankful that I have escaped so far.

Our army has fallen back to within about 25 miles of Atlanta.[2] The Yanks have flanked us and caused us to fall back. We invariably repulse them when they attack us. But they wo'nt come up and give us a general battle. If they would I believe we could whip them. The army is in fine spirits and have full confidence in themselves if we could have a fair fight. We get plenty of bacon and bread to eat.

I have not got you[r] last two letters. Ide sent them to me but I left the hospital before they reached me. But I understand that you have a fine son and you were doing well. Thank God for that. Emmaline wrote to me to tell you that she thought you had quit all such as that and for you to come over and see her and she would give you a good piece of advice as she was capable of giving it on that point.

I must close as we expect to start shortly. Continue in prayer for me and believe me yours truly

Grant Taylor

PS Our duties are very heavy. We have to fight march and work nearly all the time day and night. But if God will be with us we will come out right at last.

---

[1] The 40th Alabama was heavily engaged on this day in the battle of New Hope Church which cost approximately 1500 Union casualties and roughly 14 for the regiment out of about 500 Confederate losses. See U.S. War Department, *War of the Rebellion: A Compilation of the Official Records of the Union and Confederate Armies* 128 vols. (Washington, D.C.: Government Printing Office, 1880-1901) I:38, Part II:850; and Albert Castel, *Decision in the West: The Atlanta Campaign* (Lawrence KS: University Press of Kansas, 1992) 221-228.

[2] On May 29th the 40th Alabama was still in the general area of New Hope Church.

June 1st 1864

My ever Dear Malinda,

Good morning to you this morning. I wrote to you two or three days ago giving you an account of my ups and downs up to that time. Since then we have had no fighting to do, that [is] our Regt. But there has been heavy fight[ing] on some parts of the lines since. Night before last I was out on picket and the order was for no man to sleep. I never was sleepier in my life and I had to stand up all night to keep from going to sleep and even standing I would sometimes dream. But last night I got a good nights rest and I feel tolerably well this morning only my side is considerably sore.

Since writing to you last Sunday I have received all your letters up to May 19th. How glad I was to get them and to hear that you were getting about again. O how I want to see your 11 pounder and what a sweet little bunch of hair you sent me. I feel very thankful to God that he has been to [so] merciful to us both.

I have drawn no money in a long time and have not got a cent in the world. I sold my overcoat while I was at the hospital for 12 dollars. I would have been compelled to through it away and I thought I had better take that than nothing. I have plenty of clothes and do not intend to get any more from home except socks. If I live I will need socks next winter. I have a plenty of them to do me until then. I will also want gloves as I have lost mine by some means.

Keep everything straight in writing with Davis for he will cheat you if he can. Continue in prayer for me and believe me your loving husband as ever. In haste

To Mrs M J Taylor [from] Grant Taylor

In the woods of Ga

June 5th 1864

Dear wife & children,

Once more I am permitted to pen you a few lines. I am only in reasonable health but I hope you & the dear little ones are well and doing well. I received your kind and welcom letter of May 26th & 27th to-day. Oh how glad I was to hear that you were well. I have received all your letters up to that date. I wrote to you last sunday and also to you and Mary on the 1st inst.[3] Hope you will get them in due time.

You said that you had heard that there had been no general engagement and that is true but there has been some awful hard battles fought by Brigades & Divisions since it first commenced at Dalton and a heap of men have been killed and wounded. Yesterday was 3 weeks ago our Division charged the Yanks and drove them some over a mile. But the next day our Brigade charged them again but when they came in range the enemy poured such a deadly fire into them that they fell like grain before the scythe and they had to retreat with heavy loss. Our Regt. alone losing more than 50 men in killed and wounded.[4] From the commencement a month ago our Regt has lost 103 men in killed and wounded.[5] Our co losing 8, seven wounded and one killed, one of the wounded has since died. The one killed was a brother to John Sanders and John was wounded pretty severely. I wrote to you and Mary when I came to the Regt and about getting into that hard fought battle so it is not worthwhile to repeat it here.

We have generally whiped them in every engagement but they refuse to fight a general battle and opperate by flank

---

[3] Mary Slaughter Parker, Malinda's sister.

[4] Reference to the battle of Resaca. John H. Curry. "A History of Company B, 40th Alabama Infantry, C.S.A.," *Alabama Historical Quarterly* 17/4 (Winter 1955) 195.

[5] Taylor's figures are exaggerated—the entire month of May 1864, reecords regiment's losses, of all kinds, no higher than 80. See *Official Records*, I:38, Part II: 850.

movements causing Gen. Johnston to fall back to prevent their getting in our rear. It is reported here to-day that they drove part of our forces 4 miles yesterday on our right, but I do not know how true it is.[6] We know nothing certain here about the opperations of the army except in our immediate command. I can scarcely credit the report though something has caused us to leave our breastworks and take one of the most fatiguing marches last night and to-day that I ever took and caused us to be throwing up a new line of works.

~~We were~~ It has been raining here for several days and the roads are in a terible condition. We were up last night until about one or two o'clock when we started. I[t] was very dark and the mud from shoemouth to halfleg deep and you never saw or herad [heard] such a splashing and falling as we had. I fell flat 4 times and to my knees 5 times. One time I slipped and sit down so hard that it knocked off several rattles and a button so that I am considerably disabled from it now. We marched until ten o'clock to-day and I never was so tired in all my life and I feel very stiff and sore from it now but we are lying in reserve resting at the present but we have no idea how long it will be so.[7] I feel that it is wearing me out. But I feel very thankful that it is no worse. If I can only get home alive I will be thankful. My trust is in God. I know he will do all things right and well. And I feel that I can trust my all to his keeping.

I am sorry to hear that you will make no wheat. It seems that it is almost useless for you to try to raise anything but it all for the best.

O how I want to see your little stranger. It seems to me that I would give worlds if I possessed them for the privilege of living at home in peace during the remainder of my days. I cannot bear to study about it much. God bless sweet little Mary. How I would like

---

[6] On June 4, the Army of Tennessee fell back once again and took up positions in the Lost, Pine, and Brush mountains five miles north of Marietta. See Thomas L. Connelly, *Autumn of Glory: The Army of Tennessee, 1862-1865* (Baton Rouge LA: Louisiana State University Press, 1971) 357.

[7] After a "very disagreeable and tiresome march," the 40th Alabama rested on Lost Mountain. See Curry, "A History of Company B," 200.

to see her one time more also all the rest. My heart yearns for the pleasures of home life agian. Will it ever be satisfied.

Oh to think how happy we were once and hardly knew it and did not appreciate it. Oh Malinda (how sweet that name sounds) do pray fervently for me, for I feel that I need a heap of prayer.

As to the baby's name. Albert is a prettier name that [than] Atlas but Atlas poor fellow is gone and he was such a favorite of mine that I prefer it. But you can do as you please for I may never come home to see it or to call it's name.

Hug and kiss all the dear children and for me and tell them it is Pa's. O! do continue to pray for my return home. Give Pap and Mother my best respects and tell them to remember me in their prayers and may God bless us all is the prayer of your distant husband and father

To M J Taylor [from] G Taylor

119

In the woods near Marietta Ga

June 15ᵗʰ 1864

Beloved wife and children,

Through the mercies of God I am permitted to pen you a few lines. I am tolerably [well] except the hurt I got from slipping down as I wrote to you in my last. But God only knows how I keep up. It has rained here nearly every day for the last two weeks and I can hardly imagine how I would feel with all my clothes dry on me. I get wet and let my clothes dry on me and of a night tumble down on the wet leaves or grass and get up wet next morning. The mercies of God alone keeps me up. Many are falling sick.

I hope you and the dear children are all well and doing well. I received your kind and welcom letter of June 2ⁿᵈ and 3ᵈ this evening. I was very glad to get it. It affords me more pleasure to get a letter from you than any thing earthly. I hope your prayers for peace and my return home may be answered soon. Oh how I do want to come home but it does no good to repine.

I am in the rear of the army helping to cook for our company. It is a hard position but I am away from the Yankey bullets. I fear the smoke will affect my eyes so I will have to quit it. They hurt badly now.

I came back the 14th. I have written you every week giving you an account of our opperations as I knew them. Hope you get them. There has been no fighting only skirmishing for two weeks. The Yanks keep trying to flank us and we have to keep moving to head them [off] which makes our duties very heavy. The roads are so bad that I do not think there will be much fighting until they get better.

This is if possible a worse time than we had at Vicksburg. We get plenty bacon and bread to eat here and good water to drink but our exposure to the weather and labor are much greater and the dangers are equal. They have worked us back to within about 25 miles of Atlanta. They know they cannot whip us back and they opperate by flank movements causing us to fall back. I do not know but I believe they will get Atlanta in a month just in that way. The boys keep in good spirits but they are getting very much jaded.

I am sorry to hear of Wats sickness but glad to hear of Jakes good fortune.[8] I am sorry to hear that your little peach trees are doing so badly. Get Leonard and Jimmy to hoe around them and work them. I fear you will make no potatoes again. The ground is too poor. I wish you could have had them planted in that good land below the stables. I hope Nealy and old Teak will get along well if they do marry.[9]

The last of this month the government will owe me ($200) but I have not got a cent now and God only knows when I will have. If

---

[8] Walter Slaughter (Co A 41st AL) was in a hospital in Richmond VA from May 7-18, 1864. Jacob Parker was captured May 16, 1864 by Union forces and sent to prison in Elmira NY.

[9] In 1864, Cornelia "Nealy" Shirley Slaughter, widow of Malinda's brother Atlas Slaughter, married Ezekiel Elledge, a man forty-two years her senior. Elledge, called "Old Teak" by Grant, had eight children by a first wife and no children by a second wife. Elledge and Cornelia would have five children of their own before his death in 1876.

you can sell any bonds you had better get some from Davis and sell them if you need money and I know you do. Buy as much wheat as you need if you can get money for bonds and can get the wheat no odds what it costs you.

I want to see your <u>blue</u> eyed stranger.[10] I hope I will some day. May God bless us all and bring peace is my prayer.

To Mrs M J Taylor [from] Grant Taylor

P.S. I send you one of the prettiest pieces of poetry. You can sing it to the tune of the "Dying Californian."

120

Camps near Marietta Ga.

June 16th 1864

Beloved wife & children,

Through the mercies of a kind God I am permitted to pen you a few lines. I am in reasonable health and hope you and the dear little ones are the same.

Well Malinda I have more sad news to write. But thank God it is not so bad but that it might be worse. On the 14th inst My Regt went out on picket. My company numbered 29 officers and all which was there was all there was in the front for duty. The next morning before day the Yanks advanced on our men and wounded Lieut. Collier badly in the elbow and John O Jacobs in the shoulder. That day up in the day they advanced again and were repulsed two or three times when they came in three lines of battle and captured all of my co. except the Capt. and 8 men and 2 of them were wounded. So you see my co. is nearly all gone. There are only 13 here now for duty. We do not know whether any that were left behind were killed or wounded. There were none that we know of. The situation that they were in rendered it

---

[10] Grant is referrring to the new baby — William Rufus Grant Taylor.

almost hopeless of getting away as they held their ground until the enemy were close on them before they were ordered to retreat and then they had to run a half mile through an old field. I suppose our boys had rather be captured than run the risk in trying to get away. About half of our Regt were either killed or captured.[11] They have put my co and 3 other pieces of companies together under Capt Pickens. I understand that the 31st Ala. were all captured the same day and in the same manner.

Ide, poor fellow was captured with the rest. He was not hurt the last we heard from him. He was behind some breastworks and said to the boys never to run but stay and fight them as long as they could. I have strong hope that he is unhurt and if so we ought to be very thankful. I feel for Betty. It will be a severe blow to her but not so bad but that it might be worse. For he might have been killed and that you know would have been a heap worse. I hope she will look at it in that light and thank God for its being as it is and no worse. Look at it as being all for the best for he is out of danger and I have no doubt but he will be treated as well as the circumstances will admit. I want you to take this letter to her and let her read it and try to console her as much as you can. I feel very lonely to-day for they never make any better men than Ide. And a brother has he been to me and I feel that I have lost a true friend.

I was not in the scrape as I am in the rear cooking for the company but they have put so many companies together that I do not expect to be [a] cook long. I started a letter to you yesterday morning written some 3 or 4 days ago. Hope you will get it. I do not know ~~much~~ what they are doing on the line to-day but fighting considerably I expect as I hear the cannons roaring heavily while I am writing.[12] My God when will this thing end. O

---

[11] The 40th Alabama was trying to halt a Union advance along Noonday Creek, and lost 146 men and nine officers in the action. Union commanders erroneously claimed to have captured the entire regiment. *Official Records*, I, 38, Part IV: 481; and Charles Royster, ed., *Memories of General W. T.* Sherman (New York: Library of America, 1990) 525.

[12] General George H. Thomas had his Army of the Cumberland artillery shelling Confederate positions on this day. See Castel, *Decision in the West*, 280.

how tired I am getting of it. How I do want to come home to live with my loved ones again.

Home, sweet home. Oh how sweet the very word sounds. Will I ever get there in peace. But I have this consolation if I never get to my earthly home. I have a home sweet home in heaven where there will be no more wars nor breaking up of fond affections and separating man and wife. But where there are joys forevermore and where I hope to meet you and many of my loved ones who have gone before. Oh I do hope that I shall one day (and it may be not many days hence) be permitted to enter that Glory land and rest from all my toils and wanderings.

Dear Malinda pray that we may be permitted to enter there if all other blessings should be denied us. Give my best respects to connexion and friends and may God bless us all is the prayer of your devoted

To Mrs M J Taylor [from] Grant
& children

PS About half of the 40th were killed or captured.

121

Near Marietta Ga

June 21st 1864

Beloved wife & children,

With pleasure I am seated to pen you a few more lines. I am in pretty good health and I hope and pray that you are all well and doing well. I received your very kind and welcome letter of June 10th yesterday evening and was truly glad to hear from you once more. I have nothing strange to write as I wrote to you last week announceing our misfortu[n]e on the 15th instant in losing half of our Regt wounded and captured while on picket and the capture of Ide poor fellow. I feel very lonesom since he was taken away.

There [are] only ten of us here now for duty. They are myself, Sergt. Ware, Wm Stevens, James Speed, T J Seymour, D P Manning, A J Cook, Rabe Parker, R M Russell, R D Brandon.[13] The remainder being sick, wounded or captured. One man was wounded in the Regt yesterday with a piece of shell in the head while asleep.

I have no army news of interest to write. There has not been a great deal of fighting lately. Some heavy skirmishing nearly every day. There has been more wet weather this month than I ever saw during the same time at this season of the year and it is still raining.

I am still cooking. Two of us are cooking for 3 companies. There are only 34 men in the 3 co.

I am sorry to hear that Jake is gone.[14] Give my love to Eliza and tell her to put her trust in God for he doeth all things well.[15] I do wish the war would end.

I believe the bigest fighting will end this year for I believe we will be past fighting large battles but I do not believe peace will be made soon.

Citizens that live between here and Dalton sometimes come to us and say that the Yanks treat our people back there as mean as they can. Where ever our army goes everything nearly is destroyed, fences burned, corn fields turned out and wheat all destroyed. My God what will become of us.

I want to see you all worse than I ever did in my life but there is no chance to see you now. Maybe the time will come when we shall meet on earth. Kiss the babe for me and also the other children. Continue to pray for me. Excuse this short letter. Give my respects to all relatives and friends and believe me your ever loving husband and father

To Mrs M J Taylor   [from] Grant Taylor
& children

---

13 Sgt. N. W. Ware, William J. Stevens, James F. Speed, T. J. Seymour, David P. Manning, A. J. Cook, probably C. R. Parker, Richard M. Russell, Richard Davis Brandon, all of Co G 40th AL.

14 Jacob Parker was captured by Union forces.

15 Jacob Parker's wife, Eliza Slaughter.

PS Sam Berry King was killed some time ago.[16]

122

In line of battle Sabbath evening   June 26th 1864
near Marietta Ga

Beloved wife and children,

Through the mercies of a kind Savior I am spared to pen you a few more lines which leaves me in reasonable health except cold and the same hurting in my side that caused me so much suffering last spring. My side has never been sound and I fear never will. I hope these lines may reach you in due time and find you all well. I have just received your welcom letter of June 15th and 16th which has just been read and contents considered which gave me great satisfaction as indeed it always does to hear from you. I hope Jimmy's and Mary's sickness will not prove serious.

As I have written twice before Ide with near all of our company was captured on the 15th June while out on picket. I gave the particulars in one of my other letters and it is not necessary to repeat it hear. As to Capt Willett and his men being killed it is not all true. Capt Willett is here unhurt and he has lost but few of his men.[17]

I have been taken from cooking since our co. was captured and put in the line. We have been lying here at this place in line of battle 4 days not fighting any and its having quit raining we have had a good rest. But skirmishing is going on in hearing everyday and even now the holy stillness of the Sabbath is being broken in upon by the shrill crack of the rifle and the booming of the cannon

---

16 Sam Berry King of McCaa's Rangers, Co D 8th Confederate.

17 Willett's Company B lost only one man killed and four wounded on June 15th. See Elbert D. Willett, *History of Company B, 40th Alabama Regiment, Confederate States Army 1862 to 1865* (Montgomery, AL: Viewpoint Publications, 1963) 68-69.

in the distance. 4 days ago two divisions of the army made an attack on the enemy. They gained some advantages but were at last forced to retire with heavy loss. It is said ~~they~~ we lost twenty two hundred men in killed wounded and missing. I do not know whether that statement be true or not but it is certain our loss was very heavy.[18]

Luke Thornton was shot in the face the ball passing out the back of his head.[19] He was still alive the last I heard from him. Lab's Regt I think was in it but I have not heard how they came out. There has been no general engagement here yet but we are losing men by the thousands. The men are getting worried out by excessive fatigue. But the Yanks must be the same.

I see it stated in the papers that they acknowledge a loss from all causes of thirty thousand since the campaign began above Dalton. They keep flanking and pressing us back towards Atlanta. We are now not more than twenty miles from that place.

I feel very lonesom since our company was captured especially Ide. Oh how I miss him. May God bless him in his imprisonment and Betty in her loneliness is my sincere prayer.

Malinda I want you to get some of those bonds from Davis if you can sell them and buy as much wheat as you need. Let the price be what it may. The bonds will never do you any good unless you can use them in that way. If you cannot get money in that way I do not know what you will do for money for as I wrote you before I have not been paid since last Jan. and for clothing and wages the government owes me $200. But I have not got a cent and hav'nt had for a month. Nor do I expect to be paid anything till this thing ends here and we can be a little quiet. You will say for me not to bother myself about you but I cannot help it. I know you have a kind protector in your father and a loving savior to watch over you for which I am thankful. Yet I cannot help but be troubled when I think how destitute you are of this worlds goods.

---

[18] General John B. Hood launched an unauthorized attack on Union troops at Kolb's Farm on June 22nd. The Confederates charged repeatedly, and suffered 1000 casualties. See Jacob D. Cox, *Atlanta* (New York: Charles Scribner and Sons, 1882) 110-113; and Richard M. McMurry, "The Affair at Kolb's Farm," *Civil War Times Illustrated* (December, 1968) 171-195.

[19] Luke Thornton is unidentified.

But I am very thankful that though you are poor in this worlds goods you are rich in love to your family and rich in your love to God where I trust we have both laid up our treasures.

Write to me how quick you get this after it is written. Continue in prayer for me. Give my respects to the connexion and believe yours as ever

To Mrs M J Taylor [from] Grant Taylor
& children

123

In an apple orchard in Ga.

July 3ᵈ 1864

Beloved wife & children,

With pleasure and gratitude to my blessed Savior I will write you a few lines this holy Sabbath morning if I have time. But the tools have come and we will have to go to throwing breastworks shortly. Thank God I am in reasonable health thou[g]h tired and sleepy and I hope you and the dear little ones are in the best of health.

We commenced marching this morning at 2 o'clock and landed here about 7. Some five miles from where we have been the last ten days.[20] We have fallen back that far to meet another flank movement of the enemy. But from the present appearance we will make a stand here for awhile at least until the enemy flanks us again. We invariably whip them when they attack us but when we attack them it is generally the other way. There has been no general engagement yet for the reason that neither party will make a general attack. There has been some very hard fighting in some parts of the army and many have been killed on both sides. Last But I believe the ya[n]kee loss has been much greater than

---

[20] The Army of Tennessee fell back from its position at Kennesaw Mountain some five miles to the banks of the Chattahoochee River. See Castel, *Decision in the West*, 329-330.

ours, because they have made many more attacks than we. Last week they made an attack on one part of the line and were repulsed. A day or two after, under a flag of truce, I heard they buried four thousand, while our loss was comparatively small.[21]

I received your welcome letter of June 21st 22nd and 23d while on the march this morning. I was truly glad to hear that you were all well. You complained of bad pens. Can't you buy new ones[?] If I had any but this one or had any money to buy with I would send you some but I have neither money nor pens.

I heard from Lab Teer and Lafayett last Wednesday night. They were both well. I saw E Sellers and Wm Peacock this morning while on the march.[22] They were well. I also met up with Cloud Barton this morning.[23] He was well and belongs to a Louisiana Regt. We have been in the same division ever since last Feb. and did not know it.[24] He informed me that Lowry Calhoun got killed up here the other day.[25]

Give Mr Ashcraft my love and tell him to remember me in his prayers.[26] Tell him to pray that I may live to come home after peace but especially that I may live so that I may go to that blessed home that my Savior has prepared for all his children.

I wish I could be at home this Summer to help you eat those nice chickens you wrote about. I get plenty of fat bacon and cornbread but you know I never could relish that kind of diet well.

I dreamed of seeing you the other night at home. I thought peace was made and I had landed home. I was so glad. But I woke up and found it all a dream. When I went to sleep again I dreamed the same dream only I thought I was home on sick furlough. I

---

[21]A frustrated Sherman threw his troops against strongly-held Kennesaw Mountain on June 27th. By the time the fighting stopped, the Federals had lost some 2000 to 3000 men while Confederate losses were about 500. Sherman later referred to the action as "the hardest fight of the campaign to that date." See Sherman, *Memoirs*, 531; and Cox, *Atlanta*, 127.

[22] Elijah Sellers and William D. Peacock (36th AL).

[23] Cloud Barton is unidentified.

[24] General Randall L. Gibson's brigade in the same division was composed of Louisiana regiments.

[25] Lowry Calhoun is unidentified.

[26] Rev. William Ashcraft (born c1824), minister at Forest Church.

hope I may get home someday. Tell Wat howdy for me and tell him to write to me. Lik[e]wise, the rest of the connexion.

Sunday evening. I am so tired I do not feel like writing for since writing the above we have been out on picket and have been hard at work, Sunday as it is, cleaning off a new picket line and throwing up works for the pickets to fight behind.

Well I am glad I wrote something to make you laugh for I am glad when I can cause you to see any pleasures for here of late I scarcely ever see or hear anything to make me feel like laughing. But it is all for the best.

There was considerably skirmishing about a mile in front of us this evening.

I will put some buttons in this letter. Maybe you will get them.

~~I must clos~~ I would willingly give your respects to Ide but alas! poor fellow he was captured on the 15th June as I have written to you before.

Always pray for me. Kiss the dear children for me and believe yours truly as ever

To Mrs M J Taylor [from] Grant Taylor
& children

I am so sorry that Jake is gone. I hope Eliza will put her trust in God for help to enable her to bear her troubles. May God bless us all and bring us peace is my sincere prayer. G Taylor

124

In line of battle on Chattahoochee River

July 9th 1864

Beloved wife and children,

Once more I am permitted to pen you a few more lines. This leaves me in better health than I have been since I was taken sick last March and I hope you and my dear children are enjoying the same great blessing.

This is Saturday evening. I wrote to you last Sunday and sent you some buttons. I hope you have got them. We fell back several miles that day as I wrote to you. We built splendid breastw[o]rks there. On Tuesday morning before day we started to fall back again and came to this place the same night which is on the Chattahoochee river some 7 of 8 miles from Atlanta. We are strongly fortified here and if the Yanks would attack us I believe with God's help we would dress them out nicely. Capt Pickens has been promoted on a generals staff and left us without any commander and they are talking of putting [page torn] company without giving us leave to choose our company which I think is very unfair.

I have no news to write more than to let you hear from me which I know is always news to you.

I have just heard the Ki's George is dead. I do not know when or where he died but somewhere in the hospital. Poor little fellow, he ought never to have come here. But he did and has found an early grave. I hope he has also found a heavenly home. Why was it not me[?] Many of our friends and relatives have died since I joined the army and yet through the mercies of my blessed Maker I have been spared for some wise purpose. Oh how thankful we ought to be. I do feel thankful yet when I look at all his mercies I feel that I am not half as humble and thankful as I ought to be. Oh! may I be more humble and thankful in future than in times past.

I have just received a letter from Hughs dated June 30th. They were all well except his wife. She had been sick for 3 weeks but had got able to be up a little. I heard from Lab and Lafayette last Monday. [page torn] was complaining but still with his command. George died in Atlanta.

Why does not Leonard and Jimmy write some to me. Their little pieces are refr[e]shing to me. Give my love to connexion and friends. Kiss the babe and the other children for me. Continue in fervent prayer for me and believe yours lovingly as ever

To Mrs M J Taylor [from] Grant Taylor

PS For your eyes alone. Malinda I have always tried to be a faithful soldier in the cause of my beloved country but if they do thrust me into a company I do not want to join, I shall not be so anxious to do my duty in future. I do not intend to desert, but I shall not make strenuous exertions to get out of the enemy's way and if you hear of my being missing after some of our scrapes be not uneasy about me unless you hear that I am killed or wounded. I believe Let none see this. I expect Dock Excuse this short unsatisfactory letter. My mind is confused and I have but little paper and when I am out I do not now where more is to come from. May God bless you all is my sincere prayer.

125

In line of battle.

July 29th 1864

Beloved wife & children,

With pleasure I seat myself to inform you that I am all right yet. My health is good but I am badly exhausted. Yesterday was some hard fighting. We were in it. One Brigade in front of us charged the enemy and were repulsed with dreadful slaughter. Our Brigade then tried them but were repulsed in a few minutes.[27] Co's B and G had 9 wounded. G had 3. Powell Baker's leg was broken just below the knee.[28] Rabe Parker slightly in the hand and Cox in the knee.[29] Old John Goodwin wounded slightly in the side.[30] Lieut [Eli D.] Vance severely in the head.[31] Bob Wells was

---

[27] The July 28th battle of Ezra Church was new Army of Tennessee commander General Hood's third and final attempt to defeat Sherman at Atlanta by attack. Hood's efforts resulted in another 5000 Confederate casualties as compared to about 600 for the Union forces. See Cox, *Atlanta*, 185; Sherman, *Memoirs*, 563-565; and Castel, *Decision in the West*, 414-422.

[28] L. Powell Baker of Co G 40th AL.

[29] C. R. Parker of Co G 40th AL. Two men named Cox were in Grant's company, J. P. Cox and John R. Cox.

[30] John Goodwin (born c1810) (Co B 40th AL).

[31] Lt. Eli D. Vance was wounded July 28 and died later in the hospital in Atlanta.

wounded and died last night.[32] Jim Bailey was mortally wounded and left in the hands of the enemy.[33]

The Yanks have not got Atlanta yet. Try to convey the word to Mrs Stevens that Bill is all right.[34] I am thankful that I am still unhurt but my trust is in God. Continue in prayer for my safety.

I have no time to write no more. Yours in great hast[e].

To Mrs M J Taylor [from] Grant Taylor

126

In line of battle near Atlanta Ga

Aug. 3[d] /[18]64

Beloved wife & children,

Through the mercies of God I am permitted to pen you a few lines informing you that I am in fine health and I trust you and the children are enjoying the same blessing.

The railroad has been cut by Yankee raiding parties between this place and Ala. which has deranged the mail.[35] But I have managed to send a letter every week by hand to some part of Ala to be mailed to you. I hope you will get them. I understand arrangements are made for hauling the mail by those cut places, if so they will be regular again.

I received your kind & ever welcome letter of July 15th on the 1st inst. I was truly glad to get one more from you and to hear that you were all so well and hearty. I am glad you get a plenty to eat. Have you ever bought any wheat or flour yet? Did you make any wheat at all and how are your hogs getting along. Have you a

---

[32] Robert Wells (Co B 42nd AL).

[33] Jim Bailey is unidentified.

[34] William Stevens, son of Thomas and Mary Stevens. William was recorded as a member of Forest Church as 'Stephens."

[35] Union cavalry had been operating against railroads linking Atlanta to the rest of the Confederacy. See Castel, *Decision in the West*, 436-443; and David Evans, *Sherman's Horsemen: Union Cavalry in the Atlanta Campaign* (Bloomington IN: Indiana University Press, 1997).

pretty good chance to make your meat next winter. And has the government taken any of your meat yet. These are little things but I would like to hear all about your little matters. Though small they are important and whatever is for your welfare is interesting to me to hear about.

I wrote to you in my last which was a hasty scroll about us charging the Yankees last Wednesday and getting repulsed. I will state also in this that 3 of co. (G) got wounded. Lieut. Powell Baker leg broke, since amputated, Rabe Parker slightly in the hand since returned to duty and a man by the name of Cox wounded slightly in the knee. Co. (B) which is Willett's had 5 wounded among whom was old Johnny Goodwin in the side slight and Lieut Vance in the head severely. Co. (G) is put with Co. (B). Bob Wells was wounded the same day and died that night. Jim Bailey was mortally wounded and left on the field. Will Wells was killed in a charge they made the Friday before.[36] There is considerable skirmishing close to us on our right and we are not surprised to be called on to go into a fight at any moment. But do not be uneasy about me. I feel that I have put my trust in my savior for time and eternity and I do not dread it near so bad as I used to. Nevertheless pray for me that I may not have a false faith and that my faith fails not and that I may be spared to come home and especially for a speedy peace.

Oh how tired I am getting of this thing. But I do not see any chance or any effort being made to settle it except by fighting and I do not believe it will ever be done in that way. May God hasten a time of peace is my daily prayer. We have had a heap of men killed within the last 2 weeks. Our Regt. is about 4 miles west of Atlanta now, but we move every day or two and sometimes 2 or 3 times each day.[37]

Tell your folks and mine howdy for me and tell them not to think hard of me for not writing to them for paper pens and ink are very high and I have no money to buy with, but when they wish to hear from me they can go and see you and thus pay a visit

---

[36] William Wells (Co H 40th AL) died July 22. William and his brother Robert Wells died within four days of each other.

[37] The 40th Alabama was then posted near the Sandtown Road.

and hear from me also. Yet I would like to write to all of them if I could. I love them none the less by not writing to them.

I answerd those letters that Mary wrote to me some time ago. Did she get it. I have written all that I know of now. Give a son's grateful love to pap and mother and tell them to remember me at a throne of grace. And may God bless us all is the prayer of your distant and loving husband and father.

To Mrs M J Taylor [from] Grant Taylor
& children

P.S. I wish I could be there to go to those good meetings with you but it is willed otherwise. But as you say it is a terable thought to think of never seeing each other on earth again. But let us trust and pray to God in faith. I saw John Williamson the other day, the man that married Josaphine Crouch. Old Mr Crouch died this spring.[38] The rest were well.

127

Line of battle near Atlanta Ga

August 4th 1864

Dear Malinda,

I am in fine health this morning though my clothes are wet yet from a wetting I got yesterday evening. But being wet is what we are used to. I wrote to you yesterday stating that we might go into battle at any minute. I had scarcely started my letter off when the enemy attacked our pickets and captured 28 of our Regt of which 3 was from Co. (G) (viz) William E Craig, Tom Dillard and Thomas Calley. And 7 were from Co B. Among whom were Mark Freeman and I Freeman a cousin of his 2 of Moses Cameron's sons and one of the Elmore's.[39] They were in such a place that they could not

---

[38] John Williamson, Josephine Crouch, and Mr. Crouch are unidentified.

[39] Marcus M. Freeman and Isham A. Freeman. Three of Moses Cameron's sons were in Co B 40th AL: James B. Cameron (born c1834),

run out with out running a great risk.[40] I wrote you this for you to go and see Mrs Craig and inform her of it.[41] I was not on pickett and the enemy did not attack the main line where we were and thus I escaped.

Truly the Lord smiles on me which encourages me to hope and put my trust in him.

Continue in prayer for me. Kiss our sweet little ones for me and ever believe me yours truly

To Mrs M J Taylor [from] Grant Taylor

128

In line of battle near Atlanta

August 11th 1864

Dear and beloved wife and children,

Thank God I am permitted to pen you one more letter. I am enjoying as good health as I ever did in my life. Although our duties are very heavy and rations are growing painfully less. I hope and pray you are enjoying the best of health.

I wrote 2 letters to you last week one dated the 3[d] the other the 4th inst. On the 3[d] just after I had started my letter off the Yanks made a charge on our picketts and captured W E Craig, Thomas Dillard and Thomas Calley of old co G and several of co B and I wrote to you about it for you to inform Mrs Craig of it and the same evening I received your very welcom letter of July 21st and 22nd. I was glad to get it and to hear that your kind father had bought you some wheat. I did not answer it as I had just sent off

---

Joseph D. Cameron (born c1840), and Moses Cameron (born c1845). There were several Elmores in Co B.

[40] Union forces had pushed across Utoy Creek at Herringer's Mill on August 3rd and captured 100 soldiers on picket duty in front of General Alpheus Baker's brigade to which the 40th Alabama was assigned. See Castel, *Decision in the West*, 454; and Willett, *History of Company B*, 77.

[41] William E. Craig (Co C 40th AL). Mrs. Craig is probably his wife Mary.

two to you. Day before yesterday I received another from you dated July 27 and 28. I am sorry to hear of your continual suffering with your jaws. Oh how it pierces my heart to hear that anything ails you or the children. I know you had a lonesome ~~night~~ time that Sunday night you had to sit up with your jaw. Why do'nt you try blue mass as you did last summer. Take as good care of your pigs as you can.

As you say last time this year I was at home. What a happy time it was then to what it is now.

I have good news for Betty. I have heard from Ide. Col. [John H.] Higley received a letter from a Lieut of this Regt who was captured at the same time. He gave the names of those captured from our Regt and among them Ide's name. All of our co. was named except Levi Hamlin.[42] I expect he was killed. He gave the names of those wounded but did not give Teer's name in the wounded list. Of course he was safe. The officers were sent to Johnson's Island [Ohio][43] and the men to Rock Island.[44] The letter was dated June 28th several days after they had arrived at their destination. Consequently the Lieut. did not know how the boys were when he wrote as they had been separated several days. I heard the letter read.

I wrote to you that Jim Bailey was wounded and left on the field but I had been wrongly informed. He was taken off and sent to the hospital ~~and~~. I do not know how he is getting along now.

Our situation is unchanged since I last wrote only the Yanks have advanced nearer our lines. They are not quite a half mile off in front of us and their Pickett line are in full view of us. Their sharpshooters and ours keep both sides pretty close in their ditches. This morning some Georgia Picketts and the Yanks made a bargain not to shoot at each other and met in an old field where

---

42 Levi Hamlin (Co G 40th AL).

43 Johnson's Island was in Lake Erie not far from Sandusky, Ohio. It had been a prison since February 1862. See Patricia L. Faust, ed., *Historical Times Illustrated Encyclopedia of the Civil War* (New York: HarperCollins, 1986) 398-399.

44 Rock Island was in Illinois.

we could see them and staid together some time. I suppose they were making little trades.[45]

129

In line of battle near Atlanta Ga

August 18th 1864

Dear Malinda,

Thank God this morning I am alive and kicking and in good health and I hope this may reach your distant hand and find you all well and doing well. I have not received any letter from you this week. I have received letters up to July 28 and answered them. I have no news of much interest to write.

Our position is unchanged since I last wrote. The two armies are in line near each other and we are as close confined to the ditch[es] as we were at Vicksburg. About all the difference is we are not surrounded, get a little more to eat and the best of water to drink. Georgia is noted for its abundance of good water.

We still hold Atlanta. Our prospects are very gloomy and our men are deserting a good deal. Some going home, others going to the Yanks.

As I wrote to you last week, we heard from our boys that were captured on the 15th of June. They were at Rock Island. Ide was with them and unhurt. A Lieut wrote back giveing all their names. All of co. G was named except Levi Hamlin. Joe Leavell and Joe Park went into the battle on the 22nd July and have never been heard of since, supposed killed.[46] Lum Wells was on pickett

---

[45] This letter stops without the usual ending. The final page is thought to be missing. The last existing page was written on a ledger sheet with "Mr. J R Crew for Central Presby^n Church to D M Young for 89 church cushions for $350, March 14, 1860."

[46] General William J. Hardee's corps struck Sherman on July 22, 1864, in what became known as the Battle of Atlanta. More than 11,000 men fell on both sides, including Union General James B. McPherson. See Cox, *Atlanta*, 176; and Long, *Civil War Day by Day*, 544.

about a week ago when the Yanks attacked them. He has not been heard of since. Killed or captured.

Excuse these scraps of paper for it is the best I can do now and I have only enough of these to write one more and one more envelope.

Dear Malinda continue to pray earnestly for me. Give my love [to] all and believe me yours truly as ever

To Mrs M J Taylor [from] Grant Taylor

130

In line of battle near Atlanta Ga.

Aug. 24th 1864

My dear wife and children,

With much thankfulness I am seated to answer to most welcome letter of Aug. 12th which I have just received & read. I was so glad to get it. As I did not get one from you last week because you did not ~~get~~ write it. I am very sorry that you are suffering so much with your teeth and are having so many pulled out but am glad it is no worse. Truly the Lord has been gracious to us and especially has blessed me. I am to-day in excellent health, never better and I hope you are all well as I am. H L Mullins is Lafayett's name. His name is Hughs L.

I have nothing of interest to write. Our position is changed but little since I wrote last week. The two armies are in sight of each other and are sharpshooting and shelling nearly all the time which keeps us confined to the trenches pretty closely. Occasionally a poor fellow is sent to his long home. There has been no fighting in several days that I know of. It is reported that General [Joseph] Wheeler with a large cavalry force has got in the rear of the Yanks tore up the railroad retaken Dalton captured one thousand head of beef cattle and a number of prisoners. I do not believe all the report, but Wheeler is no doubt in the rear.[47] I wrote in my two last about hearing from Ide. Also about Jo Leavelle and Jo Park being missing. Mr Porter has been within a half mile of me and less for several weeks and yet I have not seen him. You may judge whether we are closely confined. We are not allowed to leave without a pass from the Gen. and then it must be urgent business. He was well a few days ago. A young man of our co. whose mother lives in Memphis [Pickens County, Alabama] get a letter from her the other day stating that Wick was taken prisoner some time ago near Pensacola in Florida.

I borrowed some money the other day and bought this paper at $6 per quire. It is very sorry. I could not get any envelopes. It seems from your writing on old letters yet [you] have not got any paper yet. I will send you a leaf but I doubt your being able to write on it unless you have a better pen than I have.

I wrot to Betty some time ago that there was no chance for her to draw Ide's money while he was alive and a prisoner. I want you to send me a little sowing thread in your next letter if you have any good on hand. Send both colered and white. You can send a right smart [amount] if you put it in rightly.

I will close. Give my best respects to enquiring friends and connexion. Continue in prayer for me. Kiss the dear children for me and believe me yours loving as ever

To Mrs M J Taylor [from] Grant Taylor

PS That tooth puller had better mind how he cuts up around you. You have never written what name you gave the babe whether Atlas or Wiley. I do want to see you all so bad.

---

[47] Some 6000 of Wheeler's rebel horsemen began a raid on Sherman's north Georgia supply lines beginning on August 13th. See Castel, *Decision in the West*, 469.

CHAPTER 10

THIS POOR LITTLE CONFEDERACY
IS ABOUT PLAYED OUT

While the battles for Atlanta still raged, Grant's regiment was sent back to the garrison of Mobile. Though he was nearer home in miles, he was not any closer to seeing his family. There illness and hunger would soon strike him again. At home wife Malinda coped with five children – one an infant – and running the farm. They were both exhausted from the war and ready for it to end, regardless of its outcome.

131

Mobile Ala

August 28[th] 1864

Beloved wife and children,

This leaves me in good health this beautiful sabbath morning and I hope and trust that you are the same.

No do[u]bt you will be surprised to get a letter from me at this place. I will explain. I wrote the other letter too late to get it off the same day. That night we were put on pickett and about midnight we were relieved and ~~started~~ went to Atlanta and got on the cars and proceeded to this place where we arrived an hour ago. We are waiting for the ballance of our Brigade to come up which it will do to-day. There are only our co. here.[1]

I know nothing of the situation here but stirring times are expected. Two Yankee vessels are in sight.[2]

I saw Ves Peebles this morning.[3] He was well. He says Bob was well also.[4] I cannot find out yet whether Wick is captured or not.

Mobile looks very natural and if it were like it was when you were here what a good chance it would be for you to come and see me. But there is no more chance for you to come than when I was at Atlanta. I felt almost like I was coming home while on my way here.

Direct you letters to Co G 40th Ala Baker's Brigade, Mobile Ala.

May God bless you all is my prayer.

To Mrs M J Taylor [from] Grant Taylor

---

[1] The 40th Alabama left the Atlanta area by rail to reinforce the garrison of Mobile on August 25, 1864. See U.S. War Department, *War of the Rebellion: A Compilation of the Official Records of the Union and Confederate Armies* 128 vols. (Washington, D.C.: Government Printing Office, 1880-1901) I, 39, Part II: 854; and See Elbert D. Willett, *History of Company B, 40th Alabama Regiment, Confederate States Army 1862 to 1865* (Montgomery, AL: Viewpoint Publications, 1963) 81.

[2] U.S. Navy forces in Mobile Bay numbered some 24 vessels of all types in the wake of Admiral David G. Farragut's victory there on August 5th. See U.S. War Department, *Official Records of the Union and Confederate Navies in the War of the Rebellion,* 30 vols. (Washington D.C.,: Government Printing Office, 1896-1927) I, 21: 624 and Charles G. Hearn, *Mobile Bay and the Mobile Campaign: The Last Great Battles of the Civil War* (Jefferson, N.C.: McFarland& Co Inc, Publishers, 1993) 100-101.

[3] John Ves Peebles.

[4] Probably Robert Peebles.

132

December [Sept] the 2 1864

beloved Grant,

Once more I am permitted to write you a few lines. Mathew, Mary, and the baby has the worse colds. I saw last Thursday night Mary was taken just like she was before when she had the croup. Next morning sent for Dr Shockly.[5] With the help of God he checked it. She has had some fever every day since but keeps up. Math coughs now like he had the croup. The rest are well. I hope when this reaches your distant hand it may finde you in the best of health.

I wrote to you last week of Wats death. Mother and Dully came to see me last Sunday. Tom Mobly and Larnes Baily Deserted and came home last week but have gon on to Miss. to join the Cavaldry.[6] I understand they are deserting by 5 hundred a day from Atlanta. I wish that evry one would do so until evry man would get home. From what I hear the General you have now is as mean as he can bee. It is a pity but what someone would point a loaded gun at him.[7]

There was a Negro burnt to death in Eutaw the other day for taking a white lady of[f] her horse and doing what he pleased with her. Mrs Godwin was thare and saw the smoke.[8]

The Yanks have Fort Morgan so I hear.[9] I never got a letter from you last week. How it cows my spirits when I dont get one evry week.

Eleven months today since you left home. How much longer will it bee before I see you. I have recieved just 100 and 1 letters

---

[5] Dr. Thomas Shockley (1822-1893), who served in Co B 40th AL, but was discharged.

[6] Tom Mobley is unidentified. Lawrence D. Bailey.

[7] A reference to Army of Tennessee commander General John Bell Hood.

[8] Probably Susan Goodwin.

[9] Fort Morgan, at the mouth of Mobile Bay, surrendered to Union forces on August 23, 1864. See Hearn, *Mobile Bay*, 131.

from you. Can it bee that you will stay away for me to get that many more. I must quit. Goodby. I remain yours, as ever,

M J Taylor

133

Holley Wood Baldwin County Ala

Sept 5th 1864

Dear wife & children,

Thank God I am permitted to pen you a few more lines. This leaves me in tolerable health though not so well as I was when I left Geo[r]gia. The weather is so warm and we have had so much marching to do since we have been down here that it is rather getting the better of me. But I hope by the Lord's blessing to be able to stand up under it.

I wrote to you on the 28th [Aug], the day we got to Mobile giving you a detailed account of our move up to that time. The same evening we were ordered back to the east side of the bay where we have been ever since. We have been moving from place to place nearly every day since we have been here. We came to this place a little before day this morning. It is a neat little vilage and a noted summering place for the grandees of Mobile in good times but sadly on the decline now. It [is] very pleasan[t]ly situated on the eastern shore of the bay some 15 or 20 miles southeast from Mobile and in sight of the city. It is said to be one of the most healthy places in the state. If we were allowed to do so this is a beautiful place to stay and rest awhile. But there is no rest for us. We will have to be on pickett half of every night. Everything has been quiet since we have been down in here. A Yankee gun-boat lay last night and part of to-day in a mile of us but this evening it moved about two miles farther off.

I cannot hear anything of Wick down here. I reckon it is true about his being captured.

This is a delicious climate in the shade if a person is not taking exercise. There is always a good breeze stirring, but in the sun or in exercise the heat is severe.

I had much rather be on the other side of the bay, it seems more like home to me, but this is the most pleasant.

I hear it reported that the Yanks have taken Atlanta. I hope it is not true. There have been a great many valuable lives lost in defence of that place to have to give it up now. It is said they fought 2 days there last week.[10] If so we were lucky in getting away from there for the present. The general belief here is that we will have peace before another twelve months shall have passed. I pray it may be so but I fear they are doomed to be disappointed. For my own part I shall be most agreeably disappointed if we do have peace in that time. I have no doubt but many of us will obtain everlasting peace before anothe twelve months shall have rolled around but I doubt our country's having peace in that time. God grant we may have it is my sincere prayer.

I have not received a letter from you since the day before I left Atlanta, but I hope you are all in good health. Dick Russel is sick here under the tree near me now with a chill.[11] Our co[mpany] is remarkably healthy.

I believe I have written all that will interest you. Give my love to Pap and mother and the connexion generally. Continue in fervent prayer for my temporal safety but especially for my spiritual welfare and may God bless us all and bring me safely through these trying times is my sincere prayer.

To Mrs M J Taylor [from] Grant Taylor
& children

---

[10] In the last week of August, Sherman's armies cut Atlanta's last remaining railroad connections and forced Hood's Confederates to evacuate the city on September 1. Union troops marched in the next day. See E.B. Long, *The Civil War Day by Day: An Almanac 1861-1865* (Garden City NJ: Doubleday, 1971) 564-565.

[11] Richard M. Russell of Co G 40th AL.

134

Holley Wood Baldwin County Ala

Sept. 11th 1864

Beloved wife & children,

Through the kindness of a merciful God I am permitted to pen you a few more lines which leaves me in reasonable health. Thoug[h] I do not feel so well here as I did while in Georgia and I hope and pray you are enjoying the best of health.

I have nothing of much interest to write. We are having a fine time here although we have to go on pickett every other night. We catch more fish than we can destroy. I came very near foundering yesterday on fish and pumpkin and potatoes. We caught the fish, bought the potatoes at $8.00 per bu[shel] and got the pumpkin by way of a slant.

The Yanks have not bothered us any since we have been here and if things could go on in the same way I would like to spend the remainder of my soldier life here. But I fear we will not be permitted to stay here long.

I thought of you while eating fish and wished you had as many as I did. If we stay around Mobile this winter maybe times will get so that you can come and see me if I cannot come home. This is the third letter I have written to you since I came to Mobile, but I have not got any from you since I left Atlanta.

I have not heard from Wick yet. I suppose it is certain that we have lost Atlanta. My God what are we coming to.

I wrote to you 2 weeks ago to send me some s[e]wing thread if you had any prepared in a letter. I am out and cannot get a spool for less than $4.00 even if I had the money. You can send me some in a letter to do me until you get the chance to send some by hand. Knit me two pair socks and a pair of gloves by cold weather and have them ready. But do not send them until I write for them. I fear I shall have to send back for your bed cover when cold weather comes on. I have but one of those old thin blankets that Mary let me have and I know it will be a bad chance to get a blanket from the government. I dislike very much to rob you of any more of your bed clothing but I expect to have it to do. I have bought 2 pairs of woolen socks and have drawn 2 pairs of cotton from the government since I left home and have worn them all out but 2 pairs of woolen. Did you ever get the letter containing some buttons[?]

I will bring my uninteresting letter to a close. Give my love to all the connexion. Continue in prayer for me and believe your ever loving one

To Mrs M J Taylor [from] Grant Taylor
& children

135

Holly Wood Baldwin County Ala

Sept. 18th 1864

Dear wife & children,

With pleasure I write these lines to you in answer to your ever welcome letter of the 4th and 9th inst which came to hand last Wednesday. This is Sunday evening. I was very glad to get it and to hear that you were all so well. The thread and scraps all came through right. I am not well to-day. I have been puny 2 or 3 days and this morning I had an old [--] ague and I feel so bad now that I can hardly write. Seven or eight of our co. are having the chills and new cases are occuring daily. I fear we will have a heap of sickness down here. We have to lie at the edge of the water on the bay on pickett every other night. The Yanks keep a respectful distance and we are having a high heeled time if we could have our health. I hope and pray that you are all as well as when you wrote.

I got a letter from Wick yesterday which I will send to you.

I wrote to you some time ago asking to know whether the government had taken any of your meat and how your hogs are doing and what is your prospect are for meat for another year. But you have not answered me yet. I would like to know how the cow does that I bought from Theron and whether you get plenty of milk and butter.[12] I have never found out how much your salt cost you.[13]

And also you never wrote what name you had given the baby whether Wiley or Atlas. I do want to see him so badly indeed I want to see you all very badly and if there ~~were~~ was any chance for you to get to where I am I would write for you to come. But there is no chance for there is no conveyance nearer than 6 miles. But may be the time will come when we will see each other. Let us hope and trust in God.

If I get much sick[er] and am sent to the hospital I shall write for you to come. Excuse my short letter as I feel too bad to write more. I feel truly sorry for old Uncl[e] Matthew.[14] It is a great loss to him but those that have must lose and death is the appointed lot of us all. Let us live so that we may meet it calmly.

May God bless us all is the prayer of your distant loving husband and father

To Mrs M J Taylor [from] Grant Taylor

Sept 19th I feel a little better this morning.

136

September the 28 1864

Beloved Grant,

It is through the goodness and mercies of God that I am permitted to write you one more letter. This leaves us all in fine

---

[12] Theron S. Teer, Grant's nephew.

[13] For more on impressment of supplies and salt shortages, see the appropriate chapters of Malcolm C. McMillan, *The Disintegration of a Confederate State: Three Governors and Alabama's Wartime Homefront 1861-1865* (Macon GA: Mercer University Press, 1986).

[14] "Old Uncle Matthew" is unidentified. This "loss" is unclear—property or life.

health, hoping it may reach you and finde you the same. I mist getting a letter last week. I also faild to send you one. I did not get home from church in time to get it in the Friday mail.

I must now tell you what a glorious meeting we had at old Forest.[15] There were 16 added to the church. I will give you thare names. Jo and Mary Barnet, old John Goodwin, his wife, and Billy, Euny, and Mary Davis, old Mr Langford and three of his daughters, Margaret Hood, old Bartley Upcurch, Mrs Clanton, Frank Ritcherson, and the old lady Barham.[16] Of all what a cite it was to see as olde a person as she was go under the water. Mrs Clanton joined by letter. Upcurch came from the old side. Mr Goodwin [was] taken under the watch care of the church. All the rest were immerst. The meeting began on Saturday and broke the next Friday. Brother Ashcraft had no help. Only Dr Nickeleson preached 2 or 3 times.[17] Maybee you dont know who that is. He is a Baptist minister and a docter that lives whare Brigges lived when you was at home.[18] He moved thare last winter. He has a wife and one childe. Reports say that Mr Clanton diede 2 weeks ago at Mobile.[19]

I heard yesterday thare was a man about Caralton that had 5 hundred bushels of corn to give to the soldiers wifes to faten thare hogs so maybee I will get a little. I wrote to you some time ago about getting knocked out of our wheat. Old man Thomas says now we may have it at 10$ per bushel.[20] Pap let me have 50$ and so I bought 5 bushels from him altho it went very hard with me to have to humar the old scamp enough to give him that after offering it to us at 5$.

---

15 Forest Church in Pickens Co.

16 The following people joined the church: Joseph P. and Mary Barnet; John and Susan Goodwin and their son Billy; Unity Taylor Davis (Grant's sister) and her daughter Mary Davis; Mr. Langford and his 3 daughters are unidentified; Margaret Hood is unidentified; Bartley Upchurch (1800-1879); Mrs. David G. Clanton (Caroline); perhaps B. F. Richardson; Lucy Barham (born c1798).

17 Dr. Nicholson is unidentified.

18 Perhaps Micah Briggs of Pickens County.

19 David G. Clanton.

20 Probably Thomas Thomas (born c1777).

October the 2nd 1864

This day twelve long long months ago you turned your back on your home and family. Oh how sad and lonly I feel when I think of it. I pray to my God that before another 12 months shal roll around that you may bee permitted to reach home well and harty to stay in peace.

The first part of this letter is one that I started before I went to Elcy Anns and forgot to take it with me to put in the [post] office as I came back. I wrote one over thare and started it to you. I recieved a letter from you written 18 and 19 of Sept containing Wiks. I am sorry to hear that you are in bad health again unless it will bee the means of you coming home. It seems from the reading of your letter that you have not been getting my letters. I wrote some time ago what my prospect was for meat this winter and that the government had not taken any of my meat. Also that I have never paid anything on my salt. I dont know that it will cost me anything. Only what we put in first the 5 lbs of meat and $10 in money. As to my hogs I have 12 shoats. They are small but I can fatten as many as I pleas.

I wrote in 2 letters that I have not decided on the babys name.[21] I wrote in my last that I had a thought of naming him Rufus Grant if you are willing.

You requested me to write all about Wats death. He had been at home 2 months to a day when he died. He got able to ride to Paps. He was taken worse on Friday and was very bad until the next Friday. Then he seemed better and said he felt more like getting well than he ever had. In the night he taken worse and diede about day Saturday morning. He was willing to die. All that pestered him was his family. A while before he died the clock struck 1 or 2. He asked what it struck. They tolde him he then said three hours more to suffer yet. He craved death rather than go back to the army. Me nor Mary was not thare when he diede altho he cald us boath. He said he wanted to talk a heep but could not.

---

[21] At this time the baby is over six months old but not yet named. Infant motality is high during this era, therefore infants were often not named until they were at least one year old.

He suffered dreadfully until just before he diede. He was buried thare close to Paps just below the lot. The tears flows from my eyes as I pen these lines to you. Pap and Mother did not take it as hard as you would think. They knew if he got able he would have to go back to the army.

Jack has been at Mr Boons sick 3 months. He has a large running sore on his thigh. Poor Jack he takes it very hard about Wat. We got a letter from him and it was the most hart wrenching one I ever read. He says as all his brothers have diede before him it is his time next.[22]

I am having one stable and crib moved to the house. I hire the Negros about to do it of nights. As to milk and butter we dont get very plenty. Hart went dry about a month ago and I have never got the one from Teers yet.[23] Dully says she is tolerable good cow. I am going to have her brought home. I taken a quarter of beef from Mrs Clanton. I am going to kill Beauty after a while.[24]

The report of Mr Clantons death is true. Old Mr Cosper is deade.[25] Babe Wells is married to a man by the name of Woods.[26] I have a hog up fatning to kill when he gets fat to eat with my turnips. Mrs Clanton is the most intimit neighbor I have.[27] She comes to see me oftener than she goes any whare els. She takes Mr Clanton's death very hard.

Continue in prayer for us all and believe me yours until death.

M J Taylor

---

[22] Andrew Jackson Slaughter was the only son of Wiley Slaughter and Lucy Ussery to survive until 1865. Prior to the war, three sons (Allen, Colvin, and Wiley) had died as children or young men. While in Confederate service, two more Slaughter sons died: Atlas in October 1862 and Walter in 1864.

[23] Hart was a cow. Elisha and Dulcena Teer.

[24] Beauty was a cow.

[25] Hiram P. Cosper (born c1780).

[26] Frances "Babe" Wells (born c1846), a daughter of Absolom Wells. Mr. Woods is unidentified.

[27] Caroline Clanton, wife of David G. Clanton.

137

Holly Wood Baldwin County

Oct 1st 1864

Dear Malinda,

To-morrow will be twelve months since I bade adieu to you and my loved little ones. How many changes has taken place during that time. How many Widows' hearts have been made to mourn and orphans made. Oh my God the grief and mourning and troubles that have been caused during the last twelve months. Will the next be as prolific of trouble as the last. Thou oh God knowest. Yet Malinda though I have been engaged in mortal combat the most terrific surrounded and attacked by disease and yet I say through all these dangers the Lord has brought me and you and the dear babes have been preserved through many dangers. Oh how thankful we ought to be. I do feel thankful. Lord help me to be more so. Will the Lord deal thus gently with us the next year or even more so or will his hand rest heavily on us. These are questions the answers to which belong to the unknown future. But let us my dear companion humble ourselves yet more humbly and implore the blessings of heaven in protecting us and in bringing me safe home before another twelve months shall have flitted by, more earnestly than we have ever done before. Yes in bringing me home.

The thought that I once had a home seems almost a myth a some thing in the brain not in reality. Many long, long, days, weeks, months, yea, even years have flown since I knew the luxury and peace of home where I was surrounded with peace plenty, friendship love. Yea love that makes home happy. I have studied and longed to be at home with you and the children more I believe since I came back to Mobile than in all the time since I left home the last time up to the time of coming here. Oh shall I ever be permitted to enjoy the peaceful the loving endearments of home on earth any more. I hope so. Me thinks I see the convulsive sobs that you gave when I parted from you and hear the wild cry of Leonards childish grief (as I turned down the road and was lost to sight from those dear ones) ringing in my ears to this day and see the big tears rolling down poor little Jim['s] manly cheeks with scarcely any noise. But why do I write thus. Why break up those fountains of grief again that I hope time has partially at least closed in your bosome. My heart is full to overflowing this evening. I could not sleep last night for thinking of you and to-day.

I am a mile from camps on pickett and I have no other resource than to pour out my soul thus to you. Yet I know it is wrong that it will cause you unnecessary pain. Yet Malinda since poor Ide was taken away I have no bosom friend to go to. I am lost. I am like some poor bird that has lost its mate and I must unbosome myself to you. But dearest friend, wife let us look up from the petty sorrows of this time serving world to those beautiful mansions which are prepared for the finally faithful and where so many of our dear ones are safely housed from the storms and snares of this sin stricken world and where we at last hope to come, and strive to be faithful to the end. Though we may be separated on earth never to meet in time though troubles may assail us and our friends be taken from us and our tears fall as rain yet we know that if we but hold out faithful we shall be permitted to enjoy those glorious mansions, with our friends that have gone before us and yea with our blessed savior, through the never ending ages of eternity. Then look up, pray, pray that our faith be not false, that we be not deceived, that we hold out faithful. Oh Malinda is not that never fading crown worth contending for. May God help us to strive is my sincere prayer.

My health has improved some since I wrote last week so that I am on duty but I do not feel well this evening. I fear I will relaps. I hope and pray that you and the children are all well and doing well. I received your welcome letter of Sept. 16th and 17th some ten days after it was written and was truly glad to hear from you once more and to hear that you were all well. I am very sorry to hear that the hogs had injured your potatoes. It does seem that fate is against your raising any potatoes.

As you say I am tired of this way of living but how can we help ourselves[?] O that this cruel war would close.

I also received your letter of Aug. 26th yesterday giving a ful account of poor Watts death. As he said that is the hardest trial of all but it is a debt we must all pay and let us hope that our loss is his eternal gain.

I am sorry that old man Thomas acted so shabby. I was feeding myself up with the thought that you had cake to eat but I suppose you are denied that luxury. As I have said before I can bear my hardships and hunger if I know you and the children have plenty. I know you have never suffered for the coarser necesities of life yet but I want you to have some of the finer.

I suppose you will have heard of Mr Clanton's death before you get this. He died over at Mobile about the 17th of Sept. I heard from Davis the first of this week. He is camped where we were when you came to see me and was right sick.[28] There are a great many of the state troops sick so I hear and a great many of our Brigade are sick also.[29]

Wick has gone from Mobile. His Regt left Mobile last Monday for Verona a station near Corinth. I did not get to see him. I have no other news that will interest you so goodby for the present

To Mrs M J Taylor [from] Grant Taylor

PS The Yanks threw a few shells from their gun boats at Point Clear a few miles below this the other morning and killed a little girl.[30]

---

[28] Though William R. Davis, Grant's brother-in-law, had not served most of the war, it appears that he is now in a Confederate unit.

[29] Confederate commanders at Mobile had asked for troops from states other than Alabama to be sent to avoid morale and desertion problems. See Arthur W. Bergeron, Jr., *Confederate Mobile* (Jackson MS: University Presses of Mississippi, 1991) 168.

[30] Point Clear was located on Mobile Bay's eastern shore.

138

Holly Wood Baldwin County Ala.

Oct 9th 1864

Dear wife & children,

Through the mercies of a merciful God I am permitted to pen you a few more lines which leaves me in tolerable good health though I have not got entirely over the chills yet. I hope you and the children are in good health. I received you[r] very welcome letter of Sept 30th day before yesterday which gratified me very much to hear that you were all well.

You ask me again about naming the baby. I sent you names. What objection have you got to them. But if they do'nt suit you, name it just what you please. If you intended to name it yourself, why did you ask me about it at all[?]

I gave a little piece of soap for as much sewing thread as I want. We have quite cool weather here now. The fleas and cold weather made me turn over at least twenty times last night. There are any amount of [f]leas here. The boys say that there are at least 3 pecks of fleas in each half bushel of sand.

Yesterday morning and this morning our artilery and the Yankee gun-boat (that I wrote to you about lying near here) exchanged a few shots. I was not allowed to go out where I could see. But I understand the boat was struck 2 or 3 times. At any rate she left but I expect other boats will come back this evening and we will have a pretty warm time to-morrow but we will be in but little danger unless they undertake to land which I do not think they intend to do just now.[31]

I understand that a good portion of Gen. Hood's army are in the rear of the enemy at Atlanta.[32] I got a letter from Jasper Porter

[31] On October 8-9, the gunboat *U.S.S. Sebago* exchanged fire with shore batteries at the upper eastern end of Mobile Bay. At 6:30 a.m. on the 9th, the *Sebago* was struck three times by Confederate shells. Two of her crew were dead and three wounded by 7:30 a.m. See War Department, *Official Records Navies*, I, 21: 676-677.

[32] During the first week of October, Hood moved north of Atlanta to strike at Sherman's long supply line from Chattanooga. See Long, *Civil War Day by Day*, 578-580.

dated Sept 25th. He was well. Some of our Regt have died since we have been down here none of our co.

I am rejoiced to hear that the Lord has again visited old Forest [church] with the outpourings of his spirit. I do wish I could be there to go to one more good meeting.

I do not know why it is that you fail so often of getting my letters. I write every week and the last two I sent by hand up in Pickens to be mailed somewhere up there.

I am trying to draw a hat and blanket. If I fail I shall have to send for my hat and something to keep me warm. Why do'nt Leonard and Jimmy ever write to me. How did Ide write that he was getting along. I believe I have written all that will interest you. Continue in prayer for me and believe me yours truly

Grant Taylor

139

October 15th [1864]

Dear Malinda,

I am sick again. After writing the other letter that evening I had a chill and I have been very sick ever since. I think I feel a little better this morning. Though I am so weak that I can scarcely hold my pen. The Dr gave a dose of pills yesterday the first I had since I have been sick. I hope I will be well some day. I am in this hole of a hospital.[33] Some ladies came in here yesterday and found me streched on the hard floor with noth[ing] but one thin blanket to lie on and to cover with and one of them sent me a good mattress. May God bless her.

I did not send you a letter last week. I wrote it and sent it by John Brandon to Mobile to mail it there but he missed mailing it so I kept it.[34]

---

[33] Many soldiers in the 40th Alabama fell ill at this time. See Willett, *History of Company B*, 85.
[34] John R. Brandon (1829-1903; Co B 40th AL).

I receved your of Sept 28th and October 2nd answering all my questions. I was very glad to get it. From what you say you have written several letters that I have never got. I write to you every week.

Continue in prayer for me. I must close. Goodby for the present.

To Mrs M J Taylor [from] G. Taylor

140

Holly Wood Baldwin County Ala

Oct 23^d 1864

Dear Malinda

With thankfulness I am once more seated to pen you a few lines this bea[u]tiful Sabbath morning. I have got about once more but I do not feel very well this morning though I expect to go on pickett this evening. I fear I shall not be much more account this winter. I hope and pray you and the dear children are enjoying the best of health.

I would try to get a furlough but there is no use in trying. The weather is quite cool here now and with our thin clothing quite disagreeable. We are all getting very bare of clothing and as blankets, there are very few among us than [that] could be called blankets of any use. Many of the boys are barefooted and some have to borrow pants to wear. As to myself I can make out very well a little while yet except bed clothes. My shoes are pretty good yet if I had some leather to put soles and heel taps on them.

Malinda I do hate to strip your beds again but if you have a good chance and can do without it, I want you to send me your coverlid if you cannot get me a blanket and I do not expect there is any chance for you to get one.[35] Also send my hat and one pair socks and gloves. We may be sent back to Georgia this winter

---

[35] A coverlid, or coverlet, was a bedspread or quilt.

again and I would like to have some more clothing before I go back. And it looks like the government will never pay us any more money or give us any more clothes. It is owing me about ($300) three hundred dollars for wages and clothing. If Pap can spare it ask him to send me enough leather to put one sole and heels on each shough [shoe] immediately if he can get the chance. I do hate to call on you all up there for anything but it seems I cannot help it without suffering greatly.

Malinda, Tom Gardiner at Bridgeville [Alabama] is selling flour to soldiers wives at 15 cents per pound.[36] Now if I were in your place and could get the money I would go down there and buy some. The five bu. of wheat you have bought will be only be a mere taste.

I have made about $20. since I have been making envelopes. I will send you an envelope in each letter as I have plenty.

I have no war news worth writing. Our Brigade is very unhealthy yet. Give my best love to Pap and mother and other relatives and believe me yours truly as ever

To Mrs M J Taylor [from] Grant Taylor
& children

PS Kiss the children for me.

141

Holly Wood
                                                    Oct. 25th [1864]
Dear Malinda,

I am not very well to-day. I have strong symptoms of chills to-day. I started you a letter day before yesterday. I received your letter and cakes sent by Mr Goodwin yesterday evening. The cakes were splendid.

---

36 Thomas Bradford Gardner (c1818-1869). He was an election officer at Bridgeville in 1866.

It looks like the fire has a spite at you since I left home.[37] But let us be thankful it is no worse.

I heard that Davis is about to ~~dy~~ die. If he should I intend to make it a plea to try to come home to see about father's estate. But say nothing about it.

I will send you two paks of envelopes by Mr James Byars who has a 20 days furlough to go home to see about his father's estate.[38]

I have no news to write as I wrote all last Sunday. Wiley Horton is having the chills.[39] Continue to pray for me. So goodby for the present.

Grant Taylor

142

Holly Wood Baldwin county Ala

Oct 28th/64

Beloved wife & children,

Through the mercies of God I am permitted to pen you a few more lines. I have been sick again with light fevers for five days but it has been lighter than the other attacks. I have missed it so far today. I hope I will get well soon. I hope and pray that you and the dear children are all well & doing well.

I received the cakes and ~~Envel~~ letter sent by Mr Goodwin which I answered in a little note sent by Mr James Byars who started home last Tuesday. I also sent you 2 packs of envelopes by him to be sent first to Jack Robinson's and then to old Mr McTeer.[40] I write this so you may know where to go after them. I also wrote to you last Sunday. So I have nothing much to write in this.

---

[37] Apparently another fire began in Malinda's house. Luckily the damage was not as great as when the kitchen burned.

[38] James Byars (1827-1900, Co B 40th AL).

[39] Corporal James Wiley Horton (Co B 40th AL).

[40] John G. Robinson (c1830-1899, Co B 40th AL). Mr McTeer (McAteer?) is unidentified.

Wiley Horton has had the chills but has missed them for a day or two. Several of the boys are sick besides myself. It is said the 42nd Regt are nearly all sick. They are six miles from us. Jim Williams was sent to the hospital in Mobile some 2 weeks ago and was thought to be past recovery. I have not heard from him since.

I received a letter from Emmaline yesterday. She and her family are in a bad condition. Enclosed is her letter.

There are some very kind people about here. I went to ones house this morning to get some milk gallons of which the lady has given away and she gave me a large dose of quinine which I believe kept the fever from rising on me to-day. She has been kind to me in several instances before. While I was at the hole they call a hospital the last time the ladies brought us some breakfast every morning consisting of light bread or biscuit butter tea or coffee and milk and one of them sent me a mattress to lie on as I had nothing but one thin blanket. God bless all such ladies. Some sell sweet milk here at $1.00 per quart.

Continue in prayer for me and believe me your loving one as ever

To Mrs M J Taylor [from] Grant Taylor

PS I have studied hard how to get a furlough but cannot fix it up.

143

[November 4, 1864]

[Top parts of papers are missing. Bottom parts of four pages remain.]

. . . like other men. I recieved your letter of the 9 and 15 staiting you were sick again. Ide said he was well and doing well. He never wrote but very little. I failde to send you a letter last week. I mis 2 mails getting any letter. I thought I would wait until

I heard from you. I got the 2 you sent up here to bee maild. They were blue envellops. I think I have got all your letters. Serena's Wiley was berried today was a week ago.[41] He had the fever and hooping cough. He was her oldest living. Poor Serene she is having her shear of trouble. Grant, it will bee our . . .

* * *

. . . not insulted because I spoke to you again about the babies name. I do not fancy neither of the names you sent. You said if I intended to name him myself why did I name it to you at all. This was the reson. I wanted you to bee satisfide about his name. (Enough of this) I expect he will go without a name until I see you. Leonard and Jim are platting Jim a hat. They have got very enough to make one. They can plat good as anybody. I allways keep them busy at something or other. We eat no idle bread here.

* * *

. . . don't you laugh at this. My hogs are growing very fast and are in very good order. Judes 9 pigs are the prettiest we ever had. How I wish you could come home and see how all comes on. We make out on what milk and butter we get finely. I have not braught my cow from Teers yet. She is very near dry. I am going to bring her home and winter the calf here. I know the cow will go back. It has rained here for the last 3 days and this morning it is very cool. Grant, if you can't draw a blanket . . .

* * *

. . . to stay before this cold winter came on. I feel mean to go to bed and wrap up warm and think whare you are. How I wish you could see the baby. He can say "dad dad" plain. He cries after me evry time he sees me. He is now getting sweet. How strange I feel

---

[41] Child Wiley Slaughter, son of deceased Walter Slaughter and his wife Serena Webb Slaughter. Walter had died earlier in 1864, and since Wiley is referred to as "her oldest living [child]," Serena has had an older child die as well. Serena will suffer the further heartache of the death of her young daughter Eliza Slaughter (born c1857) before 1868.

to think I have a child you never saw. [General] Hood was the man I heard was so mean to his men. I have no ware [war] news to write. I must close. Write long letters and give me all the news. I remain your distant praying wife

M J Taylor

144

Holly Wood Friday

Nov. 4th 1864

Dear Malinda,

With pleasure and gratitude to God I seat myself to write you a few more lines. I wrote you last Friday that I had had the chills again but had missed them that day. The next morning before day I relapesed with an ague that shook me at least three hours which terminated in the straigh along [with] fever. I was very sick till Wednesday when I got better and am able to poke about now. This last was the hardest of all my sickness this fall. I do not mend up much between attacks and so many of them are getting me to look badly. I expect I expect I look wores [worse] than you ever saw me. I hope you and the children are well.

I received your welcome letter of Oct 21st a few days ago and was much rejoiced to hear of your continued good health. O if I could only get home I might enjoy the same great blessing. But God has willed otherwise and I pray for grace to enable me to submit willingly.

I am rejoiced to hear that the good Lord has again visited your section of country with the outpourings of his spirit. I pray that the good work may continue till all are humbled and brought to a knowledge of the truth. I wish I could have been there to have enjoyed it with you. I haven't heard but one thing they call a sermon in about 9 months. True we have a chaplain that preaches every Sunday since we came to this place. But he is such a poor excuse that I wo'nt go to hear him. He either puts me to sleep or puts an undefineable nervousness on me [that is] perfectly unbearable. Hence my unwillingness to hear him. I heard him frequently while at Mobile before.

You remind me to recolect that twelve years back from the night of 21st Oct we were married. Ah well do I remember that blissful night and to think of our changed condition. Separated hundreds of miles (and me languishing out my life in an ungenial clime and hopeless cause) perhaps never to see each other's faces ag[a]in in life with no chance of helping ourselves. Oh how sad, sad uwfully sad it makes my poor heart almost to bursting. If I were somewhere that you could come to see me. But you cannot get here without walking at least six miles and then you have no money to bear your expenses for it would take a pocket full of our trash.

I wrote to you two weeks ago to send my hat one pair socks gloves and coverled or blanket if you could get one, by the first chance. John Brandon left here last Monday to go home on ten days furlough. I told him to bring them. He said he would if he could and would go by and see you. I did not send any letter by him because I was not able to write one. I also [wrote] to you to ask Pap to send me a sole and 2 heel taps for each shoe if he could spare it, but you will not get this letter until after Brandon shall have left to come back. I am nearly barefoot for the want of leather to mend my shoes. We drew plenty of shoes yesterday but most of them were too small and there were barefooted men enough to take the remainder.

I am glad your hogs are doing so well. I hope you will make plenty [of] meat.

I would have gone before the board yesterday for a furlough but it failed to meet. I hardly think I would have got [one] although I heard that the Dr said he intended to try to get me off for 30 days. There are too many sick they think for them to begin to furlough. I do not know when the board will meet again and when it does meet I expect I shall be too far recovered to go before it. I am now in our hole of a hospital. Over half of our co. is now sick with chills.

Leonard and Jimmy's letters were very nice and I was glad to get them. It makes me proud to think they can write to me. But I am to[o] feeble to write anything to them now.

Excuse this long unimportant letter. I have no news to write. The weather is r[i]ght cool now but there has been no frost here yet. Read this badly written letter if you can. I [am] too nervous to write well.

And O do pray with with all the fervency of soul you have for your distant and afflicted,

Husband

PS: I have no feare of your ever doing like Mrs Davis.[42]

145

November the 12 1864

Dear Grant

I started you a letter yesterday by mail. J R Brandon calde here this morning to tell me what you wanted. He says he met clothing going in as he came home. He seems to think you all have drawn blankets so I hardly know what to do about sending you my coverlid. May bee it would bee best not to sende it until I hear whether you have drawn or not. I was spining your glove thread today. Do not think me negligent about your gloves for I have so many cears on my minde. I never heard until a day or 2 ago that J R Brandon was at home. The baby has been so pewny I coulde not go to see him. He is going to start back in the morning.

I did not know until yesterday that you could [not] get lether to fix your shoes. I cannot sende to Paps and get it befor Mr Brandon comes along back this evening. I will sende your hat and socks and a few cakes this time. If you dont draw a blanket I will watch and the first chance I will sende the rest of your things.

Lab got home a day or 2 ago. I dont know on what termes.

The baby seemes better this morning. I recieved no letter from you today. Mathew sendes you one of his little teeth. Grant I had

---

42 Mrs. Davis is unidentified.

rather you could eat your cakes at home. Excuse me for not having your gloves ready. I close by saying I hope to meete with you some day.

I remain yours as ever

M J Taylor

Old Mr Ishum Parkers wife is deade.[43] Little Mary sendes you a kiss in this ring a love. [a circle is drawn on the letter.]

146

Holly Wood Baldwin County

Nov. 16th/64

Dear wife and children,

Thank Almighty goodness I am permitted to pen you a few more lines which leaves me up but not very well. I am on duty again but from the head-ache I have this evening I think I shall take the chills again soon. I hope you and the children are well and doing as well as you could under the circumstances.

I have not received a letter from you in nearly 3 weeks. The last one was dated Oct 21st and contained Buddy and Jimmy's letters. I am sorely puzzled to know the cause unless you mailed them on Saturday and they came by way of Montgomery and the Rail Road being washed up between here and there has prevented the mail from comeing from there here. When you send a letter to Mobile mail it on Friday and then it will come by Columbus [MS] and get here sooner.

I did not write to you last week because I was looking for John Brandon back but he has not come yet. I was waiting to see if he would bring me a letter and the things I wrote for some time ago. I have a chance to send a letter by hand to-morrow by one of Bob

---

[43] Sarah Pate, wife of Isham Parker (born 1799).

Jones' brothers who has been retired from the service by losing his left arm in Ga. last summer.[44] I have no news only many of our men are still sick with chills and fever.

I have been working for a fu[r]lough but as yet I see very little chance. Capt Latham says he intends to get all off home that have not been there since we came to Demopolis last fall if he possibly can and there are only four in Co G but what have been there. So if the Yanks will let us alone and I live may be I will get there some time this winter. But I have but little hopes of it.

I must brag on my dinner that I have just eaten. We had bread bacon as many fish as we wanted and a slice of potato pie fixed up all right with butter sugar and spice. There were nine of us in the mess and you ought to have seen us hide the victuals. But that was not a common meal by no means.

May God bless you all is the sincere prayer of your loving husband and father.

To Mrs M J Taylor [from] Grant Taylor
& children

PS It is reported here that old Lincoln is elected again. If so we may look for nothing short of freedom, death, or subjugation.[45]

Nov 18th Dear Malinda I am not very well to-day. I have considerable fever. I was on pickett again last night. As soon as a man gets able to go he is put on pickett every other night.

I received your welcome letter of Nov. 4th to-day. You ask me if I was insulted about your mentioning another name for the baby. God bless your soul, no. I only meant that if those names did not suit you, you could name it to suit yourself. Let us not disagree about a name as it is probable I shall never get home to call it by no name. I sent

Brandon got back this evening and brought me a letter. I am so sorry that the babe is sick. I do pray God to spare it until I see it

---

[44] Bob Jones is unidentified.

[45] President Lincoln won a second term against Democratic challenger George B. McClellan on November 8, 1864. See Long, *Civil War Day by Day*, 594.

once at least. I am very sorry Brandon could bring me nothing for when it is cold I suffer for want of covering and would suffer much more but I generally bed with some one who has got a blanket. As for drawing the clothes that Brandon spoke about there was nothing sent but coats pants and shoes and not near enough for a suit to each man and they played a snatch game over them. I was sick at the hospital and was not able to be here to snatch with the rest and so I got nothing until all was gone but shoes that were too little for any and I was permitted to draw a pair of them and sell them as I wrote in the first of this letter. A man named Locke drew a coat and as he had a better old coat than I did he let me have it.[46] I am nearly naked for pants but if you had any for me I would not send for them for I am determined not to tax your energy with making me any more pants or shirts. I need my gloves when on pickett and I have almost as good as no hat. If I had any idea that we would draw hats and blankets by Christmas I would not send to you for them. But I have no idea we will draw for I think this poor little confederacy is about played out.

You said you heard we could get leather to mend our shoes (or did you mean that you did not know that you could get leather from Pap). I will tell you how we get leather here. We pick up old shoes and tear them up secret or some of the boys get a chance and steal a saddle skirt and sell to the rest of us. That is the way I got leather to fix mine and you see what a price I paid for it. The above [is] a secret.

I do not think hard of you for not having my gloves done. I try to get along without thinking hard of any body much less you. But I cannot help it when I see how big headed officers can domineer over their superiors in every thing but office.

I suppose old Abe Lincoln is elected again. You need not build any hopes of peace soon for there will be none. I do not know of any chance you will have of sending my things soon unless you could come and bring them and that you cannot do for you have not got the money. If you could come and inform me in time what time exactly you could cross the bay I could meet you six miles

---

[46] Perhaps M.P. Locke of Co G 40th AL.

from here at Spanish Fort[47] and assist you down here. There have been several men's wives came in that way. You would have to take a boat at Mobile and come over to Blakely and then get on a little boat and come to the fort. Nothing short of going home would give me so much pleasure. But then my health is so bad I might not be able to meet you. May be it will all come right some day.

Bless Math's little tooth. How I do want to see you all. Kiss little Mary for me and may God bless us all is my sincere prayer. I will send you 20 stamps in this letter by Dick Russell who starts home on a sick furlough of 40 days day after tomorrow. Jones started before I knew it and so I did not send a letter by him. Goodbye for to-day.

Nov. 20th I am not well this morning. I [feel] very much like having a chill. There is no chance to get a furlough for the chills and they have stopped giving well furloughs for the present. What do you do for money[?] The government owes me over $300. I will send you 8 sheets of paper by Dick Russell who will either carry it to you or inform you wher[e] you can get it. He will mail this at Pleasant Ridge. I send you all the paper I have. I will get more in a day or two.

Malinda I think if Pap will do it you had better let him take Leonard next year and learn him how to work. If he will not do that send them to school all you can.

The other day I saw Mr Cobb and Talt Colvin.[48] Mr Cobb was well. [He] Has got to be a lieutenant. Colvin was not very well. I also saw Jim Clayton.[49] They all belong to the state troops and are on the other side of the bay.

~~I am glad~~ Leonard and Jimmy I am mighty Glad to hear that you are so much help to your ma. I hope you mind her in all things and are good boys in all things. If you want to please me do all you can to make your ma happy. O hope I will get to come

---

[47] Spanish Fort was ten miles across the bay from Mobile. See Hearn, *Mobile Bay*, 47.

[48] Mr. Cobb is unidentified. Tarlton Colvin (born c1820).

[49] James Clayton (born c1818) of Pickens Co.

home some day and I want you to write to me some times.
From your loving Pa.

Grant Taylor

147

The Village

Nov. 24th 1864

Dear wife & children,

I am not well this morning. I have had the chills ever since the 20th. I have missed my chill thus far to-day. I am at our hole of a hospital again. This is the fourth attack.

I sent a letter to you by Dick Russell last Sunday to be mailed at Pleasant Ridge contain[ing] 20 stamps. I also sent 8 sheets paper by him. He will either carry it to you or to Betty's. He will His furlough will be out the 1st of Jan. He said if you did not get to send my things he would try to bring them. But he will let you know or about Christmas you can go down to see Betty and find out.

You need not send my gloves for I picked up some old sock legs and got Jo Lancaster to knit me a pair this week.

John Sanders has got a furlough for 40 days and is waiting for this letter in a great hurry. I cannot write but little.

There are a great many having the chills. We have had three hard freezes in the last three nights.

Continue to pray for me and believe me yours lovingly as ever

To Mrs M J Taylor [from] Grant Taylor

148

November the 24th 1864

Beloved Grant,

It is through the kinde hand of god that I am permitted to pen you one more letter. This leaves us all in fine health. I hardly know whether I hope you are well or not for I think maybee if you remain sick they will let you come home after a while some how or other. I cant keep from looking for you now. I recieved your ever welcom letter written Nov 4. How glad I am when I get a letter from you. I never got one weeke before last. I also failed to start you one last week. Pap fell down stares last week and came very near breaking his neck. The heel of his s[h]oe caught on the top step and throwed him head long to the floor. He was laid up some time. He is up again now.

Jack was here last Thursday. He had leave of absence for a few days but he says he is not going back until he gets ready. He is at Larance Bailys whare Cate is.[50] He is fat as a bear. I wrote to you in my last of Lab beeing at home. He came without leave or lisens. He was married to Mint Gray last week.[51] Dully and Lish were very much opposed to it.[52] The[y] would not go to the wedding nor wont let her come thare. They don all they could to keep him from having her. Bill Gray and Martha Speed was maried the week before.[53]

Me and Mary went to Caralton last Monday and drew 30 dollars a piece. I will get an order in a week or too [two] to have the corn hald to me that I will draw. I dont know how much I will draw. They gave me this money to buy corn with until I could draw. I have tride the Bailys and Thomasas and cant get as much as ten bushels to feede my hogs on until I can draw.[54] I am going

---

[50] Lawrence D. Bailey who was serving in Co B 42nd AL by the end of the war. Catherine (surname unknown; 1833-1904), wife of Andrew Jackson Slaughter.

[51] Albert "Lab" Teer came home without leave to marry Araminta C. Gray (c1846-1920), daughter of John W. and Mary Gray.

[52] Elisha and Dulcena Teer, Lab's parents.

[53] Bill Gray and Martha Speed are unidentified.

[54] Bailey and Thomas are unidentified.

to sende to Crofford tomarrow.[55] He is selling at 2 dollars. Just to think I went all the way to Caralton after 30 dollars and it snowed on me nearly half the way and now cant buy as much as ten bushels of corn with it when there are thousands of bushels close around me. It looks harde and you of[f] fighting for thare property. Some times I think you are simple for staying in the army another day. Thare are thousands deserting evry day. I am almost temted to persuade you to come home and never go back. Do all you can to get a ferlow. It does seem to me if I was in your place I could querk around and get one. If no how els tell a fib. Jack writes out his own ferlows sometimes and why cant others do the same.

I supose Lincon is elected again but I dont know that it makes it any worse for him to bee elected. Maybee him better than the other one. I disremember his name. Cant you see I have a new pen. I gave a dollar for three in Caralton.

November the 25 1864 We all eat a very harty breakfast this morning. One month from today is Cristmas. God grant you may bee at home to spend one more Cristmas with me. The baby can sit alone can take any thing in his hand and grabs olde tom when he comes in his way.[56] I have never been angry enough with him yet to slap him one time. You know he is a good child.

Liz Brooks and olde Griffy Burns is married.[57] Billy Burns, Dobson Knox is dead. Also Jane Mahaffy.[58]

I killed my shoat week before last. Have not killed my beef. I wont this year. I can do very well without him. Last Tuseday and Wednesday was as cold wether as I ever felt. Oh how I thought of you. I am very sorry J Brandon could not carry your things. If you have not drawn blankets yet I will sende you my cover lid the first chance. Also the rest of your things.

I am going to hire olde Mr Danel to do some worke for me.[59] He is a very good hand and works at one dollar a day. I want him to make me a new gate build a hen house and lot and fix up my

---

[55] James D. Crawford.

[56] The baby, William Rufus Grant Taylor, is grabbing for a cat, Tom.

[57] Liz Brooks and Griffy Burns are unidentified.

[58] Billy Burns and Dobson Knox are unidentified. Perhaps Sarah Jane Mahaffey (born c1842).

[59] Mr. Daniel is unidentified.

yard fence. He is a brothern law to olde Billy Clemmons.[60] I have one stable moved to the house. Mage[e] will move one crib next week.[61]

Grant you ought to hear Mary singing ware [war] songs. She can sing them correct as I can. How I wish you could come home and see how all comes on. Can it bee that you will still bee in the army this time next year. But I ought not to complain for we have been wonderfully blessed and I feel thankful to god for it.

I will close by saying may God still extend his mercies is my daily prayer. A due [adieu] to you.

M. J. Taylor

Grant, I am so fat my clothes will hardley meet on me and little Mary is fat as a hog. We eat so many potatoes. We have eaten my crop up to about ten bushels. Nearly evry day Mary says what if Pa was to step in. What do you recon I would do[?] Leonard has just stept in with a large rabbit that he caught whare he was cutting wood. When this you see remember me.

MJT

149

The Village Ala.

Dec. 3[d] 1864

Dear wife & children,

Through the mercies of God I am spared to pen you a few more lines which leaves me in delicate health yet. Though I have had no chills in ten days yet I am weak and do not improve in flesh. I fear I never will be stout any more. I have never got entirely over the Pneumonia I had last spring. My side is always sore. I am still in the hole of a hospital yet. I hope you are all well by this time. I

---

[60] William Clemmons (1804-1898) of Pickens County.
[61] Magee is unidentified.

have got no letter from you since the one sent by Brandon. I am getting very anxious to hear how the baby has got.

Our Regt is all gone to Spanish Forte except a few picketts. It is said the reason of the removal is they are looking for an attack.[62] But whether that be the cause or not I do not know. We are waiting for a wagon to move the hospital there also. We have no houses or shelter of any kind there for the Regt or hospital and it has been raining heavily this morning. I sent a few lines by John Sanders last week to be mailed at Plesant Ridge as I did one by Dick Russell a few days before.

A Yankee flag of truce boat lay near here last night. She came to bring blankets and clothing for their men whom we have prisoners and to take potatoes to our men who are confined on Ship Island.[63] It looks curious to see men engaged in killing each other so to meet and be so friendly. This war is a shame, a disgrace to civilization. Oh! would to God it would end.

I dream of seeing you nearly every night lately and sometimes I dream of seeing some of the children. I have also dreamed of seeing father and mother several times since I have been sick. I wrote to you in my last that there being no chance to get a furlough for the chills and they have stopped granting well furloughs for some cause, meanness though I suspect. I see no chance now of ever coming home unless I run away and I dislike doing that. But I do not know what I may be driven to. I certainly shall not do it unless I see there is no chance to get there in any other way befor another summer's campaign begins. The boys are generally very much out of heart and say it is no use to fight any longer.

Continue in prayer for me and believe as ever yours devotedly,

To Mrs M J Taylor [from] G. Taylor
& children

---

[62] Federal pressure on Mobile and the rest of Alabama increased in December. See Hearn, *Mobile Bay*, 143-144.

[63] Over 800 Confederate prisoners were held on Ship Island in the Gulf of Mexico in December, 1864. See *Official Records*, I, 21:758.

Dec. 6th. I feel pretty well to-day. I received your letter of the 1st and 2nd inst yesterday. Can Baily starts home in the morning.[64] I send this by him. We have moved to Blakely 12 miles from Holly Wood.[65] We are waiting for orders. I do not know where we will go from here. You say you borrowed $30 from Pap and bought corn. If you can draw corn why did you buy[?] I have some whiskers but not as many as usual. I wish you could get to nuzzle them. We were moving last week so I did not get to send this as I intended. I have never received but one letter since the one sent by Brandon. Yours in hast[e],

G Taylor

150

Magnolia Race Track near Mobile

Dec. 10th 1864

Dear Malinda,

With pleasure I avail myself of one more opportunity of writing you a few lines which leaves me feeling tolerably well again and hoping you and the children are in the very best of health.

I sent you a letter by Can Baily stating that we were at Blakely waiting for orders. We stayed there till day before yesterday when we came over to Mobile and marched to this place 6 miles from Mobile down the bay. We are comfortably quartered in good houses but they have no chimneys and we have to build our fires in the yard and as the weather has been cold and windy and we have nothing but pine wood to burn we make a sooty appearance.

I received your [letters] of 24th and 25th Nov. after the one of Dec. 1st and 2nd. You speak of having to go to Carrolton through the snow to draw money to ~~draw~~ buy corn. I know you have hardships to bear. Only to think what you have to bear it wrings

---

[64] Kennedy Bailey (1832-1879; Co B 42nd AL.

[65] Blakeley was another heavily fortified part of the Mobile defenses. For a description, see War Department, *Official Records*, I, 49, Part I: 949.

me to the very heart and then to have to live on charity. No not charity for what little you draw is justly due you for they dont pay me anything. I tell you such a state of things is almost more than I can bear and if there were any way to help myself and you I would get out of it. But I see no chance as yet.

I think you have decided unwisely in not killing your beef for it is very uncertain whether you will be allowed to keep it for another year. I would advise you to kill it yet if it is fat enough and kill all your hogs but Judes nine shoats if you can get corn to fatten them. For I tell you if soldiers pass there much or camp near there they will kill them for you. You can sell the meat if you have more than you want and there is no danger of your getting more Confederate money on hand than you need for present use. How does your sheep come on. You will have more yearlings that will do to kill next fall. It is useless to try to keep much stock on hand for if [you] winter them the government or the soldiers would take them from you.

I heard that some cavalry stole $30 and some other things from Pap, is it so? I am truly sorry Lab threw himself away as he did.[66] I believe I have written all that will interest you.

Our co[mpany] drew 8 blankets the other day but there were enough without any to take all them so I did not get any. I got a splendid pair of pants.

Give my love to all and believe me as ever yours in the bonds of love.

To Mrs M J Taylor [from] Grant Taylor

PS I do so wish I could come home and see how all comes on but there is no use in wishing.

---

[66] Grant is probably referring to Albert Teer marrying Araminta Gray.

CHAPTER 11

I INTEND TO COME HOME...OR BE CAUGHT AND BROUGHT BACK IN THE ATTEMPT

As the Civil War entered its fourth year neither Grant nor Malinda Taylor had any hope of a Confederate victory. Desperate to see her and the children Taylor even considered transferring to a cavalry regiment stationed closer to them. When the 40th Alabama received orders to leave Mobile and move to North Carolina in the fateful spring of 1865 Pvt. Taylor went home instead. The reluctant soldier was on his way back to his regiment when the war ground to a welcomed end.

151

December the 10th 1864

December the 10th 1864

Beloved husband,

It is through the kinde hand of God that I am permitted to pen these lines to you. This leaves us all well and harty hoping it may finde you in good health once more. As long as they wont let you come home if you have to bee away I had rather you could keep well. If I knew I could get you by coming down thare I would go after you. Grant, I am tempted to persuade you to come home any how until you get well. I heard today that the Yanks were deserting and coming over to our side evry day. I dont know how to believe it.

I have 7 hogs up to kill. They are fatning finely. I wrote in my last about buying 30 bushels of corn from Mr Crofferd at 2 dollars. I can draw 5 bushels to the head for my pork hogs and I am allowed 2 hogs apiece for each of my family of stock hogs and 3 bushels to each head to feede them and 30 bushels for my horse and 10 bushels to the head for my family. It all comes to 100 and 61 bushels.

Dec the 16th Dear Grant, We are all in fine health today. I recieved your letter braught [by] Can Baily. It seemes thare is no chance for you to come home. Well Grant, Mary maries tonight to Mr John H Davis.[1] He lives in Miss[issippi]. He is a widower with one childe. His father has a very nice property. He is about common size, light hair, blue eyes, yellow whiskers and moustache and favors Gilbert Taylor only some better looking. He has been wounded 7 times. He is a very nice looking man. I trust to God she is doing well although he is rude and wicked. He is [a] Cavaldryman. He wil get to [be] with her a month or two. Mary will live whare she lives now until the ware ends.

James Powel is shot through him somewhare.[2] I did not hear. He is [in] Tenn. Lab is at home yet. Oh Grant you dont know how bad I want to see you. I think you will shurly will get to come home during this winter.

I mist close and fix to go to the wedding. Pray for us all and mankinde evry whare and may God give us peace is my earnest prayer.

M J Taylor

---

1 John H. Davis (born c1841). John Davis and Mary Slaughter eventually had 6 children, but the Slaughter family obviously never liked him. In his will, Mary's father Wiley Slaughter carefully left money to her Parker children but nothing to her Davis children. John and Mary left Alabama to live in both Arkansas and Texas after the war.

2 James Powell (Co I 7th AL Cavalry).

152

Spanish fort Ala.

Dec. 17th 1864

Beloved Malinda,

Once more I am permitted to pen you a few more lines which leaves me in reasonable health hopeing these lines may reach you and find you all well and doing as well could be expected under the circumstances.

We moved back on the east side of the bay last night. The Yanks keep sending raiding parties around which keeps us moving. Also I do not expect we will be still but a few days at one time this winter.

I have no news to write only it is reported that the Yanks have taken Pollard and cut the railroad between this and Montgomery but the report is not confirmed.[3] Sickness has somewhat subsided among us.

I have not received any letter from you this week. If you can, send my things by Dick Russell but if you cannot send them by him try to send them by Baily if he can bring. But as I wrote to you some time ago you need not send me any gloves as I have had me a pair knit out of some sock legs that I found.

I do not think we need build any hopes upon my getting to come home this winter for I have no idea that there will be any more well furloughs granted from here this winter.

Last Sunday and Sunday night was swinging cold weather. Every thing was frozen hard. I was on pickett and I tell you I had a cold time of it.

There is more goods in Mobile now than there was two years ago except calico. Paper is from $8 to $17 per quire, calico $18 per yd, dinner at the Market House where we got it when you were down at 50 cts each, is now $5. Potatoes from five to $10 per bu. Common sized apples $1 each, small biscuits $3. per doz. Pork out

---

[3] Pollard, Alabama was constantly threatened by Union forces operating from Pensacola since it was a key railroad junction. See Charles G. Hearn, *Mobile Bay and the Mobile Campaign: The Last Great Battles of the Civil War* (Jefferson, NC: McFarland & Co Inc, Publishers, 1993) 142.

in the country where we were camped $2.75 per lb. Small ginger cakes $1.00 each and one dollar in gold will buy $25 in Confederate money.

Dec. 18th While writing the above orders came for our Regt to go to Pollard. We hurried to the boat and went 6 miles to Blakely where we were ordered back to Spanish Fort. The boat turned round and back we came and landed here about sundown. They are running our Regt around considerably.

I do not feel so well this morning. I have a very bad cold. We have warm spring like weather now. Give my love to all. Kiss the children for me. Continue in prayer for me and believe me yours truly

To Mrs M J Taylor [from] Grant Taylor

153

December the 23rd 1864

Dear Grant,

It is pleasure that I am permitted to write to you again. This leaves us all well truly hoping it may finde you the same. I recieved your letter written Dec 10th. I was glad to hear you was in better health as long as they wont let you come home. I was glad also to hear you could sleep in howses. You say you make a sooty appearance. I would like to see you if you were as black as the pot for I know I have never wanted to see you so bad before.

The baby has one tooth, can sit alone, and is ceartainly the best childe that ever lived. How strange I feel when I think of having a childe nearly 8 months olde that you never saw.

The Cavaldry stolde a pair [of] new jeanes pantes 40$ a pocket knife from Pap and a bed quilt from Mother.[4]

---

[4] Confederate cavalry units were scattered over much of north and central Alabama at this time. See James Pickett Jones, *Yankee Blitzkrieg: Wilson's Raid Through Alabama and Georgia* (Athens: University of Georgia Press, 1976) 40.

I wrote in my last about Mary going to get maried last Thursday night. Well she did marry that night. Thare was about 30 thare and we all enjoid ourselves fine. Mr Jack Dannel maried them.[5] She maried a man by the name of Davis that lives in Miss. He is a widower with one childe. He is not 30 years olde. He belongs to the cavaldry. He will have to go back to his command shortly. We know nothing against him only he is no professor.

You said something about me killing Brandy yet but it is two late to kill him now.[6] One reason that I did not kill him was he had a hooked place [wound] on his sid and you know how I am about eating anything of that sort. I also wanted to sende the most of him to Tusk[aloosa] to get thread and as my good olde Pap was good enough to buy a bail of nice six hundred thread and give it to me I thought I would not kill him this year. He also found leather and shoed all my little fellows around. You said for me to kill all my hogs but Judes shoats if I could get corn to fatten them.[7] I only have 4 others whitch I thought I woulde save for another year and not have to kill [for] so much little meat. As to my sheep they are doing very well.

This is some of the paper you sente me by D Russell.[8] I also got the 2 pack of envelopes you sent by J Byars.[9]

Grant another Cristmas is nearly here and you are still absent. I was so in hopes you would spende this Cristmas at home but it seemes that I will have to spend it again without you. I pray before another Cristmas shall role around that you may bee permitted to get home safe and sound and mankinde evry whare is a prayer from an honest hart this night.

I am going down about Betties next week to see Dick Russell about carr[y]ing you some thinges. I have you such a nice pare of gloves. I feel like I want you to ware them.

I make some money now cutting coats. My price is 3 dollars. I have a good [piece] to cut these times. I made 3 dollars in about an hour Saturday evening and 3 this evening.

---

5 Jack Daniel is unidentified.

6 Brandy was a cow.

7 Jude was a pig.

8 Richard M. Russell (Co G 40th AL).

9 James Byars (Co B 40th AL).

I have one [corn] crib and stable moved to the house. In Cristmas week I expect to hire the Negros to builde me a lot and make a new yard fence and new gate. I had 25 bushels corn halled to me last week. I wrote to you some time ago what I could draw was 100 and 61 bushels. My hogs are getting pretty rounde.

Betty Teer that lived at Mitchells has got a bastard.[10] I believe I have gon through [the news] for the present.

Grant I heard twice that you would bee at home in a week or two and you dont know how it lifted me up but your letter never said anything about it. Goodbye,

M J Taylor

154

Spanish Fort Ala

Dec. 29th 1864

Dear wife and children,

Once more I am seated to pen you a few lines which leaves me in tolerable health. I have had no chills for some time.

I wrote to you in my last that we were back on the eastern shore of the bay at this place. We only stayed over there a little over a week. They are expecting an attack on Mobile every day but I cannot see that there is any more danger now than when we first came here. But still it would not surprise me in the least for Mobile or this place to be attacked any day and for us here to be captured. For I do realy think we are in as complete a trap for that purpose as could be.[11]

---

[10] Malinda distinguishes this Betty Teer from Grant's sister by stating that this Betty Teer lives at Mitchell; she is unidentified.

[11] Union General Edward R. S. Canby was preparing a force of over 40,000 troops for a final assault on the city of Mobile in December, 1864. See U.S. War Department, *War of the Rebellion: A Compilation of the Official Records of the Union and Confederate Armies* 128 vols. (Washington, D.C.: Government Printing Office, 1880-1901) I, 39, Part I: 342-343, 584, 593; and Hearn, *Mobile Bay*, 146.

I heard to-day or rather yesterday that Jeff Davis was dead. I do not wish him dead but I believe his death would be a great blessing to the Confederacy. I also heard that [General Nathan Bedford] Forrest's men had killed him. Now if that be so I am sorry of it.[12]

I received your kind and ever welcome letter of Dec 10th and 16th last night and was truly glad to hear from you once [more] as I had not received any from you in over three weeks. I was also glad to hear of your continued good health. As to my coming home I have no idea that there will be any more furloughs given here this winter except a few to the sick and God grant I may not be sick enough to get one. Although I want to come home as badly as I can yet not bad enough to want to be sick to get one. For camps is the last place to be sick in.

I hear it reported here that a good many of the Yankee prisoners whose term of service is out are taking the oath and joining our side because Lincoln will not exchange them. But we hear so many lies that we never know what to believe.[13]

I wrote to you some time ago that I thought you had done bad business in not killing your beef this fall and I say yet if it is fat enough you had better do it yet. Also if you can get corn to fatten them you had better kill all your hogs but Judes nine [or] ten. Chances to one either the government or soldiers will get them and your beef before next killing time. You can sell the meat if you do not ~~wish~~ need it. For there is no danger of your getting more Confederate money on hand than you need.

I am almost sorry that Mary has married. Not that I have anything against the man for I know nothing of him or do not wish her to see happiness, but that I want her to be happy and there are but very few John's such as John Parker was in this sinful world.

---

[12] This rumor was false. President Davis was safely in Richmond. See William C. Davis, *Jefferson Davis: The Man and His Hour* (New York: Harper Collins, 1991) 577-579.

[13] The prisoner exchange cartel between the Union and the Confederacy broke down in 1863 over the issue of treatment of black soldiers captured by the rebels. See James M. McPherson, *Battle Cry of Freedom: The Civil War Era* (New York: Oxford University Press, 1988) 792-793.

God grant her last husband may be as good as her first. Give him my respects and tell Mary that I wish her much joy.

I would ask you to send me some meat by Baily but his Regt is over about Mobile and it might be uncertain about getting it. But send my clothes by him if you cannot send them by Russell. He can send them over to me or write to me and I can go over to Mobile after them.

We are living very hard here now. About as hard as we ever have. We have no money to buy with and if we [had] there is nothing to buy nearer than Mobile. But there are a few cows in the woods and we press one of them occasionally and think it no great sin. There is some talk of paying us, but I fear it will be all talk and no cider.

Have you ever got your envelopes and paper yet[?] Write to me when you get them.

It is now between midnight and day and I am standi sitting by a little fire guarding some prisoners who are all asleep. A portion of the Regt charged the Commissary on Christmas eve and took a barrel of Whiskey and they the Col. has put 13 of them in the guardhouse and here I am sitting up guarding them while they are asleep. I was 2 miles off that night on pickett and by their taking it I missed my Christmas dram next morning but I do not blame them. O that I could have been at home to spend this Christmas with you and the children. Where will we all be next Christmas[?]

I must quit for want of paper and light. Good night my dearest ones

To Mrs M J Taylor [from] G Taylor
& children

155

Spanish Fort Ala

Jan. 4th 1865

Dear Malinda,

Again I am permitted to pen you a few lines which leaves me in tolerably good health and I hope and pray that you and the dear children are enjoying the best of health. I received your ever welcome letter of Dec. 23^d night before last and truly glad was I to get it as I always am and glad to hear of your continued good health.

I have no news to write only everything appears quiet. I do not know why it is that they do not furlough some of us now unless it be meanness for it does seem to me that they might let some of us go home now. I do not know how the report got out that I was coming home in a week or two for I am sure there has been no prospect of it.

You regret very much having to spend another Christmas without me but you cannot regret it more than I did. And think there is another year added to the date of my letter. At first I wrote 1862 on my letters to you and then [18]63 and I asked myself if I would live through that year and still be in the army. Time answered in the affirmative and yet through [18]64 the Lord has spared my life and now we are beginning another new year and still I have to ask the same question. Will I live through this year and still be in the army[?] I pray Almighty God that I may live and that I may spend most of this year at home with you and the children.

And now I will write you a secret which I want you to keep. It is this. If I live God being my helper I intend to come home next April if I do not get a furlough before then and they do not pay me off or I will be caught and brought back in the attempt. Unless you think I had better stay and bide my time for a furlough. But I do not think I can start into another summer's campaign without seeing you and the children. But do not look forward to that time with too much certainty for circumstances may render it impossible for me to get there then.

I recon I feel as curious as you do to think I have a child that can sit alone which I never saw.

Your reasons are good for not killing your beef and hogs provided you can keep them for another year. But that is extremely uncertain.

If you get a good chance send me some meat and butter for we are living very hard. We do'nt even get bread enough. But if [I] could get meat plenty the bread rations would do very well.

Give my respects to enquiring friends and connexion. Kiss the children for me and believe me ever yours truly

To Mrs M J Taylor [from] Grant Taylor

156

Spanish Fort Ala

Jan. 11th[18]65

Dear wife and children,

Once more I have the pleasure of writing you a few lines which leaves me in fair health hoping you are all enjoying the best of health.

Well Malinda, Dick Russell has come back and brought me nothing and says you never came to see him. He also says he would have brought my things if you had brought them. What was the reason you did not carry them down to him[?]

General [Alpheus] Baker and other officers are in favor of putting negroes into our brigade as soldiers. They propose to put one negro for two white men and make them cook, wash, and make fires for us but we would have to drill and fight side by side with the stinking things. They are to be set free if they fight well at the end of the war if we gain our independence. The question is causing a great deal of excitement. The men, I believe, are generally opposed to it and a great many declare they will go home if they are put in ranks with us. That is my notion. And then to think we have been fighting four years to prevent the slaves from being freed, now to turn round and free them to enable us to carry on the war. The thing is outrageous.[14]

But the big bugs say things have changed that we must bring the negroes in and make them fight or we will be made slaves of ourselves. Well if we are reduced to that extremity that we must depend on the slaves for our freedom (and many of our leading men say we are) we are in a bad condition and I say if the worst comes to the worst let it come and stop the war at once and let us come home for if we are to depend on the slaves for our freedom it is gone anyway. Then why not stop the war before it goes any further[?] Gen. Baker in a speech the other day to our Regt said without the help of the nigger we were certainly whipped and I and I have seen several pieces in the papers to the same effect.

Everything seems quiet here so far as fighting is concerned. The 42nd Ala Regt is on the other side of the bay below Mobile. I have not received any letter from you since the one dated Dec. 23[d]. No prospect of our being paid that I know of.

Give my respects to enquiring friends and connexion. Kiss the children for me. Continue in prayer for me and believe me truly yours as ever

To Mrs M J Taylor [from] Grant Taylor

PS If you have a good chance şend me something to eat.

---

[14] Plans for arming slaves and bringing them into Confederate combat units had been discussed as early as January of 1864. A bill authorizing such enlistments passed the Confederate Congress after much debate on March 13, 1865. See Emory Thomas, *The Confederate Nation 1861-1865* (New York: Harper and Row, 1879) 262-264, 294-296; Robert F. Durden, *The Gray and the Black: The Confederate Debate on Emancipation* (Baton Rouge: Louisiana State University Press, 1972) and most recently Craig L. Symonds, *Stonewall of the West: Patrick Cleburne and the Civil War* (Lawrence: University Press of Kansas, 1997) 181-202.

157

Spanish Fort Ala.

Jan. 18th [18]65

Dear Malinda,

Thank God I am spared to pen you a few more lines which leaves me in pretty good health and hoping you and the children are the same. I received your letters of Dec. 30th and Jan. 5th last night. I was very glad to get them and to hear that you were all well.

Well Malinda you ask me not to think hard of you for letting the youngsters have a party at your house. Well I do not think hard of you, but I am sorry you did not have moral courage enough to give them a decided refusal when they wished to play. I have never had a little thing to grieve me so or touch the chore [core] of my heart so painfully as that did when I first heard of it (for I heard of it several days ago). You know I always had serious objections to having parties at my house and more especially at such a time as this for several reasons and not the least of them is that designing persons both men and women use such times to carry on their sinful communications. I have heard young men brag about staying at parties up there till late in the night and then go home with the girls through the old pine fields alone and you know that the morals of the people were never so low as now. And from what I can find out some of the girls that were at your house have none of the best of characters. I know they are talked very slight[l]y about by the young men. And may God preserve me or you from doing anything that could be turned into a cloak for such meanness.

And then another thing is people are so ready to talk about women living alone as you are. You need not think your former good name will screen you if a disgraceful talk should be started about you, for I tell you nay, though you may be ever so innocent which I doubt not you would be.

So I will let this pass. But dear Malinda for the love I bear you never lack for courage, true courage to say no when they attempt to force another thing of the kind into your house. And also for the sake of your blessed Savior. May God of his goodness enable you to stand firm in the future is the prayer of your grieved but not angry husband.

As to going to the cavalry I have no idea I can get a transfer. I know I cannot get one to go with Jack and if I could get one to go with Wick I would have to go to the Army of Tenn. and be under old Hood and I do not like that.[15] But I intend to take a furlough when my 3 years is out if I can get away from here and then I may go to the cavalry after I stay at home awhile. I have no news to write. Goodby.

G Taylor

Jan 20th. I am well to-day. Since writing the above I have been trying to make a swap and get in the 8th Ala Cavalry but I am not certain that I will make it. Nor will I find out for several days. The Regt is 5 miles from here. I am trying to get in the same co. that Jasper and Milton are in. Their officers are swapping off their dismounted men. I expect Jasper will be sent to the 42nd. I cannot get a transfer and can only get to the cavalry by swapping. That is the reason I cannot go to Wicks or Jacks Regt. Hold Mary to her promise. If I get to swap I will get to come home after Button.[16] It is rumored that our Brigade will be sent to South Carolina. I hope it is not so. Continue in prayer for me. May God bless us all is my prayer.

G Taylor

Jan. 18th 1865 Dear Leonard I received your letter last night and I was very glad to get it but you do not write so well as you

---

[15] After a disastrous campaign in Tennessee, General Hood resigned as Army of Tennessee commander on January 13, 1865. See E.B. Long, *The Civil War Day by Day: An Almanac 1861-1865* (Garden City NJ: Doubleday, 1971) 623-624.

[16] The 8th Alabama Cavalry, commanded by Lieutenant Colonel Henry J. Livingston, had recently been stationed in the Tuscaloosa area. Taylor would need "Button," a horse, if he planned to transfer to the 8th, as Confederate cavalrymen had to supply their own mounts. See *Official Records*, I, 45, Part I: 1233.

used to. I am afraid you do not practise much. I wish I could be at home to help kill and eat your hogs. I am sorry you have so nearly forgotten how I look and I am afraid you will forget me entirely before you see me again. But I hope to come and see you some day and while I am gone you must be a good boy. Do not use any bad words or do anything you would be afraid or ashamed to tell me or your ma about. Help your Ma all you can and be a good boy generally and believe me your ever loving Pa.

To L F Taylor [from] Grant Taylor

158

Spanish Fort Ala

Jan. 24th 186[5]

Beloved family,

Through the mercies of God I am permitted to pen you one more letter which I expect will be my last from this place. For we have been under marching orders with two days cooked rations for 3 or 4 days. It is said we are ordered to Montgomery but all the men believe we are going to South Carolina.[17] We are very low spirited and a great many say they are going home. As for myself I hate the idea of going to S.C. nearly as bad as I did leaving home after I came from Vicksburg and you know something about how I grieved at that. But I do not see any chance to avoid going. I feel like all hope of getting home till the end of the war is at an end. But do not grieve my dear family. The Lord of all the earth will do right.

---

[17] Confederate leaders desperately worked to send troops to South Carolina in January, 1865, in order to stop General William T. Sherman's devastating march through that state. See Thomas L. Connelly, *Autumn of Glory: The Army of Tennessee, 1862-1865* (Baton Rouge LA: Louisiana State University Press, 1971) 520-522.

"Why this sadly weeping,
Beloved ones of my heart?
The Lord is good and gracious,
Though now he bids us part.
Oft have we met in gladness,
And we shall meet again,
All sorrow left behind us.
Good night, till then!"

Yes my dear ones good night till then. Till when? Till we meet either in this low ground of sorrow or in that blessed abode beyond this vale of tears. Where the wicked cease from troubling and the weary are at rest.

I am well in body but sick at heart and I hope you are all in the enjoyment of the best of health.

If you do not send my things before you get this letter do not send them until you hear from me again, unless you can send them by someone who will be certain to bring them to me. I am almost as good as out of socks and if I do not get some from some source I am bound to suffer. There is some talk of paying us some money but I do not believe they will pay us till they get us to where they are going to take us for fear we will go home. And I doubt their ever paying us.

One of our gunboats was burned to the water's edge a few nights ago at Mobile. I do not know the particulars.[18]

I wish now you had come to see me last fall.

Give my love to all the connexion. Pray fervently for me. And Oh kiss my sweet children for me, for in all probability I will never get to do it myself. I cannot help but grieve. My heart feels like bursting for I did have some hope if we stayed here of coming home this spring. But now all hope is snatched away only in deserting and I cannot bear the idea of that yet although we are treated like dogs.

---

[18] A possible reference to the *C.S.S. Baltic*, one of only four remaining Confederate ships operating in Mobile Bay by 1865. See William N. Still, Jr., *Iron Afloat: The Story of the Confederate Armorclads* (Columbia, S.C.: University of South Carolina Press, 1985) 212.

May God bless us all and bring good to us out of this painful thing is the prayer of your loving but sorrowing husband & father.

To his family [from] G Taylor

Direct your letters as usual till further orders.

159

Magnolia Race Tracks near Mobile Ala.

Jan. 26th 1865

Dear Malinda,

This leaves me well hopeing you are all well also. I wrote to you day before yesterday stating that we were ordered to Montgomerey but yesterday we were ordered to Mobile and to-day we came back to this place. But I have no idea how long we will stay here. I also wrote not to send my things till you heard from me again. But now send them if you can. If Baily brings them tell him to deposit them somewhere in Mobile and let me know. That is if our Regiments are separated when he comes like they are now. His Regt is at Spanish Fort.

I wrote also that I had been trying to get into the 8th Ala. Cavalry, but I do not expect I will succeed, or I am afraid I will not. I gave you all the news the other day so I have nothing now to write but as I have a chance to send this into Pickens [County] by Lieut. Collier I thought I would write a few lines to inform you of our move.

Continue in prayer for me and excuse bad writing for I am writing by a very sorry firelight. Yours affectionately,

To Mrs M J Taylor [from] Grant Taylor

[On January 29th, the 40th Alabama left Mobile for Montgomery on the steamer *Saint Charles*. The regiment moved across Georgia and was in South Carolina by the first week of February. By mid-

March, it was in North Carolina in time for the desperate battle of Bentonville on the 19th. Afterwards it was consolidated with the 19th, 37th, and 42nd Alabama Infantry regiments. By late March, this unit was guarding a ford on the Yadkin River. Private Grant Taylor was obviously at home and not with his command during this period. No evidence has appeared showing that he obtained a legal furlough before leaving his regiment.]

160

Demopolis Ala

March 25th 1865

Dear wife and children,

This leaves me in good health hoping you are the same. I landed at this place last night and will leave for Selma in a short time.

I failed to get on a boat at Steele's Bluff or on the stage at Eutaw so I lumbered [26 miles] out for this place on foot. I feel pretty much exhausted. I am all right so far. I have not been under guard yet. I have got transportation to Montgomery.

I will send this by a gentleman who says he is going by Martin's.[19]

I have no news to write. Yours as ever

To Mrs M J Taylor [from] Grant Taylor

The 40th Alabama was still in North Carolina when Taylor began his journey to rejoin it. It had moved to Salisbury, North Carolina, on picket duty until the Army of Tennessee officially surrendered on April 26, 1865. The 40th Alabama itself did not turn in its weapons and head for home until May 5th. Though the men began the trip home together, they soon disbanded and were left to their own devices to get home.

---

[19] Martin is unidentified.

EPILOGUE

After all of the words, sentences, and pages written during those past three years, there is no letter detailing the reunion of the Taylor family. Normal life would have quickly resumed for the husband and wife with their five children. In the post-war years, Grant and Malinda had three more children: son Lavalgas in September 1866, daughter Sally in July 1869 and son Walter in May 1870. Sadly, their daughter Sally died young. In 1876, the Taylors left Pickens County and moved to adjacent Greene County. They continued with their strong religious convictions and church connections. Grant became a founder and charter member of Prairie Baptist Church (now West Greene Baptist Church).

Shortly after 1880, the Taylors moved to Beebe, Arkansas, and lived at 402 W. Illinois Street. Grant and Malinda had many heartaches during these years. In 1883 while visiting his daughter, Malinda's father Wiley Slaughter died and was buried in Beebe. Then, in July 1884 at age twenty, Willie, the son born during the war, died in a train accident. A few years later in May 1887 at age seventeen, their son Walter died in a mill accident. Of their eight children, five lived to adulthood. Sons Leonard and Lavalgas married and lived in Arkansas, son James served as a Baptist missionary in Brazil for thirty-two years. Son Matthew and daughter Mary lived and raised their families in Greene County, Alabama.

Malinda died at age sixty-four in 1897 and was buried in Beebe. After her death, Grant returned to Greene County, Alabama. He lived alone near son Matthew and daughter Mary. Grant Taylor died in 1908 at age eighty, but he was buried next to his beloved Malinda and their two young sons in Arkansas. His marker incorrectly gives his death year as 1907.

Grant and Malinda Taylor were among the fortunate ones. They both survived the trauma of the war—on the home front and in the field. Their war time story of fear and faith, hunger and hope, will endure through their letters.

BIBLIOGRAPHY

Alabama Department of Archives and History. *Civil War Pension Records and Muster Rolls, 40th Alabama Infantry Regiment*. Microfilm.

Alabama 1907 Census of Confederate Soldiers, Perry and Pickens Counties. 3, 5. Cullman AL: Gregath Company, n.d.

Barefield, Marilyn. *Pickens County, Alabama 1841-1861*. Easley, SC: Southern Historical Press, 1984.

Bearss, Edwin C. *The Campaign for Vicksburg*. 3 vols. Dayton, Ohio: Morningside Press, 1985-1986.

Bergeron, Arthur W. Jr. *Confederate Mobile*. Jackson MS: University Presses of Mississippi, 1991.

Blomquist, Ann K. *Taylors and Tates of the South*. Baltimore, MD: Gateway Press, 1993.

Brown, Virginia and Helen M. Akens. *Alabama Heritage*. Huntsville AL: Strode Publishers, 1967.

Carter, Samuel III. *The Final Fortress: The Campaign for Vicksburg 1862-1863*. New York: St. Martin's Press, 1980.

Castel, Albert. *Decision in the West: The Atlanta Campaign*. Lawrence KS: University Press of Kansas, 1992.

Catton, Bruce. *Grant Moves South*. Boston: Little, Brown and Company Inc., 1960.

Clanahan, James F. *The History of Pickens County, Alabama 1540-1920*. Carrollton, AL: Clanahan Publications, 1964.

Connelly, Thomas L. *Autumn of Glory: The Army of Tennessee, 1862-1865*. Baton Rouge LA: Louisiana State University Press, 1971.

Cox, Jacob D. *Atlanta*. New York: Scribner and Sons, 1882.

Cozzens, Peter. *The Darkest Days of the War: The Battles of Iuka and Corinth*. Chapel Hill NC: University of North Carolina Press, 1997.

_____. *This Terrible Sound: The Battle of Chickamauga*. Urbana IL: University of Illinois Press, 1992.

_____. *The Shipwreck of Their Hopes: The Battles for Chattanooga*. Urbana IL: University of Illinois Press, 1994.

Curry, John H. "A History of Company B, 40th Alabama Infantry, C.S.A.," *Alabama Historical Quarterly*. 17/4 (Winter 1955): 159-222.

Daniel, Larry J. *Soldiering in the Army of Tennessee: A Portrait of Life in a Confederate Army*. Chapel Hill NC: University of North Carolina Press, 1991.

Davis, George B., Leslie J. Perry, and Joseph W. Kirkley. *The Official Atlas of the Civil War.* Washington DC: Government Printing Office, 1891 [rpt 1983].

Davis, William C. *Jefferson Davis: The Man and His Hour.* New York: Harper Collins, 1991.

Delaney, Caldwell. *The Story of Mobile.* Mobile AL: Gill Press, 1962.

Dodson, W. C. "Errors Concerning Ector's Brigade." *Confederate Veteran* XIII/40 vols. (1905) 457.

Durden, Robert F. *The Gray and the Black: The Confederate Debate on Emancipation.* Baton Rouge LA: Louisiana State University Press, 1972.

Eaton, Clement. *A History of the Southern Confederacy.* New York: Free Press, 1954.

Evans, Clement A., ed. "The Fortieth Alabama Infantry," *Confederate Military History,* 5/13Atlanta: Blue and Grey Press, 1899.

Faust, Patricia L., ed. *Historical Times Illustrated Encyclopedia of the Civil War.* New York: HarperCollins, 1986.

Fleming, Walter L. *Civil War and Reconstruction in Alabama.* New York: Columbia University Press, 1905.

Forest Baptist Church of Christ records, Benevola, AL. Birmingham AL: Samford University.

Gandrud, Pauline. *Alabama Records.* 245 vols in series. Easly SC: Southern Historical Press, 1981.

Hearn, Charles G. *Mobile Bay and the Mobile Campaign: The Last Great Battles of the Civil War.* Jefferson, NC: McFarland & Co Inc, Publishers, 1993.

Hendrix, Beasey S. Jr. *Tuskaloosa's Own, A Short History and Muster Roll of Confederate Units from Tuskaloosa County, Alabama.* Tuscaloosa: Colonial Press, 1988.

Hughes, Nathaniel C. Jr. *General William J. Hardee: Old Reliable.* Baton Rouge LA: Louisiana State University Press, 1965.

Johnson, James Dolphus Jr. *Early Settlers of Pickens County, Alabama.* Cullman, AL: Gregath Publishing Company, 1992.

Jones, James Pickett. *Yankee Blitzkrieg: Wilson's Raid through Alabama and Georgia.* Athens GA: University of Georgia Press, 1976.

Junkin, Betty. *Deaths, Marriages and Confederate Soldiers, Pickens County, Alabama 1841-1931.* Gordo, AL: 1990.

Long, E. B. *The Civil War Day By Day: An Almanac 1861-1865.* Garden City, NJ: Doubleday, 1971.

Lonn, Ella. *Salt as a Factor in the Confederacy.* Tuscaloosa AL: University of Alabama Press, 1965.

Losson, Christopher. *Tennessee's Forgotten Warriors: Frank Cheatham and His Confederate Division.* Knoxville TN: University of Tennessee Press, 1989.

Marshall, Mrs. S. M. *Greene County, Alabama Records.* Columbus, MS: Blewett Company, 1980.

Martin, Bessie. *Desertion of Alabama Troops from the Confederate Army: A Study of Sectionalism.* 1932; reprinted New York: AMS Press Inc, 1966.

McDonough, James L. *War in Kentucky: From Shiloh to Perryville.* Knoxville TN: University of Tennessee Press, 1994.

McGuire, Mrs. C. P. *Records of Pickens County AL.* Tuscaloosa AL: Willo Publishing Co., 1970.

McMillan, Malcom C., ed. *The Alabama Confereate Reader.* Tuscaloosa AL: University of Alabama Press, 1963.

_____. *The Disintegration of a Confederate State: Three Governors and Alabama's Wartime Homefront 1861-1865.* Macon GA: Mercer University Press, 1986.

McMurry, Richard M. "The Affair at Kolb's Farm," *Civil War Times Illustrated* (December 1968) 171-95.

McPherson, James M. *Battle Cry of Freedom: The Civil War Era.* New York: Oxford University Press, 1988.

_____. *For Cause and Comrade: Why Men Fought in the Civil War.* New York: Oxford University Press, 1997.

Miller, Francis T. ed. *The Photographic History of the Civil War.* Ten Volumes. New York: Review of Reviews, 1911.

"Monument at Livingston, Ala.," *Confederate Veteran* XVII. Nashville TN, 1909.

Moore, Albert B. *Conscription and Conflict in the Confederacy.* New York: Macmillan, 1924; Columbia, SC: University of South Carolina Press, 1996..

Musciant, Ivan. *Divided Waters: The Naval History of the Civil War.* New York: HarperCollins, 1995.

Pickens County Genealogical Society. *Pickens County, Alabama Cemetery Records.* Gordo, AL: Pickens County Genealogical Society, 1984.

"Pickens, John Henderson, Capt.," *Confederate Veteran,* XV (1907) 86.

Pickens Republican (Pickens County, AL).

Pollard, Michael B. *Pemberton: A Biography.* Jackson: University Press of Mississippi, 1991.

Prairie Baptist Church records. Birmingham, AL: Samford University.

Royster, Charles, ed. *Memories of General W. T. Sherman.* New York: Library of America, 1990.

Schroeder-Lein, Glenna R. *Confederate Hospitals on the Move: Samuel H. Stout and the Army of Tennessee*. Columbia SC: University of South Carolina Press, 1994.

Sears, Stephen W. *To the Gates of Richmond: The Peninsula Campaign*. New York: Tickner and Fields, 1992.

Still, William N. Jr. *Iron Afloat: The Story of the Confederate Armorclads*. Columbia, S.C.: University of South Carolina Press, 1985.

Symonds, Craig L. *Stonewall of the West: Patrick Cleburne and the Civil War*. Lawrence: University Press of Kansas, 1997.

Tebeau, Charlton W. *A History of Florida*. Coral Gables FL: University of Miami Press, 1980.

Thomas, Emory. *The Confederate Nation 1861-1865*. New York: Harper and Row, 1979.

Census of 1850, 1860 and 1870. Tuscaloosa County, Pickens County, Greene County, Alabama.

U.S. Bureau of Census. "Roll M432-13, Pickens County, Alabama." Population Schedules of the Seventh Census of the United States, 1850. Washington, D.C.: National Archives, 1967.

U.S. Bureau of Census. "Roll M653-20, Pickens County, Alabama." Population Schedules of the Eighth Census of the United States, 1860. Washington, D.C.: National Archives, 1967.

U.S. Bureau of Census. "Roll M593-36, Pickens County, Alabama." Population Schedules of the Ninth Census of the United States, 1870. Washington, D.C.: National Archives, 1967.

U.S. War Department. *War of the Rebellion: A Compilation of the Official Records of the Union and Confederate Armies*. 128 vols. Washington, D.C.: Government Printing Office, 1880-1901.

U.S. War Department. *Official Records of the Union and Confederate Navies in the War of the Rebellion*. 30 vols. Washington, D.C.: Government Printing Office, 1896-1927.

Walker, Peter F. *Vicksburg: A People at War 1860-1865*. Chapel Hill NC: University of North Carolina Press, 1960.

Watson, William. *Life in the Confederate Army: Being the Observations and Experiences of an Alien in the South During the American Civil War*. Baton Rouge LA: Louisiana State University Press edition, 1995.

Weise, O'Levia Neil Wilson. *Cemetery Records of Greene County Alabama and Related Areas, The Journal of Mrs. Mary Marshall*.

Wiley, Bell I. *The Life of Johnny Reb: The Common Soldier of the Confederacy*. Baton Rouge: Louisiana State University Press, 1978.

_____. *The Life of Billy Yank: The Common Soldier in the Civil War*. Baton Rouge LA: Louisiana State University Press, 1978.

Willett, Elbert D. *History of Company B, 40th Alabama Regiment, Confederate States Army 1862 to 1865*. Montgomery, AL: Viewpoint Publications, 1963.

Wooster, Ralph A. *The Secession Conventions of the South*. Princton NJ: Princeton University Press, 1962.

Wynne, Lewis N. and Robert A. Taylor. *This War So Horrible: The Civil War Diary of Hiram Smith Williams*. Tuscaloosa AL: University of Alabama Press, 1993.

INDEX

Porter, Mr. 17, 25, 29, 37, 38, 47, 82, 83,
    88, 89, 95, 100, 102, 104, 129, 132,
    195, 277
Porter, Thomas 84
Porter, William Jasper 30n, 43, 76, 84,
    120, 121, 188n, 195, 224, 292
Powell, James 314
Powell, John 100, 191, 193
Powell, Mrs. 208, 241
Prairie Baptist Church 79n, 330
Price, Gen. Sterling 119

Rachel 5, 6, 10, 21, 30, 44, 49, 56, 73, 80,
    84, 86, 93, 104, 144, 150n
Ralph AL 4n, 34n
Red River 163
Resaca GA 250
Reynolds, Mrs. 224
Rich, Mr. 97
Richardson, B. F. 286
Richardson, Ivy 143
Richardson, Mr. 37, 66
Richardson, Mrs. 37
Richardson, Rhoda 143n
Richey, Mary A. 63
Richmond VA 49, 55, 68, 95, 101
Riley, James 43, 44, 49, 50, 53, 55, 57, 59,
    62, 70, 71, 72, 73, 74, 75, 76, 81, 83,
    86, 90
Riley, Sarah 72
Ringgold GA 200
Roberson, Rev. 86
Robinson, John 296
Robinson, Mr. 212
Rock Island IL 220, 274, 275
Roebuck, George 66, 151
Rogers, James W. 138, 188
Roper Hotel 115
Rowe, James 224
Royal Street 115
Rudolph, D. R. 120n
Russell, Richard M. 117, 262, 282, 305,
    306, 309, 315, 317, 320, 322

Saint Charles steamer 328
Saint Jordan 92
Salisbury NC 329
Salmon, Jane 5, 8n, 12n
Salmon, Tom 8, 12, 89, 92, 122
Salmon, William T. 5, 8n, 12n, 14, 15,
    22, 30, 66, 84, 87, 92, 93, 102
Sam 9

Sanders, Ezekiel 82, 89
Sanders, John W. 140, 183, 184n, 203,
    238, 253, 255, 306, 309
Sawyer, Charles C. xii
Scott, Rev. William 27
Sellers, Elijah 17, 18n, 25, 37n, 47, 51,
    67, 69, 83, 195, 266
Sellers, Lizy 87
Sellers, Mrs. 83
Sellers, Nancy Drummond 49
Selma AL 95, 188, 189, 329
Seymour, T. J. 262
Sherman, Gen. William T. x, 146n
Shiloh 2, 13n, 100
Ship Island 310
Shirley, James 41
Shockley, Dr. Thomas W. 22, 103, 280
Shorter, John G. 118n
Sipsey River 84, 91, 99, 169
Slaughter, Allen 288n
Slaughter, Andrew Jackson 2, 23, 53,
    64, 69n, 71, 76, 79, 81, 85, 88, 90, 91,
    103, 105, 108, 111, 119, 120, 121,
    154, 156, 158, 161, 164, 165, 167,
    169, 173, 175, 246, 288, 307, 308, 325
Slaughter, Atlas J. xii, 2, 8, 20, 23, 29,
    37, 42, 79, 89, 95, 108, 113, 117, 120,
    154, 177, 179, 215, 258n, 288n
Slaughter, Catherine 69, 307
Slaughter, Colvin 288n
Slaughter, Cornelia Shirley 179, 208,
    258
Slaughter, Eliza (child) 298n
Slaughter, Eliza A. 45
Slaughter, Lucretia Ussery 26, 37, 41,
    103, 108, 127, 164, 174, 179, 208,
    210, 211, 212, 222, 246, 257, 272,
    280, 282, 288, 295, 316
Slaughter, Serena Webb 208, 298
Slaughter, Walter xii, 16, 23, 41, 45, 57,
    89, 95, 113, 117, 120, 127, 154, 164,
    185, 186n, 191, 193, 195, 206, 208,
    214, 217, 246, 258, 267, 280, 287,
    287, 288n, 290, 298n
Slaughter, Wiley 5, 26, 31, 37, 41, 49, 58,
    79n, 92, 96, 97, 98, 102, 103, 107,
    108, 109, 115, 117, 121, 127, 144,
    147, 149, 160, 164, 181, 208, 211,
    217, 222, 230, 246, 257, 272, 282,
    286, 287, 288, 288n, 295, 300, 301,
    304, 305, 307, 310, 312, 314n, 316,
    317, 330